MONSON
Free Library and Reading Room
ASSOCIATION

NO. 33619

RULES AND REGULATIONS

A fine of two cents a day shall be paid by every person keeping a book more than two weeks, and the right to the use of the Library shall be forfeited until all dues are paid.

Every person who draws a book shall be responsible for all loss or damage to the same while it is out in his or her name.

All books shall be returned to the Library on the call of the Librarian or Directors.

GENERAL LAWS OF MASS., CHAP. 266, SEC. 99

Whoever willfully and maliciously or wantonly and without cause writes upon, injures, defaces, tears or destroys a book, plate, picture, engraving or statute belonging to a law, town, city or other public library shall be punished by a fine of not less than five nor more than fifty dollars, or by imprisonment in the jail not exceeding six months.

TWENTY CENTURIES OF CHRISTIANITY

BOOKS BY PAUL HUTCHINSON

THE NEXT STEP: A STUDY IN METHODIST POLITY, 1922

THE SPREAD OF CHRISTIANITY, 1922

CHINA'S REAL REVOLUTION, 1924

THE STORY OF METHODISM, 1926
  with Halford E. Luccock

WHAT AND WHY IN CHINA, 1927

THE STORY OF THE EPWORTH LEAGUE, 1927

THE UNITED STATES OF EUROPE, 1929

THE MEN WHO MADE THE CHURCHES, 1930

WORLD REVOLUTION AND RELIGION, 1931

STORM OVER ASIA, 1932

THE ORDEAL OF WESTERN RELIGION, 1933

FROM VICTORY TO PEACE, 1943

THE NEW LEVIATHAN, 1946

THE NEW ORDEAL OF CHRISTIANITY, 1957

BOOKS BY WINFRED E. GARRISON

ALEXANDER CAMPBELL'S THEOLOGY, 1900

WHEELING THROUGH EUROPE, 1900

AFFIRMATIVE RELIGION, 1928

CATHOLICISM AND THE AMERICAN MIND, 1928

RELIGION FOLLOWS THE FRONTIER, 1931

THE MARCH OF FAITH, 1933

INTOLERANCE, 1934

AN AMERICAN RELIGIOUS MOVEMENT, 1945

THE DISCIPLES OF CHRIST: A HISTORY, 1948
  with Alfred De Groot

WHENCE AND WHITHER THE DISCIPLES OF CHRIST, 1948

A PROTESTANT MANIFESTO, 1952

CHRISTIAN UNITY AND DISCIPLES OF CHRIST, 1955

THE QUEST AND CHARACTER OF A UNITED CHURCH, 1957

Centuries of Christianity

A CONCISE HISTORY

PAUL HUTCHINSON

WINFRED E. GARRISON

NEW YORK   HARCOURT, BRACE AND COMPANY

FOREWORD

Paul Hutchinson wrote the article "The Onward March of the Christian Faith" for that issue of *Life* (December 26, 1955) which ended its series "The World's Great Religions." A publisher suggested that he expand the article into a book. He gladly undertook this congenial task, but death overtook him suddenly before he had proceeded far with it. His family asked me to carry it to completion. I have done this with the feeling that I have been not so much writing my own book as finishing his.

Though he and I had no consultation about any part of the project other than an hour of very specific talk while the *Life* article was being written, the book is truly the product of collaboration, for we had been collaborating in many matters for a long time. We were colleagues for more than thirty years on the editorial staff of the *Christian Century*, he as managing editor and then editor, I as part-time literary editor and editorial writer while my chief work was with the University of Chicago. Without an exception that I can remember, our differences of opinion were mutually supplementary rather than contradictory. The congeniality of our minds was such that our agreements were often unspoken.

I have reason to hope, therefore, that what I have done with the beginning of Dr. Hutchinson's book manuscript in carrying the story on from the fourth century to the twentieth is not too unlike what he would have done, though, of course, I have followed my own light. Not to make him responsible for anything he would not have written —or would have written better—it should be stated that the first eight chapters of this book are Hutchinson; the remaining eighteen, Garrison. The editors of *Life* kindly gave permission to make free use of the Hutchinson article. The borrowings from it are considerable in the first eight chapters, very slight from there to the end. The closing sentences of the book are to be ascribed to Dr. Hutchinson, since they became his final testament of faith.

Dr. Hutchinson had sketched a preface for the book, apparently before beginning to write it. This draft scarcely fits the book now, but one paragraph of it ought to be preserved:

> Not long ago the *New Yorker* published a cartoon which showed a harassed salesman in a bookstore confronted by a determined matron demanding "an unbiased history of the Civil War from a Southern point of view." With the best intentions in the world to achieve objectivity, those who write the history of Christianity can hardly claim a greater degree of success. There is, in church history, a Roman Catholic point of view, an Eastern Orthodox point of view, a Protestant-Anglican point of view (with Calvinist, Lutheran, and Anabaptist refinements), and none of us who write in the field can escape from the one in which we are at home.

The history of Christianity bristles with controversial issues and diversities of interpretation and evaluation. The authors can only say that they have tried to be as objective as they could—from a Protestant point of view. One thing is clear, they both write from a standpoint within the Christian movement, though not within the same denomination. They believe that Christianity is important, that its influence has been on the whole beneficent, and that its main affirmations about God and man are true. If this gives them a slanted view of its history, so be it. Here we stand. We can do no other.

WINFRED E. GARRISON

CHRONOLOGICAL TABLE

c. B.C. 4   Birth of Jesus

c. A.D. 29   Crucifixion

   c. 35   Conversion of Paul

   47-57   Paul's missionary journeys and letters to Thessalonica, Corinth, Galatia, and Rome

     49   Jerusalem Council

   64-65   Persecution by Nero; martyrdom of Peter and Paul

     70   Destruction of Jerusalem

     96   Persecution by Domitian

    170   Persecution by Marcus Aurelius

    250   Persecution by Decius

    303   Last persecution of Christians, by Diocletian

    313   Constantine's Edict of Toleration

1182-1226	St. Francis of Assisi
1198-1216	Pope Innocent III
1233	Inquisition established
1225-74	St. Thomas Aquinas
1265-1321	Dante
1284-1303	Pope Boniface VIII
1309-77	Papacy at Avignon
1328-84	John Wyclif
1377-1417	The Great Schism
1415	John Huss burned; Council of Constance
1480	Spanish Inquisition established
1498	Savonarola burned at Florence
1516	Erasmus; first printed Greek New Testament
1517	Luther's Ninety-five Theses
1521	Diet at Worms
1522	Zwingli began reforms at Zurich
1529	Diet at Speyer; "Protestants"
1530	Augsburg Confession
1534	Henry VIII broke with Rome, excommunicated
1536	Calvin's *Institutes,* first edition
1540	Jesuit order officially recognized
1545-63	Council of Trent
1553	Servetus burned at Geneva
1560	Elizabethan Settlement
1572	Massacre of St. Bartholomew's Day, France
1603-25	James I
1629-40	Great Puritan migration

CONTENTS

I

The Beginning

Among all the religions by which men seek to worship, Christianity is the most widely spread, embraces the largest number of adherents, and makes the most stupendous claims for the divinity of its Founder and the finality of its teaching. Of the two and a half billion human beings on earth, nearly 800 million—one out of every three—are ordinarily listed as Christians. They are either Christians by personal avowal or live in cultures saturated with Christian ideas and practices. In one sense or the other, they are part of Christendom.

The churches in which Christians worship have, during their nearly two thousand years since Jesus Christ lived and died, developed such an astonishing diversity of belief and ritual that it is sometimes difficult to recognize that they all acknowledge the same Lord. The glittering spectacle of an Easter Mass in St. Peter's, the stillness within the bare walls of a Quaker meeting-house, the squatting circle of Congo tribesmen listening to the white-haired medical missionary as he preaches in a jungle clearing, the chanting monks cut off from the world on the forbidden peak of Mount Athos, a hundred thousand Mar Thoma devotees gathered in a dry river bed to join their prayers under the blazing sun of South India, thousands pressing forward in London's Wembley Stadium at the appeal of a spotlighted evangelist, wraith-like figures kneeling in perpetual adoration before the altar in a Quebec convent, a sea of dark faces swaying while the tide of the spiritual rolls across them: "It's me, O Lord, standin' in the need of prayer"—how can these, and hundreds of other differing manifestations, all be accounted parts of the whole to which we give the name of Christianity?

Some will deny that they are. But there is justification for the habit of including all such diversities in the inclusive reckoning. All, under whatever form, acknowledge one God; all declare their loyalty to one Lord; all find in one Cross the symbol of their faith. The differences they present to the world are endless, confusing even to themselves, often enfeebling. Considered from the outside, it is manifestly not true, as one of their most-sung hymns affirms, that

> We are not divided, All one body we,
> One in hope and doctrine, One in charity.

Often in their dealings with one another, charity has been the element most painfully missing. But in their ultimate allegiance they are one. They are Christians.

Inevitably the questions rise: Where did this Christian religion come from? How did it spread? Why has it taken so many forms?

The answers make up one of the most dramatic, and in some parts romantic, stories known to history. It cannot be told here in all its ramifications; this, as the subtitle of this book states, is simply a short account, confined to the high spots and the most memorable personalities and events in the long record. From the days of St. Luke, who wrote his account of the Acts of the Apostles sometime in the first Christian century (the fact that over most of the world time is dated B.C. or A.D. is itself of historical significance), down to the present, thousands of scholars have labored to uncover all the facts which go to make up the complete story. Before Christianity was a hundred years old some despairing soul, adding a postscript verse to the last-written Gospel, sighed that "even the world itself" would not be large enough to contain all the books that could be written to fill out the Christian record. When one considers the vast libraries of such scholarship that have been accumulated since then, this hardly seems an exaggerated prophecy. In the brief compass of this account, however, many details connected with events and many names familiar to church historians must be passed over. Here we are trying only to recall a few of the men and women who bore leading parts in making Christianity what it is today, trying to catch them in characteristic moments which suggest their importance to the record, and to note the great movements of thought and action of which these notable personalities were either the movers or the agents.

JOHN THE BAPTIST

Christianity is the religion that springs historically from Jesus of Nazareth. If, for the sake of brevity, one ignores the long Jewish background—although this had so deep an influence on those who became the first Christians that it must not be forgotten—the emergence of Christianity can be dated from the appearance in the Judean wilderness, about the year 28, of John, an ascetic whose fiery denunciations of the morals of Palestine's ruling classes, coupled with prophecy of imminent judgment at the hands of an outraged God and the equally imminent coming of the Messianic agent of this judgment, drew crowds to the Jordan valley to hear him.

John is identified in some of the New Testament narratives as a cousin of Jesus. But that has little bearing on his importance to the birth of Christianity. What mattered was that he was a direct spiritual descendant of the line of great Hebrew prophets. He may well have been, before he took up his solitary preaching mission, a member of one of the Essene or other Jewish monastic reforming communities which excavation and decipherment of the lately discovered Dead Sea scrolls are uncovering to modern eyes. His requirement that those who believed his message should be immersed by him in the Jordan as a symbol of their confession and repentance fastened on him the name by which he is known to history—

John the Baptizer, or Baptist. The early Christians regarded him as the great forerunner of their Master, and the New Testament represents John as himself having that conception of his mission. But there was at least a small band of followers of John who continued a separate existence for some years after the formation of the first Christian churches.

With his fierce assault on the privileged, whom he called a "generation of vipers," it did not take John long to land in trouble. Herod Antipas, the Roman puppet tetrarch of Galilee, not relishing John's comments on his personal morals, threw him into prison, and presently, inflamed by incestuous passion for the Princess Salome, cut off his head. The circumstances of his execution have made an irresistible appeal to scores of dramatists, composers, artists, and Hollywood script-writers.

Before John's arrest, however, there appeared among those seeking baptism from him a man from the Galilean hill town of Nazareth. His name was Joshua; in the Greek form, Jesus. He was about thirty, a member of the Jewish tribe of Judah. The Gospel According to St. Matthew states that through "Joseph the husband of Mary, of whom was born Jesus," he could claim descent from the great national hero, King David (Matt. 1:16). Tradition holds that up to the time he joined the crowds flocking to hear John he had been supporting himself, and helping to support the large family of his widowed mother, by working as a carpenter.* The same tradition asserts that John recognized in his cousin the Messianic judge and deliverer whose coming he had been predicting, and that he demurred at the idea of baptizing him "for the remission of sins." But Jesus insisted, the rite was performed, and later it came to be believed in the church that immediately after his baptism Jesus saw "the heavens opened . . . the Spirit of God descending like a dove," and heard a voice from heaven, "Thou art my beloved Son." Thus, symbolically, the torch of religious reformation was passed along from the Baptizer to the Man of Nazareth.

* The Roman Catholic Church denies that the Virgin Mary bore other children. It holds that the word translated "brothers" in most English versions of the New Testament (see Matt. 12:46-50) should be rendered "cousins."

JESUS OF NAZARETH

What we know about Jesus comes from the letters (Epistles) that the Apostle Paul and other early Christian leaders wrote to Christian churches in their formative years; from the Acts of the Apostles, an account by St. Luke, a physician and St. Paul's traveling companion, of the missionary activities and preaching of some of the first-generation Christians; and from the four Gospels that open the New Testament. Such references to Jesus as appear in the secular literature of that age—a few sentences in Josephus, Pliny the Younger, Tacitus, and, possibly, Suetonius—throw no light on his career. (Josephus knew much more about John than about Jesus.) The evidence in all these records is so confusing, pays so little attention to chronology, and in part is so contradictory that it is impossible to be sure about many facts in the Nazarene's life. At the close of the work that established his eminence as a theologian, *The Quest of the Historical Jesus*, Albert Schweitzer wrote: "There is nothing more negative than the result of the critical study of the life of Jesus. . . . We are experiencing what Paul experienced. In the very moment when we were coming nearer to the historical Jesus than men had ever come before . . . we have been obliged to give up the attempt and acknowledge our failure in that paradoxical saying: 'If we have known Christ after the flesh, yet henceforth know we him no more.' " Biblical scholars will widely agree with the verdict of the Encyclopaedia Britannica: "Any attempt to write a 'Life of Jesus' should be frankly abandoned. The material for it certainly does not exist."

Yet there are some facts. At the very least it can be said that some men and women who lived in Palestine and in other parts of the Mediterranean world during the Roman reigns that stretched from Augustus to Titus believed certain things about Jesus to be true, and their belief had such profound effects that it changed the course of history. What were these history-making beliefs?

They believed that Jesus was an actual historical person who lived at the time and place indicated in the Gospels, and that, after the imprisonment of John, he left Nazareth, apparently to take up the mission of spiritual awakening his cousin had been forced to lay down. They believed he traveled about Palestine, most of the time in his native Galilee, more briefly in Judea, for an indeterminate period in the region between the two. For perhaps as much as three years, but more likely for about half that time (the Gospels tell of events on not more than fifty days), he healed, he worked wonders, he taught. He gathered a following which varied greatly in size, apparently depending on the amount of healing he was doing. Out of this following he screened a dozen men for especially intimate companionship and instruction. He was remembered as a man who loved the open, drew many an illustrative teaching from the ways of nature, made little of family ties, could be forbiddingly stern with pretense and the pretentious but infinitely tender with the sorrowing and needy. One of the firmest beliefs in the early church was that he had a natural gift for winning the trust of children.

These contemporaries believed that as Jesus grew more convinced of his Messianic role and as his moral judgments grew more rigorous, he came into conflict with the conservative religious forces of his nation. The Roman procurator, Pontius Pilate, was induced to regard the Nazareth prophet as a threat to public order, even a possible revolutionist (the Gospels suggest that it was the word "king" which stuck in Pilate's mind when he was examining this prisoner) and he was crucified. But his followers believed that he rose from the dead. They declared that, in a resurrected and glorified form, he appeared to many of them. They must have believed it, for within fifty days after Jesus had been executed, what had been a despairing and disintegrating band of disillusioned dreamers—vividly portrayed in St. Luke's haunting story of the walk to Emmaus—was transformed into a company of zealots who would dare any fate to proclaim that this resurrected Jesus was in fact God's promised Messiah, or, in Greek, the Christ—the Anointed One sent by God. "Upon this conviction, that their Master had risen from the dead, the Christian religion is historically founded." Some day, those contemporary believers in Jesus as the Messiah expected, this resurrected Lord would be "revealed from heaven" in a flaming spectacle of judgment, when punishment would be meted out to the wicked and his own followers would share in his glorious reign. That day, they thought, was not far distant; for the first few years most of those early disciples of Jesus looked for his return before their own deaths.

II

Peter, Paul, and the Apostolic Age

In the company of Jesus' twelve specially chosen disciples—reduced to eleven by the treachery of Judas Iscariot—the one who stands out is Simon, better known by the affectionate name, Peter, given him by his Master. In a famous passage in Matthew 16:18, 19, Jesus is reported to pun on the name and its Greek meaning—*petros*, rock. In a rush of praise after Simon had declared his belief that his Master was "the Christ, the son of the living God," Jesus bestowed his accolade: "Blessed art thou, Simon Bar-jona: . . . Thou art *Peter*, and upon this *rock* I will build my church; . . . And I will give unto thee the keys of the kingdom of heaven: and whatsoever thou shalt bind on earth shall be bound in heaven; and whatsoever thou shalt loose on earth shall be loosed in heaven."

It can be plausibly contended that these few words, not found in the other Gospels, have influenced history, for good or ill, more profoundly than any other single recorded utterance. Because the Roman Catholic Church has seized on them as possessing such supreme importance, claiming that through them both the institution of the papacy and the authority of its priests to absolve from sin can be traced back to the very words of Christ, the passage has

been often questioned. Some have claimed that it is an interpola-
tion, inserted years after Matthew was written to justify the by-
then growing ascendency of the bishop of Rome among Christian leaders. Others say that it was not intended as any grant of
peculiar spiritual powers to Simon, but was simply an affirmation
by Jesus that faith in Him as the Christ, which had just been
publicly declared for the first time, was the faith on which the
community of His followers would be founded and grow. Although these questions will never be settled, probably a majority
of contemporary Protestant scholars regard this passage in Matthew as authentic, but they would not agree that there is anything
in it to indicate that Jesus intended any precedence He conferred
on Peter among the Twelve to pass on to the later bishops of
Rome. And so far as conferring on Peter any measure of spiritual
infallibility is concerned, any reader has only to proceed in that
chapter of Matthew for another four verses to find the Master's
praise of His impetuous follower turning to blistering rebuke:
"Get thee behind me, Satan: thou art an offense unto me: for thou
savorest not the things that be of God, but those that be of men."
It is to be noted also that the binding-and-loosing formula is repeated just a little later (Matt. 18:18) but with a significant difference, for here it is in the plural, "Whatsoever ye shall bind"
addressed not specifically to Peter but to all the apostles.

The textual evidence for a divine instruction as to the nature
of the Christian church, its government and its powers, is, to say
the least, ambiguous. But that ambiguity has made a lot of history—
some of it very dreadful history.

THE APOSTLE PETER

The other apostles, as this band of Jesus' intimates came to be
known, are shadowy figures. But Peter, headstrong, blundering,
violently temperamental, easily influenced by his surroundings or
by the words of others, yet always ardent and—after one terrible
experience while Jesus was on trial—always courageous, Peter is
unforgettable. As has been said, it is Peter to whom the New Testament accords the honor of first openly saluting Jesus as the Mes-

siah. Paul told the Greek Christians at Corinth that it was to Peter, after the crucifixion, the risen Lord first appeared (I Cor. 15:5). And when, fifty days after the resurrection, the followers of the new faith made their first attempt to win a public hearing, it was Peter who preached the sermon on that memorable Pentecost.

We do not know a great deal about Peter's subsequent career, for he had no biographer who traveled with him, as did Luke with Paul, to keep a record of his preaching journeys. We learn, however, from the early chapters of the Acts of the Apostles and from statements in Paul's letters, that Peter spent some time with the church in Jerusalem and the churches that were springing up in many Gentile cities in Asia Minor. Finally, in some unknown fashion, he reached Rome, where Catholic tradition holds that he was the first bishop. There he is believed to have suffered martyrdom under Nero in A.D. 64. There is some reason to expect that before long his burial place in the present Vatican—at that time the site of Nero's gardens—will be authenticated.

Everything about Peter's career in Rome is legendary, but legends are often valuable in their revelation of character. There is one story, for example, which tells how the apostle was induced by other Christians, when Nero's persecution started, to escape the emperor's wrath by fleeing. But as he plodded along the Appian Way he met a Figure whom he recognized as One with whom he had once traveled the roads of Galilee. *Quo vadis, Domine?* ("Where are you going, Lord?") he asked. "To Rome in your stead," the Figure answered. Whereupon Peter, in remorse only a little less bitter than he had tasted after his denial in the high priest's courtyard, turned around and marched back to his death. It was possible for pliable Peter to be persuaded by others to go wrong. Paul told the Galatian churches about that (see Gal. 2). But he could recognize his mistakes, repent of them, and correct them.

Another legend deals with the manner of Peter's martyrdom. After he had been condemned, it asserted, the apostle asked that, as a last favor, he might be crucified head down. In this way he sought to show his sense of unworthiness to be put to death in the same fashion as had his Lord. True or not, it is at least in character with all that is known of St. Peter. Origen tells us that by the third century this story had become familiar to Christians every-where.

THE OTHER APOSTLES

Of the others in that original company of apostles, almost nothing can be said with confidence. Tradition has apportioned to all of them missionary journeys and a roster of places of martyrdom so geographically distributed as to arouse suspicion. One of the most remarkable and least improbable of these legends ascribes to St. Thomas, "the doubter," a mission to India, where he is revered as founder of the large Mar Thoma churches which still flourish, and where he is supposed to have suffered martyrdom near Madras. The Apostle James, by the testimony of the New Testament, is known to have been put to death in Jerusalem about A.D. 44 in a local persecution under Herod Agrippa I.* The name of St. John, "the beloved," is linked by hazardous tradition with Ephesus, where it is possible that he wrote that Fourth Gospel which some scholars do, and more scholars do not, ascribe to his authorship. There is a legendary picture of him as a very old man, nearly if not quite a centenarian, being carried on a litter through the Ephesian church, murmuring his blessing over the kneeling congregation: "Little children, love one another." The closing verses of the Fourth Gospel, by whomever written, certainly indicate that St. John lived to a great age.

As for what happened to the other apostles, we have nothing to go on but conjecture. And the materials for intelligent conjecture do not exist. It may be noted that even according to the most con-

---

* The martyred Apostle James is not to be confused with James "the brother of the Lord" (Gal. 1:19; 2:9 and Acts 21:18) who later held the leadership of the Jerusalem church and suffered martyrdom just before the remnants of that church fled from Jerusalem in the face of Titus's approach. After the fall of Jerusalem, what was left of the Jerusalem congregation established headquarters east of the Jordan and chose Simeon, another relative of Jesus, as its head. This suggests that the Palestinian tradition, had it prevailed, might have fastened on Christianity a system of hereditary rule like that of the later Islamic caliphate.

servative opinion only three of the twelve apostles had any part in writing the books of the New Testament and that these wrote only about one-third of its total contents. Most modern scholars would reduce the direct contribution of the Twelve to a very much lower figure, in fact, almost to the vanishing point.

SAUL OF TARSUS

There is another figure, however, who stands right alongside St. Peter in the story of the first Christian century—the Apostolic Age. This is St. Paul, the man who has been credited, though with some scholarly dissent, with having written a great part of the New Testament. In his brilliant study of early Christianity, the recently retired Bishop of London, Dr. J. W. C. Wand, has explained its rapid expansion from a Jewish sect into a world religion by the fact that "the Christian society was born at the place where two worlds met, the East and the West, the Semitic and the Graeco-Roman, the Jew and the Gentile." This meeting and mingling of cultures was very nearly incarnated in the Apostle Paul.

Paul was not an apostle in the sense of being one of the Twelve. The probability is that he never saw Jesus during his earthly career; if he had seen him, it is unlikely that his epistles would have failed to say so. It is possible, though not probable, that Paul did not reach Jerusalem until after the crucifixion.

Born in the Cilician city of Tarsus, a Pharisaic Jew of the Dispersion, acquainted with the Greek Stoic teaching which was popular in his native city, Saul, as he was known before his conversion, possessed the immense advantage of birthright Roman citizenship when he went to Jerusalem to complete his rabbinical education under the famous Rabbi Gamaliel. One lesson, however, he seems never to have learned from his mentor—tolerance. In Acts 5:38, 39 it is recalled how calm Gamaliel remained in the face of the rising Christian challenge which so excited other rabbis. Young Saul became as wrought-up as any of the Pharisees over what he construed as an attempt to undermine the teaching and authority of the old Hebrew law. Soon he was going all out to suppress the new teaching, even taking part in the stoning of Stephen, the first Christian martyr.

Then suddenly, probably about the year 35, as Saul was riding to Damascus with a commission to destroy a company of Christians that had sprung up there, he underwent the shattering experience so vividly described in Acts and in the apostle's own letters. From there, having adopted the name of Paul (meaning "little" or "the little one," though there is no New Testament evidence of any overwhelming modesty on his part), he went on to become the great missionary to the Gentiles. In doing this, as we shall see, he had to maintain against strong elements in the Jerusalem church and many Jewish Christians outside Palestine his right to be accepted as an apostle. This he did on the ground that he had received his commission to preach to the Gentiles directly from Christ, and it is interesting to discover, in I Corinthians 15:8, that Paul claimed to have seen the risen Lord several years after the crucifixion as truly as had Peter and the others who were in Jerusalem at the time of the resurrection. Nor does this passage suggest any difference in the nature of these appearances of the postcrucifixion Christ.

Paul was the great, though by no means the only, missionary of that first century. His indefatigable journeyings can be traced largely, though not completely, in the Acts of the Apostles, with a little additional information from his own Epistles. He went from one major city in the Roman Empire to another until he had covered almost all of Asia Minor, Greece, and various Mediterranean islands. Early Christian testimony declares that he preached as far west as Spain. Finally, however, he was beheaded (as a Roman citizen he could not be crucified) in Rome, if tradition is dependable, at about the same time St. Peter was martyred. The church in Rome thus acquired the distinction of being the one church in the West to have had the advantage not only of receiving the teaching of two apostles, but also of being the venerated place of their martyrdoms.

In Peter and Paul the Christian religion can be seen beginning to develop along both the great avenues which give it permanent importance. It develops as an institution (the church) and as a teaching, a theology, a faith. The institution is named first because the theology came out of it, not the institution out of the theology. The New Testament—Gospels, Epistles, Apocalypse—is a product of the Christian community. None of it was written until there were Christian churches scattered over a great part of the Roman world. The New Testament, as we have it, is the recollection of Jesus as it persisted in the churches for a hundred years after his death, plus what were believed to be authentic writings by apostles and others. Several books crept into the New Testament because they were erroneously ascribed to apostles, and a few not claiming apostolic authorship were kept out that might perhaps profitably have been let in.

With Peter, the rudimentary original nature of the Christian institution and the Christian teaching stands out. The early chapters of Acts show Peter rushing about to set up emergency forms of organization in Jerusalem. These were improvisations, and some of them did not work out well—for example, the choice by lot of a twelfth apostle, Matthias, who promptly sank from the record without leaving a trace. Peter's teaching, as shown in the long report of his sermon on the first Pentecost and in I Peter (which he probably wrote; something which cannot be said for II Peter), was just as rudimentary. Jesus was the Messiah, sent by God, rejected by his nation but certified by his resurrection, who was soon to return to lift into a glorified and eternal state of bliss all who acknowledged him as Lord and were baptized in his name. The tremendous questions regarding the nature of Christ, his relation to God and to humanity, which were to rend later generations and still torment men's minds, seem scarcely to have occurred to Peter.

Paul was of a different stripe. He was no Galilean fisherman being carried to immortality by the intensity of his devotion to a Master with whom he had once lived on terms of personal intimacy. Paul was a sophisticated Roman citizen and product of Greek-Hebrew culture. When he reached Athens, he was quite able to preach the Christian gospel there in terms to challenge the minds of Greek intellectuals, though the truth he had to preach, of a God crucified for man's salvation, he admitted to be "foolishness" to Greek thinking.

Paul was a tireless founder of churches, and in these churches there sprang up all sorts of competing interpretations of what the Christian teaching was. So he wrote letter after letter to straighten out the thinking, and at times the behavior, in these churches. Such of these letters as survived are the real beginning of the attempt to formalize, rationalize, put down in logical argument the Christian faith. So much so that it has been charged that Paul, not Jesus, is the real author of what we know today as Christianity, that differences and divisions among Christians have resulted from obscuring the simple moral precepts of the Galilean with the sophisticated metaphysical speculations of this man from Tarsus.

There were more objections of that kind a few years ago than there are today. One reason is the discovery that, while the New Testament contains ample evidence of vigorous disagreements between Paul and Peter and James and others on questions of church order—on such a matter, for instance, as the necessity or otherwise of circumcision for Gentile converts—it gives not the slightest hint that any apostle ever took exception to Paul's *doctrinal* teaching. If one had, we can be confident that the apostle to the Gentiles would have said something about it. It would probably have been something drastic. The argument from silence can never be conclusive, but in this instance it is certainly to be taken into account.

But more to the point in laying at rest the charge that Paul substituted his own speculations for "the simple gospel" of Jesus is our increasing realization that what Jesus taught was by no means confined to simple moral precepts. To be sure, there were such precepts and a considerable admixture of "sweetness and light" in the teaching of Jesus. (This is assuming that we have the substance of that teaching in the first three "Synoptic" Gospels.) But along with the Beatitudes and the rest of the Sermon on the Mount, along with his assurance of God's fatherly love and care, must be set the predictions which Jesus uttered of impending catastrophe, of coming judgment and punishment, and only after these terrifying experiences, after an implacable separation of sheep from goats, would a new age come. "Simple gospel?" That is hardly what a careful reader finds in Matthew, Mark, and Luke. (The Fourth Gospel, John, is itself a theology thrown into biographical form.)

So when Paul, writing from twenty to thirty years after the crucifixion, tried to give the Gentile converts in his churches a satisfying interpretation of Christian teachings, naturally the first questions he had to answer were: Who *was* this Jesus Christ? By what authority did he make his tremendous declarations about the relation of God to the world and man, and about what was to be the ultimate outcome of that relationship? When Paul tried to answer those inescapable questions—inescapable if Christianity was to survive—the theology that was to take hard-and-fast form in the later creeds was born. When Paul wrote his letters to the new Christians in young churches, he was not reciting what they had been required to believe in order to become Christians; he was telling them what he thought they ought to believe in order to get the full value of the Christianity which they had already accepted.

III

Life in the Earliest Churches

How did it come about that Christianity spread so rapidly and so widely throughout the empire of the early Caesars? There is something almost magical about that expansion. In the year 33, a Galilean teacher with a handful of followers is put to death as a common malefactor in an out-of-the-way corner of Rome's sprawling dominions. Close your eyes then for the passage of three centuries, and when you open them a religion that worships this Galilean as its divine Lord has covered the Mediterranean world with its churches, has won converts by the thousands from every level of society, perhaps ten per cent of the total population, and has even brought the emperor to the point of placing its symbols in his imperial standards and to accepting baptism! What explanation for such a dramatic transformation makes sense?

To a considerable degree, as many writers have pointed out, the way had been opened for the swift permeation of the Graeco-Roman world by the waning vigor of its old faiths. The temples of the Roman and Greek gods were still open; the prescribed sacrifices were still offered in them. But there was a general feeling that what virtue the ancient forms of worship had once possessed was rapidly seeping out of them. Both Roman and Greek literature from the time of Cicero on is filled with mourning for the passing of the "good old days," and with exhortations to return to the virtues of the fathers, now largely vanished. This pervasive sense of unfulfilled spiritual desires encouraged the importation from Egypt and the East of a number of so-called "mystery religions."

By the time Peter and Paul started on their missionary labors, Rome was filled with these new fads in religion, existing alongside the official cult of the state gods and goddesses, commanding devotion from their initiates and exerting an alluring fascination on thousands. Such a great emperor, for example, as Hadrian (117-138), who spent little of his reign in Rome, eagerly sought initiation into whatever cults he encountered as he moved about his vast domain. This sense of the weakening hold of the old gods and of the need to find satisfaction in strange new rites was as deeply felt in the other cities of the empire as in Rome.

Indeed, the time had come when a moral decline in all the lands clustered around the Mediterranean showed the need for a new spiritual lift to higher levels of conduct. Not that the Graeco-Roman world was bereft of moral ideals. Far from it. Socrates, Plato, and the other great Greek philosophers had taught principles of conduct which remain an imperishable legacy. The Stoics held up standards that were loftier than the mine-run of human beings have ever lived up to anywhere or at any time. Nevertheless, the corruption which, as Lord Acton says, goes with power was working havoc in Roman society, while the outlying cities of the empire sometimes seemed to be vying with one another to win notoriety as centers of vice. As one reads today the history of the Caesars, or the comments of contemporary satirists on the society they observed about them, the smell of putrefaction rises from page after page. Read Juvenal and Martial and Suetonius's *Lives of the Twelve Caesars.*

Into this morally sick world Christianity came like a breath of fresh air. It had a theology of a God-man who opened a way of salvation that was more arresting than any of the myths of the older faiths. It had baptismal and eucharistic rites as conducive to the curiosity of outsiders as any rites of the mystery religions.

(Some of the wild rumors that gained general credence concerning these rites were to make bitter trouble for the Christians.) But primarily, it had an object lesson to show that pagan world in the form of communities in which people of all kinds—a few aristocrats, numbers of artisans and tradesmen and housewives, even numerous slaves—were living the sort of daily lives which their neighbors instinctively wished they were living. Edwyn Bevan writes:

> It can hardly be doubted that the attraction of Christianity from the very beginning was social. It was not as a disembodied truth uttered into the air that the Christian "Good News" laid hold of men; it was through the corporate life of the little Christian societies in the cities of the ancient world. The life and spirit of these societies was indeed what it was because amongst them the Christian Good News was believed, but it was the life and spirit which gave the Good News its power. Men coming into contact with such a group felt an atmosphere unlike anything else. Each little group was a center of attraction which drew men in from the surrounding world. In that way, probably, more than by the preaching of any few individuals, the church grew. (Edwyn Bevan, *Christianity*, Oxford University Press, 1932.)

Someone has said that Christianity is not taught so much as caught. That was certainly true in the world of the first Christian century, and it remains true.

THE CHRISTIAN COMMUNITIES

What was life like in those earliest Christian churches? Well, such evidence as we have indicates that they differed from one to another in details of organization and in their practices. But in the main they seem to have been little groups who came together out of a common acknowledgment of Jesus as Messiah and Lord, and were welded together by their sense of being different from and regarded with suspicion by their surrounding Jewish or Gentile communities. They had an initiatory rite, baptism. What symbolic meaning it had for the earliest Christians we cannot be sure, but one fact appears certain—baptism was supposed to be accompanied or followed by an experience known as "the gift of the Holy Spirit," which would give the one baptized an inner power to live up to the high standards of conduct that were required of all believers.

The formula of creedal affirmation for all who sought entrance into this company was, in the earliest days, very simple. The New Testament shows that all the candidate for baptism had to avow was his belief that "Jesus is Lord," and then go on from there. But the fellowship in the little groups, who sometimes called themselves "the Brethren" and sometimes "Followers of the Way," was very close. They met together daily. There was constant concern for the physical needs of all members; collecting and distributing for their poor was one of the principal activities within their groups. Groups in more fortunate circumstances took up collections for the relief of other groups, sometimes hundreds of miles away, who were having hard going. For a brief time at the start the Jerusalem group practiced a sort of voluntary social communism (Acts 2:44, 45).

Within these Christian groups, which gradually came to speak of themselves as *ecclesiai*, a Greek word we translate as "churches," the standards of personal morality were very high, though the level of actual practice was sometimes shockingly lower. The early Christians were, after all, recent converts from a corrupt pagan society. They had some bad habits to overcome, and that took time. There were even times, as when St. Paul counseled his converts to follow his example and remain unmarried in order to concentrate on their religious duties, when there was a tendency to regard celibacy as the highest form of moral life. Fortunately, that extravagance withered. But no sexual indulgence outside the marriage relation was countenanced, no loose living of any kind, while in all business and social dealings the most exacting standards were enjoined.

The fact that mattered most, however, was not that these early "Nazarenes," as their Jewish critics called them, taught these lofty precepts of conduct, but that, by and large, they actually lived up to them. St. Augustine later was to claim that Christianity's distinguishing virtue lay not in its possession of any moral precepts which were very different from or superior to the precepts of the Hebrew religion or of the greatest Greek philosophers, but that it gave innumerable ordinary men and women the ability to live out a code of conduct to which formerly only a few philosophers had attained.

One other thing distinguished these early Christian churches. This was their habit of meeting for a communal meal, at which bread and wine were shared. Exactly what symbolic meaning was at first attached to this act is a matter for debate. St. Paul speaks of the bread and wine as being the Body and Blood of the Lord, but how he meant those terms to be taken, or how those in his churches understood them, who can tell? There is no reason to doubt, however, that the apostolic tradition asserted that Jesus, at the Last Supper, made a similar reference to the bread he broke and the wine he poured out. It was natural, therefore, that from the earliest days the Christian groups should have gathered in these commemorative meals at which bread and wine formed the central elements, though it took more than a thousand years to develop fully the dogma of transubstantiation.

This common meal, in which only baptized believers participated, led to some of the most damaging slanders circulated against Christianity. The very fact that Christians tended to live by themselves and to celebrate their most sacred rites in private encouraged the rumormongers. Three charges in particular were made when Christians were brought before magistrates: atheism, incest, and cannibalism. The first grew out of their refusal to venerate any images or to cast incense on the altars dedicated to the emperor's genius. More will be said about that when we come to the persecutions. The second was downright libel, and easily proved so. But the cannibalism charge had this faint shadow of a factual basis— that the Christians were alleged to "eat their God" in their secret communal meals.

We have a reflection of the trouble this charge caused those early Christians in a famous letter which Pliny the Younger wrote Trajan about the year 113. Pliny had been sent out as governor of Bithynia and found himself called on to try Christians against whom these scandalous charges had been leveled. When he examined them, he found the accusations so baseless and the general conduct of the accused so blameless that he wrote to the emperor for instructions as to what to do. Far from indulging in licentious living or secret orgies, he told Trajan, this is what he had found out about them:

> . . . They declared that the sum of their guilt or error had amounted only to this, that on an appointed day they had been accustomed to meet before daybreak, and to recite a hymn antiphonally to Christ, as to God, and to bind themselves by an oath, not for the commission of any crime, but to abstain from theft, robbery, adultery and breach of faith, and not to deny a deposit when it was claimed. After the conclusion of this ceremony it was their custom to depart and meet again to take food; but it was ordinary and harmless food and they had ceased this practice after my edict in which, in accordance with your orders, I had forbidden secret societies. I thought it the more necessary, therefore, to find out what truth there was in this by applying torture to two maidservants, who were called deaconesses. But I found nothing but a depraved and extravagant superstition, and I therefore postponed my examination and had recourse to you for consultation.

Pliny seems to have been fairly certain that the Christians were guilty of something. He wasn't sure what it was. But at least he had found out that it was not cannibalism or immorality.

From such descriptions of life in the early Christian churches it must not be concluded that all was harmony within them. One of the "church fathers" wrote that these congregations made their deepest impression because their fellowship was so warm. "Behold," he quoted their pagan neighbors exclaiming, "how these Christians love one another!" There were times, however, when the internal disputes waxed hot.

DEBATES AND DISPUTES

One of the first of these concerned circumcision. The original Christian congregation in Jerusalem held that all the requirements of the Jewish law applied to its members. If Gentiles were to become Christians, then they must be circumcised—an act peculiarly abhorrent to Greeks—just as Gentile proselytes to Judaism had been required to undergo circumcision. St. Paul and others who were active in missionary work among Gentiles challenged this claim. Their argument was that Christ had brought an end to the period in which the old Mosaic law had to be observed in all its details. This was a new era, a "new dispensation."

This debate raged throughout the churches almost as long as the Jerusalem church retained its ascendancy. Where Jews as well as Gentiles became converts, the churches in Gentile cities were shaken by the same hot arguments. For a time St. Peter had trouble making up his mind which side he was on. Paul accused him face to face of wobbling. But at last he came down decisively on the side of those who held circumcision no longer a binding command. And James, "the Lord's brother," head of the Jerusalem church, finally, though apparently without much enthusiasm, accepted the same view.

Behind this internal struggle over circumcision was the more basic and important struggle over whether the new faith was to be just another reforming sect within Judaism or a universal religion. There is a widespread notion that the teaching of Jesus had answered that question, but this is not so. As a matter of fact, there are one or two statements attributed to Jesus that could have been used as arguments by those who regarded "the Way" as a cleansing and reviving movement to be kept within Judaism. It was Paul who insisted on Christianity's universalism, who declared that in the Christian fellowship there was "neither Greek nor Jew, barbarian, Scythian, bond nor free." And again Peter, after a period of hesitation, came decisively to the support of this position. The critical phase of this struggle was soon over. Paul dealt with the basic issue in his epistles to the Romans and to the Galatians, but does not mention it in writing to the Ephesians just a little later. After that the extreme "Judaizers" were cut off, or cut themselves off, from the main stream of Christianity and became the vanishing sect of the Ebionites.

Nor was it only over such fundamental decisions that disputes broke out in those earliest churches. There were differences of opinion over doctrine and over the ways in which church activities should be conducted. Sometimes congregations threatened to split over loyalty to various leaders. The first purpose of one of St. Paul's most famous epistles was to patch up the party quarrels that had rent the church at Corinth between the adherents of three teachers—Apollos, Peter, and Paul himself—and those who tried to bypass such disputes by saying that they belonged to none of these factions but that "I am of Christ." Human nature is a pretty constant quality, and those who deplore the divisions among Christians today should at least remember that there have been disagreements within the Christian community from the beginning, and also that the responsible leaders strongly rebuked all the partisans, including their own.

Yet with all the internal quarrels, throughout that first century the feeling grew among Christians that they were not simply another Jewish sect, but that their local groups of believers, or *ecclesiai*, together constituted something entirely new. Instead of coining a new word for this new thing, they used an old word and gave it a new meaning. They called it the *ecclesia, the* church. In the secular Greek of the time, this word meant a public meeting of any kind or a gathering of citizens. In the Greek translation of the Old Testament (the Septuagint) it was used to translate the Hebrew word *Qahal*, which meant an assembly of the people. The Christian *ecclesia* was not a mass meeting that went out of existence when the meeting adjourned; it was a continuing reality. It was not a "new Israel," but a new "people of God" taking that place after Israel had forfeited it, yet inheriting much from the Hebrew tradition. The Messiahship was a Jewish concept expressed in the prophetic expectation of a Messiah who would restore Israel. Christianity was a new religion founded on faith in Jesus as the Messiah who would redeem the world, or so much of it as would accept redemption through him. As the preponderance of adherents swung to the congregations outside Palestine, pushing the Jewish members into a smaller and smaller minority, this feeling of non-Jewishness increased. After the Romans all but wiped Jerusalem off the map, the center of activity shifted finally to the great Gentile cities. For a long time Antioch, the Syrian metropolis, was the most vigorous of all the congregations, and the Book of Acts tells us that it was in Antioch the disciples of Jesus were first called Christians.

That name, first applied by their pagan neighbors, stuck. As the new religion spread, the name spread. By the time the Roman writer Suetonius came to write his life of the Emperor Claudius, he explained the edict that banished Jews from Rome in A.D. 52 on the ground that they were a constant source of turmoil in the city, "continually making disturbances at the instigation of Chrestus." (Like many a modern newspaper reporter, he didn't quite spell the name correctly.) In his life of Nero, Suetonius called the adherents of this "novel and mischievous superstition" Christians. At the end of that first century, both within and without the young churches, the name was in general use.

THE NEW TESTAMENT

One more important development had begun before that first Christian century ended. The Christians had produced most of the writings that were later to be collected to form the New Testament. At the start, the Bible used in the Christian groups was the Bible of Judaism, the Old Testament. Christian teachers read it and interpreted it as prophecy that had been fulfilled by Christ. But along with the Hebrew Scriptures (in a Greek translation), those earliest congregations listened to letters from their most important leaders, in which practical advice for their own conduct mingled with recollections of things taught by Jesus. At the same time, as the number decreased of those who could testify by word of mouth to what they had heard Jesus say, there was a demand that these recollected sayings should be written down.

We need not here go into the long story of how all these oral recollections, later written memoranda, letters to churches, and letters to individuals shook down into the New Testament. Tradition asserts that, of the three Gospels that open the New Testament, the one attributed to Mark was written by John Mark, Peter's nephew and secretary, to keep in permanent form Peter's memories; that the one attributed to Matthew was the collection of sayings and biographical material that grew up in the church at Antioch, possibly influenced by the apostle whose name it bears;

and that the Gospel According to Luke, Paul's companion, was compiled originally by that gifted physician-writer for the guidance of the congregations in Greece. Much later—probably not before the end of the century and possibly as much as two or three decades later—a Fourth Gospel emerged, tradition says in Ephesus, which cast the recollections of Jesus' contemporaries into a wholly different framework. (Some interpreters of the Dead Sea scrolls have found grounds for a conjecture that the Fourth Gospel may have been the first in order of writing.) This Gospel was a sort of dramatic argument to prove not only that Jesus was the Christ, the Messiah for whom Judaism looked, but that he was the Logos, the Divine Word of Greek philosophy, the pre-existent Source of all creation and the Sustainer and Sacrificial Redeemer of all created beings.

Scholars have argued for centuries about this Fourth Gospel—who wrote it, to what extent the words it puts in the mouth of Jesus were actually spoken by him, and, more importantly, to what extent the ideas it ascribes to him of his own nature and attributes were actually his. That argument still rages and, like many others concerned with the early churches, it is safe to predict that it will never be settled. Any reader of the New Testament, however, can see with his own eyes that the portrait of Jesus in the first three Gospels differs fundamentally from that in the Fourth; one who approached the four books without prior acquaintance would find it difficult to believe that the writer of the Fourth Gospel and the writers of the first three were talking about the same man.

Slowly, these collections of Christian writings came to be regarded in the early churches as having equal standing as Holy Scripture with the books of the Old Testament. Thus, what is called a "canon" of the Bible, Old and New Testaments, grew. This was not an easy or simple task. There were dozens of "Gospels," "Acts," "Epistles," and "Apocalypses" having some sort of claim to inclusion, and it was long before all the books now included were unanimously accepted. The gradual fixation of the canon came about by the usage of the churches, not by the act of any council or central authority. By the middle of the second century it was generally agreed that some Christian writings were more authoritative than others and that there could be a collection of these which would constitute a canon of Christian Scriptures. By the end of the second century there was general agreement on most of the contents of such a canon. The test was reputed authorship by an apostle or by a companion of an apostle so as to preserve the apostolic teaching. Marginal differences remained until late in the fourth century.

Scholars are predominantly of the opinion that the churches of that formative period were not infallible in determining apostolic authorship. The Epistle to the Hebrews, for example, was included (fortunately) on the ground that it was written by Paul, but nothing is now more certain in the field of Biblical scholarship than that Paul did not write it. It is highly improbable that II Peter, II and III John, and Revelation were written by apostles. But when one compares the books that were accepted into the canon with the scores of competing writings that did not make it, the level of spiritual perception among those early Christians is seen to have been remarkably high.

Much later a difference of opinion arose in regard to the limits of the Old Testament canon. If the Protestant layman will examine the "pulpit Bible" on the lectern in almost any church, he will probably find between Malachi and Matthew several books that are not in the Bible he has at home. These are labeled "Apocrypha." In Roman Catholic Bibles this material is not thus set apart, but is treated as an integral part of the Bible. These books were not written in Hebrew but in Greek, and were not in the Hebrew canon. St. Jerome included them in his great Latin translation, the Vulgate, and until the sixteenth century they were regarded by all Christians as having equal rank with all other parts of the Old Testament. Modern Protestant scholars have a growing appreciation of their literary and religious value. It is some comfort to reflect that, while these differences exist in regard to the Old Testament, there is no doubt whatever as to what books constitute the New Testament.

IV

The Blood of the Martyrs

For two hundred and fifty years after the martyrdoms of Peter and Paul, Christianity spread steadily over the Mediterranean world, its expansion not much affected by periods of official repression which sometimes blew up into vigorous persecutions. This was the period during which the church enrolled some of the most illustrious names on its roster of martyrs. But there is a widespread misconception about the number of these martyrs, as well as about the extent of the persecutions. During those first three centuries before Christianity became the established religion of the empire, not all Christians were thrown to the lions. Neither did every Christian go to bed every night fearful lest, before morning, there would come that dreadful knocking on the door and he would be hustled off to stand trial before the magistrate. It was not like that at all. On the contrary, most of the time most Christians lived in security, and the churches went on gathering their converts without interference. Persecution was the abnormal, not the normal, thing.

This is not to deny that there were persecutions, nor to minimize the trials of the martyrs. But official attempts to curb the

Christians, as well as mob outbreaks against them, were largely local affairs, touched off by some local incident—at times nothing more than the attempt of an unpopular Roman governor to work off the anger of the populace on a convenient scapegoat—and they seldom lasted long. Nero's famous persecution in 64 was of that sort. Even Tacitus, the Roman historian, was fairly certain that the Christians, who suffered so horribly then for a short period, had nothing to do with the burning of Rome, but were the victims of the emperor's need to turn suspicion from himself.

There was another period of persecution by Domitian just before the end of the first century, which is reflected in the bitter accusations and dire threats against "Babylon" (Rome) in the closing book of the New Testament, the Revelation of John, written at that time. The virtuous Stoic Emperor Marcus Aurelius (161-180) was a conscientious persecutor. Polycarp and Justin Martyr were his most famous victims. But we have no proof that any effective general law of the empire was enacted against the Christians before the opening of the third century, when Emperor Septimius Severus made it a crime to baptize a new convert. There were several more brief and scattered persecutions during the even briefer reigns which cluttered up the record of that anarchic century, the fiercest and most general being that under Decius. But the all-out, merciless effort to stamp out Christianity in every part of the empire was not to come until the opening of the fourth century, and we have not yet reached that point in the story.

EMPEROR WORSHIP

Such persecution of Christians as there was in the first three centuries resulted in most instances from difficulties over emperor worship. As has been said, the grip of the old Roman gods was slackening throughout the period of the empire. The Romans were normally tolerant in regard to religion, chiefly through indifference. But from Augustus on there rose a cult of homage to the emperor proclaimed a god. Temples were built in all the principal cities of the empire to this living divinity, and in these stood the altars on which the loyal citizen was required to sprinkle incense to the emperor's Genius. To the Roman authorities, this was more an act of patriotism than of religion. Or perhaps it should be called a religious act performed as a proof of patriotism. Something much like it was required in the Japanese Empire before World War II, when the divinity of the Japanese imperial house was the fundamental tenet of State Shinto. It made almost as much trouble for Christians in Japan and Korea as did the demands of emperor worship for the Christians in the Roman Empire.

On the whole, Roman policy was remarkably tolerant in dealing with the religions encountered as the legions overran that world around the Mediterranean. If the national religions of the conquered countries would add homage to the emperor to their other rites, Rome almost never interfered. On the contrary, it was more likely to find a place for the foreign religion in the swarm of new deities whose cults were brought to Rome. And in one notable instance, Rome even dropped the requirement of emperor worship. The Jews, with their fanatical loyalty to their One True God, and their readiness to turn their land into a blood-soaked waste before they would acknowledge any other deity, were exempted.

If Rome was willing to make an exception in the case of the Jews, why was it not willing likewise to exempt Christians from spilling incense on the altars of the divine emperors? At the start, the Roman authorities not unnaturally regarded the Christians as just one more sect of Jews, and this may help to explain why general persecution was so slow in starting. The Christians, however, raised the problem of toleration in a form more exasperating, from the Roman viewpoint, than the Jews ever had. The Jews, after all, were a sort of closed corporation, a people set apart from others by the mark of circumcision, who lived and worshiped largely by themselves, and did no active proselyting. The Christians, on the other hand, were ceaseless proselyters. They were avowedly out to make Christians of the entire population of the empire, and the rapidity of their spread showed that this was no idle dream. Not only did they, like the Jews, refuse to worship the emperor as a living god, but they were doing their utmost to induce every subject of the emperor to join them in that same refusal.

The problem for the empire, in other words, was more political than religious. While sacrifice to the Genius of the emperor remained the test of patriotism, could the state authorities afford to wink at the contumacy of these unpatriotic Christians? The trouble in which the Christians consequently found themselves was not wholly unlike the trouble in which, during the war years, that aggressive sect known as Jehovah's Witnesses found itself in the United States over the matter of saluting the national flag.

Logically, the Roman state of the Caesars should have cracked down everywhere and at all times on the Christians. It did nothing of the sort. The Roman proconsuls and local magistrates were not looking for trouble; when their jurisdictions were peaceful they were glad to leave well enough alone. At the same time, the Christians went out of their way to try to prove that they were good citizens. They lived quiet, moral, indeed model lives. The epistles read in their meetings, written by Paul and other leaders, admonished them to render proper obedience to those in civil authority. If they would not pray *to* the emperor by scattering incense on his altars, they never failed to pray *for* him in their meetings. In every respect except that single matter of incense-burning they were exemplary citizens.

Moreover, some of them were influential citizens. As early as when St. Paul was writing his letters, he included salutations to the church at Rome from "Erastus the chamberlain of the city," and to the church at Philippi from "the saints . . . that are of Caesar's household." A Roman consul, so close a relative of the emperor that his sons were named to the imperial succession, was among the converts before the first century ended. By the reign of Diocletian, when the Great Persecution was ordered, the wife and daughter of the emperor were rumored to be catechumens. Certainly by that time the imperial household and the Roman military and administrative service were honeycombed with Christians.

Face to face with an actual situation of this sort, logic usually gave way to caution in Rome's dealing with this new faith. The

Christians were openly recalcitrant when it came to participating in this one prescribed loyalty test. For this reason they were always, legally considered, in contempt of Caesar and therefore liable to punishment. But by the middle of the second century no official who considered persecuting them could be sure how close to his own household the purge might come. So Rome, on the whole, moved cautiously. "This curious vacillation on the part of the Roman government," writes Edwyn Bevan, "striking now and again with atrocious violence, and then for long periods letting the Christian community grow unchecked, suggests that the government was really puzzled what line to follow, when confronted with the new and mysterious phenomenon."

Nevertheless, there were martyrs, and their blood, as the familiar saying put it, was the seed of the church. When persecution came, not all Christians proved courageous enough to stand up against it. One problem that agitated those early churches was what to do about the apostates who, having sprinkled incense on the altars of the emperors when their lives were at stake, after the persecution died down repented of their weakness and asked to be taken back into the Christian fellowship. Yet there were enough who sealed their faith with martyrdom to make a deep impression on pagan observers. During some of the later persecutions there even came periods when a sort of psychological mass mania for martyrdom swept through some of the churches, and Christian leaders felt constrained to expostulate against the idea that there was merit in going out of one's way to provoke magisterial action.

There has been some disparagement of the courage of those early martyrs on the ground that, since they were expecting the end of all things to come with the return of Christ at any moment, it made little difference to them whether they lived much longer. St. Paul, who was himself to be one of the earliest martyrs, told the Philippian Christians that he was in a dilemma between wanting to die and "be with Christ, which is far better," and to live and carry on his work as a missionary. On the whole, he had concluded that it was better to go on living, but he acknowledged the urge to welcome death.

It is ridiculous, however, to try to discount those early Christian martyrdoms on such grounds. Life was sweet to those Christians, just as it is to us. Deliberately to choose death, when a simple gesture could insure life, required a courage, a constancy, and a faith that went down to the very roots of their being. This those Christian martyrs had. And as we read their stories, it is not hard to understand what the effect must have been on a world that no longer believed in much of anything or that no longer was committed to any convictions worth dying for.

EARLY MARTYRS

The heroism of some of those martyrs, who left a testimony which has survived, can reach across the centuries to move us even at this far distance. Such a man, for example, was Ignatius, the bishop of Antioch at about the turn of the first century. When he was being taken to Rome, where death awaited, he forbade the churches to attempt to have his sentence lifted in these memorable words: "I write to all the churches and charge them all to know that I die willingly for God, if you hinder not. I entreat you, do not unseasonably befriend me. Suffer me to belong to the wild beasts, through whom I may attain to God. I am God's grain, and I am ground by the teeth of the wild beasts, that I may be found pure bread."

Then there was Polycarp, whose story has been left us in a letter written by his church to other churches after his death. Polycarp had been a disciple of the apostle John. He was a close friend of Ignatius. When a local persecution finally sought his life he was bishop at Smyrna. For a few days his church tried to hide the aged bishop, but he was finally tracked down and brought before the Roman proconsul in an amphitheater crowded with a blood-lusting mob shouting for his life. Who even today can read unmoved the account of this old man's death as his fellow Christians told it in *The Martyrdom of Polycarp?*

> And the Proconsul tried to persuade him, saying, "Have respect to thine age," and so forth, according to their customary form; "Swear by the genius of Caesar," "Repent," "Say, 'Away with the atheists!' " Then Polycarp looked with a severe coun-

tenance on the mob of lawless heathen in the stadium, and he waved his hand at them, and looking up to heaven he groaned and said, "Away with the atheists." But the Proconsul urged him and said, "Swear, and I will release thee; curse the Christ." And Polycarp said, "Eighty and six years have I served him, and he has done me no wrong; how then can I blaspheme my King who saved me?"

The Proconsul threatened death under the fangs of wild beasts; the mob kept shouting for the lions. Finally, as Polycarp had predicted, he was condemned to be burned at the stake.

And now things happened with such speed, in less time than it takes to tell; for the mob straightway brought together timber and faggots from the workshops and baths, the Jews giving themselves zealously to the work, as they were like to do. . . . They were about to nail him to the stake, when he said, "Let me be as I am. He that granted me to endure the fire will grant me also to remain at the pyre unmoved, without being secured by nails."

When he had ended his prayer the firemen lighted the fire. And a great flame flashed forth: and we, to whom it was given to see, beheld a marvel. . . . The fire took the shape of a vault, like a ship's sail bellying in the wind, and it made a wall around the martyr's body; and there was the body in the midst, like a loaf being baked or like gold and silver being tried in the furnace.

"The blood of the martyrs was the seed of the church."

V

The Creeds

During the three hundred years of which we have been speaking—
roughly from the Crucifixion to the council of Christian bishops
at Nicaea in 325—whether Christians were enjoying a respite from
state interference or were being forced underground, there gradually emerged a formulation of Christian teachings (though never
complete agreement) and of the ways in which congregations
should be governed. Legions of scholars have disputed for centuries, and are still disputing over this problem of congregational
government. How "primitive" was the organization of congregations with ordained pastors (elders, presbyters, priests) under the
rule of apostolically consecrated bishops? When did the informal
gatherings described by such an early church father as Justin
Martyr (*c.* 100-165) become the strictly prescribed sacramental
and liturgical services that have come down to our time?

Justin, in his description of Christian worship about the middle
of the second century, wrote:

> On the day that is called the day of the sun, there is an
> assembly of all who live in the towns or in the country; and the
> memoirs of the Apostles or the writings of the prophets are

read, as long as time permits. Then the reader ceases, and the president speaks, admonishing us and exhorting us to imitate these excellent examples. Then we arise all together and offer prayers; and, as we said before, when we have concluded our prayers, bread is brought, and wine and water, and the president in like manner offers up prayers and thanksgivings with all his might; and the people assent with Amen; and there is the distribution and partaking by all of the Eucharistic elements; and to them that are not present they are sent by the hand of the deacons. And they that are prosperous and wish to do so give what they will, each after his choice. What is collected is deposited with the president, who gives aid to the orphans and widows and such as are in want by reason of sickness or other cause; and to those that are in prison, and to strangers from abroad; in fact to all that are in need he is a protector.

How and when did the Christian churches pass from such simplicity as this to the elaborate, fixed liturgies and the sharply distinguished orders of church officials that we find in the third century and later? These are questions for which the Roman Catholic, the Greek Orthodox, and the other Christian churches have their own answers. Accord is never likely, because the evidence is so sparse and so capable of many interpretations. A Roman Catholic historian, Philip Hughes, writes that "the sources from which the historian must reconstruct the story of the primitive church are, from the point of view of his task, far from ideal. . . . Nowhere, save in the Acts of the Apostles, is there, for nearly three hundred years, anything that can be called a contemporary historical record."

As someone has said, the history of Christianity between the time when the first Christian congregation fled from Jerusalem, just before Titus captured that city in 70, and a century later is like a plunge into a tunnel. We know it came out at this end with a fully articulated institution—churches, the equivalent of dioceses, bishops, minor clergy, sacraments, feasts, and all the rest—together with a proliferating and subtle theology. But we really do not *know* a great deal about what went on in the tunnel. Not as much as it is sometimes claimed we know.

CHRIST AS GOD

Our best source as to what Christian teaching had become by the close of the second century is Irenaeus, whose *Adversus Haereses (Against the Heretics)* has been preserved complete in a Latin translation and in large fragments of the original Greek. In a way, Irenaeus summed up in his career the world-embracing character of early Christianity, for he was a Greek, born somewhere in Asia Minor. He studied under Polycarp at Smyrna, then moved on to Rome, and finally wound up as bishop in Lyons, a distant post in Gaul, where he complained that his ministry in Celtic had ruined his Greek. He wrote to confute the ideas of various schools of Gnostics, who, as their name implies (the Greek word *gnosis* means "knowledge"), claimed to possess a secret, superior knowledge, passed on by some of the apostles to selected initiates, concerning the relation of God to the universe and this world, the nature of Christ, and the means by which Christ saved those who believed in him.

The purity of Irenaeus's Greek may have suffered from his sojourn in Gaul, but he was still capable of giving his contemporaries this explanation of the mystery of the Incarnation, and the salvation made available to man through the church's provision of the sacraments: "By His own blood the Lord redeemed us; and gave His soul for our souls, and His flesh for our flesh, and poured out the Spirit of the Father upon the union and communion of God and man, bringing down God to man by the Spirit, and raising up man to God by the Incarnation, and bestowing on us incorruptibility in a real and true sense at his advent, through communion with himself."

In such a declaration as this we find one of the hundreds of attempts that were being made throughout this period to answer the questions the pagan world persisted in asking of Christian missionaries who penetrated it. The Greek mind, in particular, could not rest without trying to fathom the metaphysical enigmas it found in Christian claims respecting Christ. During the apostolic age Jesus had been worshiped as Lord and Master, a Saviour who bore a relation to God unique among mortals. But Professor John Knox, of Union Theological Seminary, whose standing as an authority is certified by the fact that he was chosen to edit the technical sections on the New Testament in the monumental *Interpreter's Bible*, says that "there is no convincing evidence that [Jesus] was called 'God' in the First Century, and indisputable evidence that he was not generally called by that name." When that ascription *did* become common, the questions became inescapable.

If Christ was God, how could he be man? Was he actually man or had the Figure who "suffered under Pontius Pilate" been some sort of wraithlike simulation of a man? What had been the relation of this Christ who had "dwelt among us" to the Creator-God before time was and in the work of creation? If he was the "Son of God," did this mean that he was not on an equality of dignity with God the Father, or that he differed in some manner from the Almighty Ruler of the universe worshiped by monotheists? Were Christians in truth monotheists, or did they worship two gods?

To discover how Christian thinkers of that time tried to solve such enigmas the reader can go to any of the almost innumerable books on the teachings of the early church fathers. They will be found in any good library. To those interested in a brief translation of the principal ideas of those church fathers in their own words, *Documents of the Christian Church*, selected and edited by Henry Bettenson (Oxford University Press, 1943) can be recommended. In the quotations used in this book, Mr. Bettenson's translations have been followed.

Whatever a modern man may think of the results at which these early theologians arrived in their efforts to "expose the inexpressible," he is likely to carry away admiration for their intellectual capacities. Their world is not ours; the scientific ideas and the philosophical conceptions they took over from the Greeks— such, for example, as their concern with the "substance" of a personality—are so foreign to our thinking that they border on the incomprehensible. But no time, including our own, has produced keener minds than that of Tertullian, the hotheaded Carthage lawyer turned theologian, whose puritanical ideals and blasting attacks on what he considered heresy have earned him the title of "the Thomas Carlyle of early Christian literature"; or of Clement of Alexandria, the great bishop-teacher who combined his love for Platonic philosophy with his Christian theological speculation; or of Clement's more famous pupil, Origen.

EARLY HERESIES: ORIGEN AND GNOSTICISM

Origen is peculiarly attractive today because of the freedom and daring with which his mind explored in all directions. He was "orthodox" as against the Gnostics in his teaching about the nature of Christ, but he was strikingly unorthodox in his beliefs in reincarnation and in universalism. There could be, he said, no eternal damnation by a beneficent God, but all beings, including the devils and Satan, would ultimately return to the equality of bliss in heaven in which they had originally existed. Along with this, he showed a modesty in putting forward his own opinions and an irenic spirit toward those who rejected them which stands in sharp contrast with the acidity of most theological debate, both then and later. The wrath of the bishop of Alexandria forced him to leave his native city during the later years of his life. He took refuge in Palestine, where the persecution of 250 caught him. Torture failed to daunt his heroic spirit, but it broke his body and he died soon after.

Origen's was the most creative and prolific theological mind produced by the church between the time of St. Paul and that of St. Augustine. He is said to have written 6,000 books of theology and Biblical exposition. This claim probably reflects the free-and-easy statistics of those days, although that indefatigable student of the next century, St. Jerome, is credited with saying that no man could in one lifetime read through all Origen's writings. In any case, there can be no denial that he left his mark for centuries on church teaching. In the Eastern churches it is still deeply felt. Yet it is of interest to note that not one of these three influential Christian teachers—Tertullian, Clement, and Origen—pure as were their lives, has been remembered by the church with the accolade

"Saint." All three illustrate the large degree to which, up to the fourth century, Christian teachers were still disagreeing with one another and diverging in what they were teaching. It was an era of relatively free thought. Doctrinal regimentation had not yet been achieved, nor had the necessary apparatus for enforcing uniformity been created.

It was only slowly that an "orthodox" body of Christian belief won general acceptance. The church fathers of the second and third centuries produced many variations in the Christian explanation as to how Jesus of Nazareth became Christ the Son, how the Son was related to God the Father, and later how the Holy Spirit was part of a trinitarian deity and related to its two other Persons. Out of these variations came the "heresies" which flourished so profusely. Gnosticism, Montanism, Sabellianism, Manicheism, Donatism, Arianism, Pelagianism, Nestorianism—today these are not much more than entries in an encyclopedia, where the inquiring reader can look them up, though some of their ideas persist in various forms and there are Arian and Nestorian churches still in existence. In the third and fourth centuries, however, these were views for which men risked exile and death. In some instances, it was only by the narrowest of margins, after church councils had voted first on one side and then the other, that these views were branded as heretical and the trinitarian view prevailed.

If one were to single out any of these heresies for passing attention, it should be Gnosticism. Gnosticism had a historic importance not so much because of what it taught (there were many schools of Gnostics and they taught so many differing ideas that it is impossible to put a finger on one set of beliefs and say, "This was Gnosticism") as because of what it produced. In general, it can be said that Gnosticism held a dualistic world view, with God set wholly apart from this evil world, which he approaches only through created intermediaries, of whom Christ was foremost, in conflict with the powers of evil which rule the world. For most Gnostics, Christ was a spiritual manifestation, not in any real sense a human being who experienced the tragedy of crucifixion or the glory of resurrection. And this superior Gnostic knowledge, which was only for a small group of the enlightened, who could grasp it, had been passed on secretly by the inner circle of the original apostles.

All this sounds fantastic; the nearest approach we have to anything like it in these days is what is loosely called theosophy. It would be a waste of time for the reader to try to straighten it all out in his mind into a logical theological-philosophical system. But it deserves to be remembered because this weird mixture of ideas, spreading among the churches for about fifty years in the middle of the second century, drove them to a more rigid, carefully defined statement of the Christian faith than had been felt necessary before. If the blood of the martyrs was the seed of the church, then the speculations of the heretics were the seedbeds of the church's creeds.

In the beginning, as has been said, all that was required of a convert seeking to enter church membership was the affirmation "Jesus is Lord." But that obviously would not cover the issues that the Gnostics, with their claims of a special knowledge passed on from the apostles, had raised. So, little by little, there came into being statements of the essentials of Christian belief which the principal churches held to be what the apostles had *really* taught, and what were therefore to be accepted by candidates for baptism as the true Christian faith. These were the creeds.

THE BEGINNING OF THE CREEDS

There were many creeds, and scholars can trace the flowing lines of battle within the churches of that time by their variations. We are not interested in tracing these changes of wording. But one who is called on, when attending a Christian service today, to join with the congregation in repeating what is known as the Apostles' Creed may catch some sense of the continuity of Christian history by knowing that as early as 175 this affirmation of faith was in use in the church at Rome:

> I believe in God the Father Almighty; and in Christ Jesus, His only begotten Son, our Lord, who was born of the Holy Spirit and the Virgin Mary, crucified under Pontius Pilate and buried; the third day He rose from the dead, ascended into the

heavens, being seated at the right hand of the Father, whence He shall come to judge the living and the dead; and in the Holy Spirit, holy church, forgiveness of sins, resurrection of the flesh.*

This creed was designed as a rebuttal of the theory that Jesus had not been a real person who had real human experiences of life and death. But if this satisfied the church at Rome and was received with respect in other churches, especially in the West, it by no means satisfied the churches in North Africa and the East, which were locked in battle with the Gnostics and other variant teachings. It was, as any reader will immediately perceive, not much more than a recapitulation of certain events that the church affirmed either had occurred or would occur. It was silent on the very questions that most plagued the metaphysical Greek mind. (And which, it should be added, continue to make most trouble for Christian theology down to the present.)

Take the phrase "only begotten Son." What did it mean? In attempting to establish the divinity of Christ there had been in the early church a doctrine of his pre-existence and his agency in the work of creation from the beginning. This runs all through the epistles of St. Paul and the Fourth Gospel. Yet if Christ had been "begotten" by the Father, did this mean that there had been when he was not, and that therefore he could not be fully God in the sense that the uncreated Father Almighty was? If that sentence seems to lack two words—"a time" between the words "had been" and "he was not"—it must be explained that the omission is deliberate. The followers of Arius, of whom more later, were careful not to say that there had been a moment *in time* when Christ had not been in existence; their contention was that if he had been begotten then he must have had a beginning like any other created thing, though this act on the part of God the Father Almighty was not necessarily related to human conceptions of time. Augustine was to say later that God created time and the cosmos together, so that the begetting of the Son was in the eternity before time existed.

* This is the wording of an early form of the Apostles' Creed as given in *A History of the Christian Church*, Williston Walker, Scribner's, 1918.

While there was intense, often violent and sometimes disgracefully acrimonious, debate among churches, bishops, priests, and even some laymen over nearly every clause in the creeds, as one looks back across the centuries and tries to peer into the dust of that theological conflict it becomes clear that the key word was "begotten." How could the Christian faith have a single unified God, as the trinitarian formula declared, if the Second Person in the Trinity had been begotten of the First? And later this metaphysical puzzle was extended to the question as to how the Third Person in the Trinity, the Holy Spirit, could "proceed from" one or both of the other two, and still be on an equality with them in a monotheistic unity?

These struggles to define a creed that would be accepted by all the churches came to a head in Alexandria just as the fourth century was opening. Alexandria was a natural spot for this decisive battle, for it was by that time the outstanding literary and philosophical center of the Roman Empire. It was the place where Roman, Greek, and Jewish thought, all to some extent influenced by the thought of Persia and other parts of Asia, met Christian thought, sometimes to challenge it, sometimes to reinforce it, and always to influence it. The dogmatic controversy in Alexandria, which was to lead to the adoption of the other creed that ranks, along with the Apostles' Creed, as normative for most of Christendom, swirled around two local priests, Arius and Athanasius. But if we are to understand the way in which the tides of their theological conflict surged back and forth, and its outcome, we must first look at the revolutionary political developments that were then taking place in the Roman Empire.

VI

Constantine

The second and third centuries witnessed an accelerating decline of the Roman Empire. In the hundred years following the reign of Septimius Severus (198-211), thirty emperors claimed the throne, and there were others whose troops draped them in the imperial purple but who never won any larger following. The Roman Senate hardly pretended any longer to go through the motions of electing the Caesars, and kinship to a reigning emperor was of little importance in determining the succession. On the contrary, the sons or near relatives of one Caesar usually found themselves in jeopardy of speedy execution or assassination when the next emperor took over.

Chaos and anarchy spread throughout the empire, and when one Caesar had been killed—few of them died natural deaths—the next was chosen by acclamation of the troops. Sometimes the Praetorian Guards stationed in Rome made the choice; sometimes it came from the armies on the various frontiers. It should be remembered that by this time these "Roman" soldiers who had seized control of Rome's fate were almost without exception Germans, Gauls, Illyrians, Asians, and Africans. As the third century drew toward its close, most thoughtful Romans were in despair. They saw the empire on a swift slide into ruin and the civilization of which it had been the political expression about to be submerged in a barbarian sea.

That, of course, was what eventually happened. But it did not happen around the year 300. It did not happen in the West for another one hundred and seventy-five years. And in the East an empire which claimed to be "Roman" continued in existence almost until the day Columbus hauled up anchor to sail to the discovery of the New World. This sudden about-face in Rome's history, from chaos and encroaching dissolution to a new access of vigor and stability, was largely the product of one reign, that of Diocletian, who occupied the throne for the twenty years from 284 to 305.

DIOCLETIAN AND CHRISTIAN PERSECUTION

Diocletian has not enjoyed what is called a "good press" at the hands of history, largely because after his reign the writing of history, or what then passed for history, was the work of Christian priests, and Diocletian was the most savage of all persecutors of the church. But judged by the anarchy he inherited and by the revived empire he passed on to his successors when he abdicated, Diocletian deserves to be ranked as one of the greatest of Rome's emperors.

Diocletian was the son of Dalmatian slaves. He embarked on a military career which brought him to the command of the army before he was forty. Raised to the purple "by the election of generals and officers," he settled any possible competition for that office from Aper, prefect of the Praetorians, by leaping on him as he stood before the tribunal of the Senate and running him through. From that moment on, this rough-handed soldier proceeded to take the disintegrating empire as it were by the scruff of its neck and shake it into new life. He not only stopped the retreat in Germany and along the line of the Danube, but even reconquered most of distant Britain and Persia.

Diocletian was more than a victorious general. He was a constructive statesman who could plan in long-range terms for the empire's future and make bold innovations to secure efficient administration. His military experience convinced him that the empire had become too unwieldy, and was under too constant attack along its frontiers, to be successfully governed from one center. Accordingly, he divided the imperial power with three others, and established four imperial courts, none of them in Rome. His own court he placed in Nicomedia, in the northwest corner of Asia Minor, across the Hellespont from Europe. From there he could keep a close watch on the always-threatening monarchs and tribes along the eastern borders.

Diocletian's contrivance to protect the empire from the anarchy created by the constant assassination of emperors at the instigation of ambitious rivals, along with the frequent internecine conflicts between rival armies when the imperial throne had thus been vacated, bears witness to the subtlety of his thinking. At first glance, it might seem that to divide the imperial rule among four men—two "Augusti," each with his slightly subordinate "Caesar" —would have been the very way to insure a constant battle over which was top dog. But the shrewd old emperor believed that the ambitions of his most likely rival could be satisfied by sharing power with him as a second Augustus, while if the Augusti adopted the most promising (and ambitious) military leaders in the next generation as their "Caesars" with the promise of succession, they would no longer be tempted to promote their fortunes by killing the older rulers. But to insure that their ambitions should be realized within a reasonable length of time, Diocletian rounded out his scheme of government by providing that the Augusti should abdicate after twenty years of rule. It was a remarkable scheme, but it worked only as long as its originator's imperious will was in command to work it.

For reasons that are still a subject for debate among historians, Diocletian, two years before the end of his highly effective reign, joined with his fellow Augustus, Maximian, to order the most terrible of all persecutions of the Christians. Various emperors a generation earlier had placed restrictions on the churches, mainly depriving them of properties which they were beginning to accumulate on a large scale. For eighteen years Diocletian, although himself a convinced and practicing pagan, paid no attention to the growing Christian power. His court was full of Christian functionaries. Great Christian churches were built in the principal cities of the empire, the largest in his capital of Nicomedia. Christians were appointed governors of important provinces and excused from sacrificing to the emperor.

Then, suddenly, the old emperor ordered his army purged of Christians. After that, an imperial edict commanded that Christian churches should be destroyed, Christian worship prohibited, and Christian Scriptures confiscated and burned. The protection of the laws was withdrawn from Christians. Christian bishops were rounded up wholesale, imprisoned, tortured, and many put to death, while the whole power of the throne was turned loose to wipe out the rest of the Christian community in blood.

One of the legends that have come down from that time tells how, when the emperor's order for the destruction of Christian churches was attached to the palace gate in Nicomedia, a high-ranking officer tore it down, and was immediately executed. The martyred officer became St. George, the patron saint of England. If he ever fought a dragon, it must have been imperial Caesar.

In 305 Diocletian, in accordance with his long-announced intention, abdicated and forced his fellow Augustus, Maximian, to do likewise. What history recalls as the Diocletian persecution was still raging. In fact, the new Augustus in the East, Galerius, who was credited by Christian writers of that period with having been the real instigator of the slaughter, was more intent than ever on pushing ahead to complete extermination of Christianity.

But the pagans themselves were growing sickened with too much bloodshed. The other new Augustus, Constantius Chlorus, in far-off Britain, who had never pushed the persecution very hard in his prefecture of Gaul, suspended all proceedings against the Christians and began to show them many signs of favor. In 311, on his deathbed, Galerius realized that the attempt to do away with the upstart religion had failed. Thousands upon thousands of terrified Christians had, to be sure, recanted, but other thousands had stood fast, sealing their faith with their blood. So eager, in fact, did many Christians prove to suffer for their faith that Bishop Mensurius of Carthage demanded that those who needlessly sought martyrdom should not be revered as martyrs. The effect on public opinion throughout the empire had been tremendous. Even the throne could no longer take the risk of continuing the torturing, maiming, killing. So, in his last official act, Galerius, reluctantly, grudgingly, issued an edict of toleration, and the last and worst persecution of Christians by Rome was at an end.

Simultaneously, a struggle for the imperial power began between the Augusti and the Caesars which we need not trace here. The fact of monumental importance for Christianity was that in that struggle the ambitious son of Constantius Chlorus—proclaimed Augustus by his father's troops when the ruler of the West died suddenly while on a campaign in Britain—launched a drive for power that carried him in the brief space of four years from the outpost of York in England to control of Gaul, Spain, and Italy, made him the sole ruler of the empire in another thirteen years, and thrust him into history's limelight as Constantine the Great.

CONSTANTINE AND THE CHURCH

Christian writers of that time, who all but drowned the actual Constantine in the floods of their adulation, have preserved a number of stories about him which probably had little factual foundation. The best known is one that Eusebius, the first church historian to follow St. Luke, says he was told by Constantine himself. As he prepared for the decisive battle at the Milvian bridge outside Rome, which was to settle the control of Italy, the emperor swore that he saw in the night sky a lighted cross with the words *In hoc signo vinces* ("In this sign thou shalt conquer") and that Christ appeared to him in a vision. Mythical as that story may have been—both Eusebius and Constantine were facile myth-manufacturers—it is a fact of history that from then on Constantine's legions carried standards with the Greek letters chi rho, the first two letters in the Greek word for Christ, surmounting a cross. And it is equally a fact that from then on Constantine was known as the friend and protector of Christianity.

What sort of man was Constantine? There have been few characters over whom historians have reached more divergent verdicts. "All great men are bad men," wrote Lord Acton, the famed British historian, and the Constantine who emerges from the pages of such a book as *The Age of Constantine the Great*, by the great Swiss historian Jakob Burckhardt, fits that verdict exactly. Burckhardt sees Constantine as boundlessly ambitious, utterly unscrupulous, "essentially unreligious" but clever in his manipulation of both pagan and Christian religions, "who persecuted what was nearest him and slew first his son and nephew, then his wife, then a crowd of friends." But, insists Burckhardt, judged by what he accomplished, Constantine is rightfully called "the Great."

On the other hand, there have been historians from the time of Eusebius on who have seen Constantine as an incarnation of most of the virtues, approximating as nearly as any ruler can the perfection of a saint. In their efforts to defend the emperor who was the first imperial patron of Christianity, these champions have swung as far in the direction of romanticism as Burckhardt did in judging him by the standards of a time not his own. A middle-ground judgment would seem to be that Constantine was as ready as any other despot of his day to protect his throne by any means, including murder, if it seemed necessary, but that he also had a political sense which enabled him to take over a realm that seemed fated to go to pieces again within less than a generation after Diocletian and to weld it into an empire which was to last, at any rate in the East, for another thousand years. How many existing governments are a thousand years old? There is at least one yardstick by which to measure what Constantine accomplished.

As to Constantine's relation to the Christian church, the evidence is obscure and conflicting. He certainly started out as a friend of the Christians. Though some scholars today throw doubt on the assertion that he issued an "Edict of Milan" in 313 granting complete toleration to Christians along with legal rights equal to those of the old pagan faith, there is still predominating evidence that he did just that. It is beyond dispute that he showed Christians favors of many sorts. This was particularly so in his treatment of Christian clerics, who were relieved from army service and taxes to such an extent that the emperor had to put a stop to the stampede of wealthy citizens to obtain ordination.

All the property that had been taken away from the Christians in previous reigns was returned; all the churches that had been destroyed were rebuilt and towering new basilicas rose under imperial orders in many cities; the imperial court, first in Nicomedia and later when it was moved to Constantinople, the rechristened Byzantium, was running over with clerics either holding, or seeking, the ruler's ear. Eusebius claims that Constantine considered himself a sort of bishop, and we know that he did not hesitate to preach to the bishops even on obscure points of theology. (The bishops were properly impressed.) The emperor's letters were sprinkled with the sort of pious salutations one Christian dignitary would use in addressing another. He encouraged his mother to tour the Holy Land seeking the locations where great events in the life of Christ occurred, and gave her what she asked to build churches and shrines at the sacred spots which the local inhabitants obligingly identified for her. Nor does this exhaust the record of Constantine's interest in the Christian church or the list of favors he showered on it.

Nevertheless, he retained the old pagan title of Pontifex Maximus to the end of his reign. He assisted in the building or refurbishing of some pagan temples. Most significant fact of all, he was not baptized until the day he died. Then only, at the uttermost extremity, he allowed an Arian bishop to pour on his head the water that made him a member of the Christian church. The reason for the delay, doubtless, was the belief that baptism washes away all prior sins. It seemed wise therefore to postpone it until the hour of death when there would be neither time nor opportunity for any more sins. The church confirmed the belief but frowned on this use of it.

How is so contradictory a record to be evaluated? Is it not a fair verdict to say that Constantine, sharp as was his political instinct, saw at the very start of his rise to power the need for some strong cultural cement to hold together his sprawling, multicultured empire, and he believed he could find that binding element in Christianity? He was impressed not only by the moral superiority of Christianity over a dying paganism, but by its ability to weld its communicants into a vigorous, self-conscious community. Primarily, his interests were probably always political —that made him a great emperor. But with whatever motives, and whatever personal hesitations, he seized on Christianity to be the cultural, ethical, and emotional fountain of energy for the "new Rome" he sought to establish, and his choice was vindicated by history.

For Christianity, the reign of Constantine marked the transition from the days in which it lived perilously and amid derision to the days of its freedom from fear and the beginnings of its social prestige. To be sure, the legal process by which Christianity became the religion of the state and paganism a proscribed faith was not completed for nearly half a century after Constantine's death. But Constantine took the decisive steps that were to culminate in the edicts of Theodosius. It is with Constantine on the throne that the process summed up in a famous sentence by Gibbon reached its climax: "While that great body [the Roman Empire] was invaded by open violence, or undermined by slow decay, a pure and humble religion gently insinuated itself into the minds of men, grew up in silence and obscurity, derived new vigor from opposition, and finally erected the triumphant banner of the Cross on the ruins of the Capitol."

Great as was the change in the fortunes of the church with Constantine's tolerance and favor, a greater change was yet to come. During Constantine's reign many professed Christianity to gain worldly advantage, but no one was compelled to do so. Christianity was still, as it had been in the beginning, a voluntary religion. Constantine frowned upon those who would divide the church, because he wanted it to be a unifying force in his empire, but he did not make Christianity compulsory. The great divide in Christian history came near the end of the fourth century when the acceptance of Christianity became mandatory and when the church, having so lately escaped from its persecutors, became a persecuting church.

VII

Athanasius and After

If Constantine hoped to find in Christianity the religion that would bind his empire in a cultural unity, as has been suggested, by the time he was firmly established in power he must have begun to wonder whether he had been mistaken. Instead of bringing his subjects closer together in a common faith, the evidence seemed to indicate that this religion was another source of division, and that the cleavages it produced struck deeper and were less susceptible to healing than any that had plagued the empire in the past.

As the emperor at last eliminated all rivals and gathered all the reins of government in his own hands, reports came to him from all quarters of the bitterness with which Christians were disputing over theological issues, denouncing and excommunicating each other, and appealing to the civil authorities to employ the punitive powers of the state against their opponents in these church battles. The same Christians who, while Diocletian and Galerius ruled, had been the victims of terrible persecution, were demanding, now that the imperial favor was extended, that their fellow Christians who differed from them on points of doctrine be suppressed, banished,

52

or ejected from their churches by the power of the state. Constantine saw no choice but to intervene to stop this constant bickering, or worse, and to make his Christian subjects agree on what their Christian doctrines were. One may regret the consequences of that imperial intervention in the affairs of the church, but one can hardly wonder that the emperor, seeking stability and unity for his realm, should have resorted to it. Though his edict had declared that both Christians and pagans might freely practice their religions, he had no firm convictions about either religious or civil liberty.

ARIUS VERSUS ATHANASIUS

The most important of these disputes over Christian teaching, as was said at the close of Chapter V, centered in the city of Alexandria. Its central figures were two priests, Arius and Athanasius. And the issue at stake involved the Christian belief as to the nature of Christ. Was the Son, the Second Person in the Christian Trinity, of the *same* substance as God the Father? Or was he of *like* substance, but in some essential way different? Arius held the second view; Athanasius the first.

Many today look back on the war of words that swirled around those Alexandrian antagonists in the fourth century with a sort of incredulity, or sometimes with downright scorn. Since the matters in dispute dealt with questions of a metaphysical sort which the human mind can never compass, for which indeed it has no adequate vocabulary, it is not difficult to conclude that the whole argument was senseless. Mere men were claiming infallible certainty where in the very nature of things they could not know and could not speak with exactness. Edward Gibbon, the historian of *The Decline and Fall of the Roman Empire*, expressed this feeling. Two Greek words, *homoousios* and *homoiousios*, became the key terms in the controversy. The first, "of the same substance" or "of one substance," was the word accepted by Athanasius. Hosius, bishop of Cordova in Spain, is credited with coining it during the Council of Nicaea. The second, "of like substance" or "of similar substance," expressed the thought of Arius, though it was not invented until several years after his death. Until this controversy arose, the Greek language had no such words because there had been no occasion to express these two ideas and the contrast between them. It had *homos* meaning "the same," and *homoios* meaning "similar"; and it had *ousia* meaning "being" or "essential substance." Out of these, ingenious theologians now constructed the two adjectives that put the issue between them in a nutshell. Gibbon, in his memorable history, passed on a sneer that in this struggle, which lasted for centuries and cannot be said to be entirely ended even today, Christians fought each other over a diphthong.

Well, so it was—a diphthong. But that diphthong carried an immense meaning. To Arius, when Christians called Christ God, it was not meant that he was deity except in a sort of approximate sense. He was a kind of minor divine being, not the eternal and uncreated Creator. He was a created Being—the first created Being and the greatest, but nevertheless himself created. "The Son," wrote Arius in explaining his position to Eusebius, the bishop at the empire's capital of Nicomedia (not to be confused with Eusebius the historian), "the Son has a beginning, but . . . God is without beginning." Against that teaching Athanasius flung down his challenge. Taking his stand where Christian thought in the West had stood, in the main, for years, he asserted that God the Father and God the Son were *one*—two Persons but having an identical substance.

At the start it looked as though Arius would win this theological battle. He was a much older man, pastor of the influential Baucalis church in Alexandria (what we would call today a congregation made up of "the best people"). He was an eloquent preacher and, though the unfriendly accounts that have come down to us accuse him of vanity and self-opinionated pride, he seems to have been highly regarded in his home city for learning, ability, and good character. Moreover, he had a flair for what we call public relations. In the opening stages of the conflict, while it was confined to Alexandria, he put his ideas into jingles which, set to simple tunes like a radio commercial, were soon being sung by the dockworkers, the street-hawkers, and the school children of the city. Later, when the controversy had involved the churches in every part of the empire, it turned out that the Arians had influential political as well as ecclesiastical connections. Recall that it was an Arian bishop in the imperial palace who finally baptized Constantine. This too augured success.

Athanasius was a very young man when he entered the lists— not yet more than a deacon. He held his views with such intensity, feeling that those who did not accept them were not simply mistaken but evil, that he never made friends or influenced people easily. But he started with one great advantage, that his opinion agreed with that of the bishop of Alexandria. It was with the bishop, in fact, that Arius began his dispute. When the controversial priest appealed to the bishop of Nicomedia, and won his backing, the theological quarrel became a test of strength between the two most important sees in the East, Nicomedia, the political capital, and Alexandria, the intellectual capital. Just about the time Constantine finally disposed of his last rival, Licinius, the debate in Alexandria came to an explosive climax. The bishop, after a local church council had formally rejected the views of Arius, expelled him from his pastorate and from the city. But he sought refuge with the powerful bishop of Nicomedia, who not only espoused the Arian doctrines which Alexandria had rejected but began to circulate them through all the Eastern churches and to press them on the imperial court.

THE COUNCIL OF NICAEA—A.D. 325

So it happened that Constantine, the patron of Christianity, who was looking to this religion to tie his empire together, no sooner became master of all the Roman world than he found this major Christian dispute on his hands, more threatening than any political challenge to the unity of his realm. He was, of course, incapable of understanding the subtleties of theological distinctions in the debate. But there was one thing on which he was determined; he meant to have internal peace. So in 325, the second year of his undivided rule, he summoned the Christian bishops to a council at Nicaea, near Nicomedia. Not all Christian bishops were invited. Less than a dozen were from the West, and the most important of the Western bishops, the bishop of Rome, was not among them. Burckhardt, with his usual jaundiced view of Constantine's relations with the church, says that "of the perhaps thousand bishops of the East only those received invitations from the imperial secretariat whose opinions could be swayed or overborne." The council had one purpose—to end the theological controversy which was rending the church and disturbing the empire by reaching an agreement on the nature of the Christian God.

Eusebius of Caesarea, who participated in that historic meeting, has painted a vivid picture of the assembling of that first general church council. He tells how more than three hundred bishops (other sources say there were exactly 318) came rushing to Nicaea with their attendants in a frenzy of excitement, many of them scarred by what they had undergone in Diocletian's persecution, with eyeless sockets, disfigured faces, twisted and withered limbs, paralyzed hands. Constantine himself presided, a glittering figure in his imperial robes, which were no longer the austere purple garment worn by the emperors in Rome but were the jewel-encrusted, multicolored brocades thought proper to an Eastern monarch.

At the start, the bishops were divided nearly evenly between those who supported the Arian view and those who favored that of Athanasius. Eusebius, who had Arian leanings, proposed a formula in words quoted directly from the New Testament, but the Athanasian party would have none of that because it seemed that the Arians might accept it and still hold their own views. The New Testament writers had never said anything about the *ousia* of either the Father or the Son. It was probably Bishop Hosius who introduced the word *homoousion*. Since he had great influence with Constantine, the imperial weight was thrown into that side of the scales. After more days of inconclusive debate the impatient emperor intervened to demand that this statement of the Athanasian view should be adopted. Only two bishops voted against it. Thus, it came to pass that, out of an assembly which partook more of the character of a political convention than a religious convocation, there emerged that Nicene Creed, which to this day is the standard of orthodoxy in the Roman, Eastern, Anglican, and some other churches:

> We believe in one God the Father Almighty, maker of all things visible and invisible;
> And in one Lord Jesus Christ, the Son of God, begotten of the Father, only-begotten, that is, of the substance of the Father, God of God, Light of Light, very God of very God, begotten not made, of one substance with the Father, through whom all things were made, both things in heaven and things on earth; who for us men and for our salvation came down and was made flesh, and became man, suffered, and rose on the third day, ascended into the heavens, is coming to judge living and dead.
> And in the Holy Spirit.
> But those that say "There was when He was not," and, "Before He was begotten He was not," and that, "He came into being from what-is-not," or those that allege that the Son of God is "Of another substance or essence," or "created," or "changeable" or "alterable," these the Catholic and Apostolic Church anathematizes.

From Constantine on, the Christian record undergoes a fundamental change. Many will contend that it was not a change for the better. "After Constantine," said the late Dean William R. Inge, of St. Paul's Cathedral, London (often called "the Gloomy Dean"), "there is not much that is not humiliating." This is, of course, too sweeping. But certainly life in a church that had vanquished its rivals, that enjoyed so many special privileges and was constantly being given evidences of the imperial favor, a church in which membership was soon by imperial decree to include all loyal subjects, was bound to differ from that in a church where membership was by individual choice and might involve martyrdom. At one swoop Christian congregations throughout the empire were swamped with hordes of candidates clamoring for baptism whose only motive in becoming Christians was to get on board the imperial bandwagon.

Such a church historian as Bevan laments that, after the church "won" its acceptance by Constantine, no perceptible change or improvement followed in Roman customs or courts. (Constantine did, to be sure, put a final end to gladiatorial contests, but these had been losing their attraction for a long time before his rescript was issued.) How could any improvement have been expected? The new Christians were, so far as thinking and habits went, the same old pagans; their desire for baptism was strictly prudential. Their surge into the churches did not mean that Christianity had wiped out paganism. On the contrary, hordes of baptized pagans meant that paganism had diluted the moral energies of organized Christianity to the point of social impotence. St. Jerome and St. Augustine both deplored the corruption of the Christian community by the sudden influx of the unconverted.

Even more distressing, as one looks back, was the alacrity with which the Christian clergy who had suffered under pagan persecution turned to persecuting their opponents. "In the hour of victory," writes Arnold Toynbee, "the intransigence of the Christian martyrs degenerated into the intolerance of Christian persecutors who had picked up from the martyrs' defeated pagan opponents the fatal practice of resorting to physical force as a short cut to victory in religious controversy." * By the time a century had passed, St. Augustine had found in the text from Luke 14:23, "Compel them to come in," a command from Christ himself for the persecution of heretics!

This persecuting zeal would not have been put effectively into practice if it had not been backed by the imperial power. Constantine began it in a small way, not to compel pagans to become Christians but to enforce unity among Christians. Even before the Council of Nicaea he had banished certain North African bishops who had adopted the Donatist position that had been condemned by a council at Arles in 314. This contended that a certain bishop of Carthage, who had apostacized during the Diocletian persecution, could not after that effectively ordain his successor. The Western bishops who were at Arles decided that the sinful character of the bishop in no way altered the spiritual powers which had been conferred on him at his ordination. The Donatist bishops, refusing to accept this decision, appealed to the throne, which answered by depriving them of their churches and sending them

* A Study of History, Oxford University Press, 1954, vol. VII, p. 439.

into exile. This did not end the Donatist schism. A century later Augustine was cheering on the imperial troops that had been called in to liquidate Donatism.

After Nicaea, Constantine stepped in again to banish Arius and to exile from their dioceses most of his conspicuous supporters, including Eusebius of Nicomedia, even though at the final vote in that council they had bowed to the imperial will. What happened after that, no one familiar with human nature will need to be told. Control of church offices was seen to depend on control of the imperial favor. The emperor's court was overrun by ecclesiastics, all competing for the imperial ear. First Constantine and then his successors found themselves pulled this way and that by theological and political factions in the church, with the result that the imperial power was forever ordering bishops into banishment and almost as often bringing them back again when some new group of ecclesiastical advisers got the upper hand in the palace.

No career better illustrates the way in which the imperial power took over actual control of the church than that of Athanasius. As a young priest he had won a resounding dogmatic victory at Nicaea over his elderly opponent, Arius. Soon after that he became bishop of the great see of Alexandria at the age of 33, and his controversial life was to continue until 373. During that time he was banished no less than five times, each banishment and return to Alexandria representing either a change in emperors or a shift in the make-up of the palace ecclesiastical clique that had the emperor's ear. There were times when Athanasius was so completely out of imperial favor that he felt deserted by all his supporters. Then it was that he uttered his famous defiance, *Athanasius contra mundum*. He would stand alone, if need be, against the world. But when the imperial favor smiled in his direction he did not lack followers. He died in such a period, again in possession of his diocese of Alexandria, with his "Nicene" doctrines accepted by nearly all the churches in the central parts of the Roman Empire, though the barbarian tribes on the borders—newly converted or about to be converted—were largely Arian. His city buried him with pomp and circumstance.

VIII

The Church under the
Byzantine Emperors

Nicaea is regarded by all Christian churches as the first ecumenical church council. That word "ecumenical," which occurs frequently of late in discussions of church affairs, seems to give trouble to many, including some earnest churchmen. There is no reason why it should. It comes from a Greek word which literally meant "the inhabited world." In other words, all the world, universal. And an ecumenical council was, therefore, one in which the Christian churches of all the world purported to be represented. The theory was that, with all the churches represented, the Holy Spirit would guide the delegates to infallible conclusions, which it would then be incumbent on all Christians to accept.

If one holds "ecumenical" to its strict meaning of universal or all-embracing, it can be argued that there never has been a genuinely ecumenical church council. At Nicaea, as we have seen, only the East had a large representation, and only a minority of even the Eastern bishops were there. The bishop of Rome was represented only by a couple of observers. Nevertheless, there is a general readiness to grant the status of ecumenicity to Nicaea and to six other councils that followed before the end of the eighth century. The most important of these, next to Nicaea, was the Council of Chalcedon, which, in 451, explicitly defined the doctrine that in Jesus two natures, one divine and the other human, completely united to form one Person who, in his earthly existence, was both in body and in soul at one and the same time God and man. This declaration at Chalcedon has, for fifteen hundred years since then, been the accepted formula as to the nature of Jesus in all except the Unitarian and Monophysite churches.

When the number of ecumenical councils is limited to seven, that implies rejection of the claim of the Roman Catholic Church that the councils it has held in considerable numbers since 787, including the history-making councils of Constance and Trent and that held at the Vatican in 1870, were ecumenical. This rejection rests on the undisputed fact that, after the seventh general council, there took place the first great division in the body of Christendom, the split between East and West, and that after that the East was never represented in the councils held in the West. The Roman Catholic contention is that after the split the Eastern churches were schismatic, and that they were therefore not eligible to participate in the conciliar proceedings of the One True Church.*

Following Constantine came the sons of Constantine. And after they had finished murdering or in other ways getting rid of one another, there ascended the throne for a year and a half a figure about whom romantic legends have clustered ever since— Julian "the Apostate."

* The same strictures apply to the use, by the non-Roman churches holding membership in the World Council of Churches, of the term "ecumenical" for its assemblies, such as that which met at Evanston, Illinois, in 1954. These churches employ "ecumenical" to mean that their World Council, established in 1948, is part of a process designed to bring about their ultimate union, and that they cherish the hope that this union will eventually include all trinitarian Christian bodies, including the Roman Catholic Church. But in a strict sense, this Orthodox-Anglican-Protestant council at the present time is not ecumenical. It is ecumenical in spirit, not in fact.

THE PAGAN REVIVAL

Julian was not really an apostate, because he was never a Christian. He was an idealistic, honest man who owed his life to the fact that, when the sons of Constantine murdered the rest of his family, he had been too young to threaten their succession. Throughout his boyhood, for his own safety he had to appear to accept the rigid Christian training to which his bloody-handed uncles ordered that he be subjected. In his young manhood, the troops in Paris declared him emperor, and he felt himself strong enough to challenge Constantine II, the last surviving son of Constantine, for the throne. He became openly what he had long been in secret; he proclaimed himself a convinced pagan and dedicated the imperial power to a pagan revival.

For Julian, Christianity was a compound of the hypocritical piety of his uncles, who had murdered his father, and the endless, venomous debates between clerics over the nature of the Godhead. He wanted to get back to the mysticism of some of the later Greek Neoplatonist philosophers and to what he romanticized as the beauties of pagan worship. One gathers that he was dreaming of lovely maidens and clean-limbed young athletes with garlands in their hair, singing praises to Apollo in the groves about his shrines while their elders gathered in the forum to continue the eager philosophic dialogue which the disciples of Plato had never finished. Such measures as Julian took against the Christians were mild; he cut off the state funds which by that time were flowing like a flood to the support of the clergy, and he excluded Christians from the teaching profession. As fast as he could, he reopened the surviving pagan temples.

But it was all over almost before it had started. After Julian had been emperor less than eighteen months he had to embark on one of the interminable campaigns that all the emperors had to fight to protect their eastern frontiers against the Persians. In almost his first engagement he was fatally wounded. Legend says that, as he lay dying, Julian murmured, "Thou hast conquered, O Galilean!" Perhaps the words are mythical; the fact was true. With

Julian's death the old paganism of Rome and Greece and the gods of the Mediterranean world died.

CHRISTIANITY—STATE RELIGION

Then, in a few swift years, came the complete triumph of the church. All state subsidies to pagan temples were ended and the temples themselves destroyed or turned into churches. Endowments accumulated by some of the old temples were confiscated. Persons attempting to celebrate pagan rites were to be arrested and fined; they were denied legal ownership of property. Pagan schools of philosophy were suppressed; before the middle of the sixth century the school at Athens founded by Plato was closed by imperial decree. By the end of the fourth century Emperor Theodosius I had not only made Christianity the state religion but had made refusal to accept Christianity tantamount to disloyalty to the throne.

It was indeed a triumph so complete, in its outward aspects, that, as we look back on it and remember the little group of despised Jews with whom the Christian expansion started less than four centuries earlier, it is hard to comprehend. But the key word in that sentence is "outward." Inwardly, in the spiritual life of the church, the adoption of Christianity by the throne was a disaster. From the time of Julian on, especially in the East, the church was to become little more than an appendage of the state, a tool and plaything of emperors. After Theodosius the Roman realm permanently split into two parts, though a theory of sovereignty over the western half held by the emperor in Constantinople was kept alive down to the time, at the very end of the eighth century, when Charlemagne put an end to that fantasy. In the Byzantine, or Eastern, Empire, where the imperial court remained, the inner rot permeated almost everywhere.

Perhaps the Byzantine emperors were not to blame. A few of them seem to have had at least a glimmering of what the Christian gospel was all about, and would have been happy had the churches in their domains, with their clergy, exemplified the spirit as well as the teaching of that gospel. But most of the emperors regarded the ambitious schemes of patriarchs and bishops with the same cynical complacency they showed toward all the other maneuverings for power that swirled around their thrones. They acquiesced in it when they did not encourage it. As a consequence, ecclesiastics grew more and more servile in their attendance on the throne, clerical preferment became increasingly a pawn of palace intrigue, and decade by decade the church in the East lapsed steadily into that Erastian torpor which has put into our dictionaries a term of reproach that still applies to the churches with a Byzantine background, "caesaropapism." The Christian church in the East paid dearly for the triumph that tied it so tightly to such a fount of corruption as the Byzantine court.

This is not to deny the presence of some devoted Christians in the upper circles of imperial pomp. St. Helena, the mother of Constantine, who has already been mentioned, was one such. The legends that have become attached to her name are mostly without foundation, and the readiness with which she accepted the identifications of sacred places shown her on her pilgrimage to Palestine suggests that she must have been more than usually credulous even in that credulous age. Yet she was undoubtedly a woman pure in character and devout in spirit, who deserved the canonization later accorded her. More typical, however, of the women of the Byzantine court in their relations to the church was the Empress Theodora, whose constant interference in church affairs contributed greatly to the demoralization of the sycophant clergy. Of the part played by another empress, Eudoxia, in hounding to his death that pure and shining light of the Eastern church, St. John Chrysostom, more will be said presently.

While the Eastern church was thus suffering internally through the corruption of its clergy by their ceaseless competition for imperial favor, it was likewise passing through a series of convulsions over doctrine. The less its spiritual vigor, the greater its attention to meticulous definitions of spiritual mysteries. Fighting over the precise Greek words to use to define the indefinable became more and more part of the struggle over ecclesiastical preferment. When one patriarch or bishop wanted to get rid of another patriarch or bishop, either to exalt the comparative importance of his own see or to build up his own personal power, the most effective way of going about it was to accuse his rival of heresy in an appeal to the throne.

Although the great Justinian, who reigned in the middle of the sixth century, was a better theologian than most of his clerical subjects, most of the emperors knew little theology but they knew the value of having what might be called a "palace party" in control of the key bishoprics. So they seldom hesitated to intervene by passing on doctrinal issues and banishing recalcitrant bishops. Soon, likewise, the bishops of Rome, who by this time had risen to pre-eminence in the West, were drawn into the same miserable business. Their influence, it should be said at once, was usually on the side of moderation and humane treatment for the defeated disputants, but their influence with the Byzantine emperors was seldom large. In the Western Empire, to which we shall return in the next chapter, there was never such subordination of the clergy to the court as in the East. Nothing ever happened in the Byzantine Empire comparable to the stern exclusion of Emperor Theodosius from the sacrament by Ambrose, Bishop of Milan, until he should do penance for the sin of massacring a crowd of demonstrating citizens in Thessalonica. Chrysostom had the courage but not the effective moral authority.

THE EASTERN AND WESTERN CHURCHES

It would take too much space to attempt here to trace all the theological issues that occupied the church councils that met in the East from the fourth century through the eighth. Nor would most readers keep the distinctions between one council and the next clearly in mind for ten minutes after reading of them. It is sufficient for our purposes to recall that throughout this long period of doctrinal debate there was a constant triangular contest going on in the East among the three great patriarchates of Alexandria, Antioch, and Constantinople, with the Western patriarchate of Rome drawn in at intervals by appeals for support from the

Eastern disputants. Ostensibly these debates were over creedal matters; actually they were usually over the precedence of the patriarchates.

In the main, Alexandria and Rome tended to support each other, and Antioch to go along with Constantinople. On Alexandria's part this reflected the jealousy that proud and ancient city felt at the rise of the upstart capital on the Bosporus. The see of Rome, too, while for the time content to extend its influence over the imperial dominions in the West, found no cause for satisfaction in the growing pretensions of the "new Rome" in the East. On the other hand, Antioch and Alexandria had long been at loggerheads, as rivals for precedence in the East. If Antioch could not gain that position, it preferred to see it go to the patriarchate in the new capital rather than to its old rival on the Nile.

These informal alliances continued to influence the decisions of church councils until, at Ephesus in 449, the patriarch of Alexandria, in order to win a momentary victory and put a candidate of his own in the bishopric of Constantinople, broke with Leo I, first of the great Roman popes.* After that there was almost always tension between Rome and all the East.

Out of these controversial councils there came also the two major Eastern heresies, the Monophysite and the Nestorian, which survive to our day in certain churches. (See Chapter XII.) The Monophysite teaching, as its name indicates, was a rejection of the decision as to the nature of Christ reached at the Chalcedon council in 451. It held that, instead of the divine and human natures joining to form one Person in Jesus, he possessed but one nature in which divine and human were indistinguishable, but its effect in actual preaching was to exalt the divine at the expense of the human. The theological issue, though subtle, was important, but the factor that contributed most to the breaking away of the Monophysite churches from the rest of Eastern Orthodoxy was the lessening grip of the Byzantine throne on the outlying portions of the

---

* Leo I denied that this gathering had been a general church council. It was, rather, he said, "a den of thieves—*latrocinium.*" The growing influence of the pope is reflected in the fact that his indignant repudiation has stuck; Ephesus 449 is remembered as the "latrocinium council."

Eastern Empire and the growing sense of national patriotism in those regions. The Coptic Church, which is the largest Christian body in Egypt today, with a related church in Ethiopia, is a Monophysite church. So is the so-called Jacobite Church of Syria, which has most of its adherents in South India. And so is the Armenian Church, which can boast one of the most heroic records of any Christian body.

As for Nestorianism, after a period of great missionary success in Persia, and later in China, its principal surviving strength is also in South India. Those who wonder what the fate of Christianity in China will be if Communist rule continues for a long time recall, with apprehension, the utter disappearance of the Nestorian churches which archaeology testifies once flourished there. It is hard to decide in what respect Nestorius, who was a patriarch of Constantinople, broke with the orthodox creed. The controversy was one of several having to do with the exact method of the union of the human and divine natures in Christ, while all parties admitted that both natures were present. The test phrase was "Mother of God" as applied to the Virgin Mary. Nestorius objected to the use of that term on the ground that God could not have a human parent, and perhaps also because he could not approve the rising cult of the Virgin Mary which this title was obviously designed to support. But the issue is somewhat blurred by the fact that he did say that he was willing to use the phrase with certain interpretations that were approved by other theologians regarded as orthodox. It appears that the phrase "Mother of God" was coined not so much to honor Mary as to assert the complete godship of her son. It represents an aspect of the Christological controversy. Granted that the Son, the Second Person of the Trinity, is truly God, does it follow, some asked, that Jesus was God at every stage of his earthly life, as infant, youth, and man, so that even at the moment of birth he was an infant God? The assertion that Mary was "the Mother of God" was a way of answering that question affirmatively. The Nestorians thought otherwise. The truth seems to be that Nestorius was deprived of his see and driven into exile by what was in essence the political triumph of the ambitious patriarch of Alexandria, Cyril, who had the support of the bishop of Rome in that struggle. The battle, which ended in the branding of Nestorius as a heretic, has been called by Williston Walker "one of the most repulsive contests in church history."

It should not be concluded from all this that there was nothing but intrigue, political maneuvering, and the pursuit of personal ambition in the Christian church under the Byzantine emperors. There were thousands of spiritually concerned men and women who, in pursuit of salvation, went off by themselves into the deserts of Egypt and the caves of Palestine where, apart from the brutal and sensual world, they hoped to achieve holiness. And there were some theologians of pure character and towering intellect who are remembered as among the most profound thinkers Christianity has known. Conspicuous among these were the three great "Cappadocian fathers"—so known from the region in Asia Minor where they were born: Basil of Caesarea in Cappadocia; his younger brother, Gregory of Nyssa; and Basil's intimate friend, Gregory of Nazianzus, for a brief period under Theodosius I patriarch of Constantinople. He gave up that post to escape its worldly entanglements so that he could concentrate on teaching and writing.

ST. JOHN CHRYSOSTOM

Honored as such men are, however, their careers are not truly indicative of the disastrous part that imperial patronage played in demoralizing the Eastern church. Much more characteristic was the tragic career of St. John Chrysostom. The name by which he is remembered (Chrysostom means "golden tongued") was given him long after his death as a deserved tribute to as eloquent a Christian preacher as ever stood in a pulpit. Born in an aristocratic family in Antioch, he became for a time an anchorite in the desert. The austerities of that life so undermined his health that he was forced to return to his home city. There he became a priest, and soon by far the most famous preacher in that whole region. He played little part in the theological disputes that were agitating the church at the close of the fourth century. Instead, his sermons were expositions of the ethical teachings of the Scriptures, both Jewish and Christian, with none of the allegorizing that, after Origen, had marked the interpretations emanating from Alexandria.

Finally his following grew so large that he was practically forced, as the fifth century was about to open, to accept the bishopric of Constantinople. There he was soon in hot water. The morally lax clergy in the capital resisted his attempts to discipline them. The populace fumed at his blistering sermons aimed at every sort of sensual indulgence. But worst of all, the Empress Eudoxia considered his attacks on extravagance in dress and ostentatious luxury in living, delivered from the pulpit of St. Sophia, as directed against herself, and she became his implacable enemy. Thereupon the patriarch of Alexandria saw his chance to humiliate the man he considered his rival in Constantinople. Working hand in hand with the empress, he secured Chrysostom's deposition and banishment. Soon this judgment was reversed and for a short time John was permitted to resume his bishopric. But when he denounced the ceremonies at the dedication of a silver statue of the empress as bordering on the idolatrous, he was again, and this time permanently, banished. He was sent into exile in a little town lost among the mountains on the edge of Armenia, the court ignoring a protest from Pope Innocent I. When his letters from there continued to denounce the licentiousness of the court and its capital, he was ordered to move on and immure himself in a village in the desolate Caucasus. He never reached there. His depleted strength gave out under the rigors of that journey and he died on the road.

That was the sort of thing which, in the Eastern church, was continually happening to those who attempted to uphold the moral authority of Christian teaching in the face of the despotic and vicious Byzantine court. It was the happy fortune of the Western church, and of Christianity in its other than Byzantine forms, that Rome was so far distant from Constantinople.

IX

The Great Divide

Let us go back to the Western church and to Constantine and the Edict of Toleration that he issued in A.D. 313 and note again the changing status of the church in relation to the state and to the religions that were in competition with what had already come to be called Catholic Christianity. The fourth century was the great divide in the character of the church, but the crest of this divide was reached only toward the close of that century.

Two mistaken ideas about Constantine must be cleared away. One is that he gave the bishop of Rome sovereignty over the city of Rome and its environs; the other is that he made Christianity the established and only legal religion of the empire. Actually he did neither. The first of these fables can be easily disposed of. A document known as the "Donation of Constantine" appeared without previous history in a medieval collection of decretals. It purported to be the original text of an edict by which Constantine transferred to Pope Sylvester absolute sovereignty over Rome and a large territory surrounding it. This seemed plausible enough, for by the time this forged "Donation" was brought to light the popes already had such sovereignty, conferred on the Roman see by

Pippin (or Pepin) in the eighth century. In 1440 Laurentius Valla proved conclusively that the Constantine document was a pious fraud and that it had been written several centuries after Constantine's time. Valla's argument was never answered and his conclusion is not now disputed.

THE EDICT OF TOLERATION

The second, and much more serious, mistake about Constantine is the idea that he established Christianity as the empire's official religion and banned pagan worship. What he did was immensely important, but it was not that. What he really did was to proclaim complete religious liberty for both pagans and Christians. Personally he favored Christianity, as has been said earlier, but he decreed that everyone in the empire should be free to worship whatever God or gods he pleased. This was exactly what such Christians as Tertullian and Lactantius had been arguing for during the times of persecution. Constantine granted their request. Here are some of the words of his great Edict of Toleration:

> Liberty of worship shall not be denied to any, but the mind and will of every individual shall be free to manage divine affairs according to his choice. . . . Every person who desires to observe the Christian religion shall freely and unconditionally proceed to observe the same without let or hindrance. The same free and open power to follow their own religion or worship is granted to others, in accordance with the tranquility of our times, in order that every person may have free opportunity to worship the object of his choice.

This was a very radical program. One may well question whether Constantine realized how radical it was. It would be centuries before the development of any doctrine of human rights or any principle of religious liberty to support such complete freedom of individual choice in matters of religion. John Locke stated it theoretically in 1689. The First Amendment to the Constitution of the United States enacted it into law in 1791. A different philosophy prevailed in the long interval before these. The edict was indeed a landmark in the fortunes of the church, for it ended the age of Christian martyrs and brought the church out of the catacombs. It would have been a turning point in the history of civilization and political theory if its generous provisions had been maintained. In the light of what followed we can now see that it marked only the moment of transition when the moving finger paused briefly at the zero point while shifting from one side to the other on the dial of persecution—from the persecution of orthodox Christians by a pagan state to the persecution of pagans and heretics by orthodox Christians in alliance with the state.

It took a little time for the persecuting impulse to pass this dead center and begin to operate in the other direction. Constantine did indeed apply the imperial influence to the unification of the Catholic Church (it was already called that) as against the divisiveness of the Arian heresy in the East and the Donatist schism in North Africa, but he did not trouble the "pagans" who continued to worship the old gods. His admiring Christian friend and biographer, Eusebius, later reported that Constantine forbade pagan worship, but actually he did nothing of the kind. Even if he had issued such a decree he could not have enforced it. There were too many pagans. The Christians were probably not more than ten per cent of the population at the beginning of his reign and still a minority, though a much larger one, at the end of it.

Fifteen years after Constantine's death a not-very-important Christian theologian, Julius Firmicus Maternus, addressed to Constantine's two sons, Constans and Constantius, who had divided the empire between them, a strong appeal for the imposition of the death penalty on all who persisted in worshiping the old gods. It is doubtful whether Maternus had much influence with the emperors, but they actually tried to do exactly what he had suggested. It was a premature and futile gesture. There were still too many pagans. Not until Theodosius I did it become politically practicable to attempt serious enforcement of decrees banning pagan worship and making orthodox Christianity the sole and compulsory religion within the empire.

A series of edicts beginning in 380 and continuing for more than half a century, through the reign of Theodosius II, achieved this result. With the increasingly rigorous enforcement of these decrees, the revolution in the character of the church became complete. It had ceased to be the voluntary association of believers; it had become the sole legal religion of the empire; its membership had become everybody. To reject this religion was thereafter equivalent to treason against the state and, naturally, was punishable by death. Church and state alike adopted the presupposition that religious homogeneity was essential to the cohesion of the social order and the stability of the civil government. This principle dominated the Middle Ages and was part of the heritage that the great Protestant state churches of the Reformation period accepted from the medieval Catholic Church. Its continuing consequences will be noted later.

Obviously a change so sweeping as the liquidation of Roman paganism and the Christianization of the Roman Empire could not be accomplished in a day, or even in a decade. The edict of Theodosius in 383 and the stronger one in 392 did not have the finality that their strong words seemed to give them. There were still too many worshipers of the old gods, many of them in high place and in public office. For example, there was Quintus Aurelius Symmachus, of noble Roman family, who was proconsul for Africa a few years before the first of these edicts and prefect of the city of Rome in the year after it. He continued his prosperous political career for twenty years after that, all the while an outspoken defender of the old gods; and his son, just as pagan as he, later held the same offices. When Rome was taken and sacked by Alaric in 410, Augustine felt it necessary to write his greatest book, *The City of God*, to answer the argument of those who blamed the adoption of Christianity for this calamity. To evoke such a formidable reply from Christianity's foremost champion, there must have been a good many persons of pagan sympathies who still held this opinion.

Nevertheless, the fate of the old religion was sealed, though it was long in dying, and the character of the new religion as a social structure was radically altered when the Christian church entered into such alliance with the Roman Empire that thereafter it had the police power of the state at its command for the enforcement of conformity and the suppression of dissent or competition.

The temper and quality of the Christian community also

changed, as might have been expected, with this change in the worldly fortunes of the church. When it became socially and politically advantageous to be a Christian (under Constantine), and still more when it became unsafe *not* to be one (under Theodosius), thousands declared their adherence to the church with little or no change in their moral or religious attitudes. St. Jerome and St. Augustine, both contemporaries of Theodosius, lamented bitterly that the church was being crowded with the unconverted who had been led to join it by merely selfish and mundane motives. The mass of Christians suffered a dilution, not to say a corruption, in quality as it swelled in quantity. This was doubtless one reason for the increase of the power and prestige of the clergy. When the laity contained so large an element that knew little and cared little about the Christian faith, who but the priests and bishops could carry the responsibility for guarding the interests of the church, administering its affairs and, so far as might be possible, disciplining its unruly laity? Many of the clergy were themselves more pagan than Christian in their motives and morals, but no doubt they averaged better than the general mass of the laymen.

It is fortunate that factors of a nonpolitical kind were simultaneously at work to strengthen the moral position of the church and to counteract the demoralizing effect of these wholesale and indiscriminate additions to its membership. There was the growing prestige and authority of the bishop of Rome. There was the mellowing effect of monasticism, with its example of complete devotion which challenged the admiration even of those careless Christians who had no taste for emulating its austerities. There was a developing cultus of ritual worship, sacraments, festivals, and the invocation of saints, all providing patterns of religious behavior that could be followed by the multitudes. There was coming into existence a technique of discipline through the practice of confession, penance, and absolution. Moreover, there were some commanding personalities—men like Ambrose, Jerome, and Augustine—who, by administrative ability, conspicuous piety, and intellectual power, impressed the imagination of their own and succeeding generations.

THE PAPACY

The papacy is a controversial topic. Roman Catholics and Protestants are never going to agree on the *de jure* status of the bishop of Rome. Fortunately it is not necessary in this historical survey to attempt any judgment on that matter. It will be sufficient to state briefly some of the undisputed facts about the gradual acquisition of an acknowledged primacy of rank and power in Western Christendom by the Roman bishop. Roman Catholics of course hold that the Apostle Peter was the first pope, and that he and his successors in unbroken line—Linus, Cletus, Clement, Anencletus, and so on—were alike endowed with supreme authority and with infallibility in doctrine and morals. It is no part of their faith to hold that the possession of these powers was either recognized by the church or claimed by the leaders of the church at Rome from the beginning. There is no quarrel between Catholic and Protestant historians as to the process by which this primacy came to be generally recognized.*

Several early Christian writers, beginning with Irenaeus in the second century, referred to Peter and Paul as founders of the church in Rome and to Linus as successor in the episcopate. There are frequent references to the primacy of Peter among the apostles, and to the office of bishops as standing in succession from the apostles. A moot question was the interpretation to be put on the "upon this rock" and the "binding and loosing" passages in Matthew 16:18, 19 and 18:18. Origen thought that the reference was to all who had such a faith as Peter had. Tertullian held that it was to Peter personally. Cyprian said the grant of authority was to all the apostles, and hence to all the bishops that came after them, but first of all to Peter. Cyprian was constantly stressing the importance of the episcopate—"the Church is the bishop

* Professor James T. Shotwell, a Catholic layman who was long an eminent professor of history at Columbia University, is coauthor of a very useful and reliable work which traces this historical process as far as the end of the fourth century with full documentation: *The See of Peter*, James T. Shotwell and Louise Roper Loomis, Columbia University Press, 1927.

and the bishop is the Church"—but at the same time he insisted on the equality of all bishops and declared that no bishop could "set himself up as a bishop of bishops." Yet even in his time (the middle of the third century) the bishops were not actually equal, for the bishops of large cities had precedence over those of smaller towns, and bishops of churches known or believed to have been founded by apostles had superior prestige.

Both of these considerations worked to the advantage of the bishop of Rome, for the historic importance of Rome cast its shadow over every other city west of the Adriatic, and no other church in the West could claim an apostle as its founder. Jealousies and disputes among the metropolitan churches in the East led to appeals to Rome in the third and fourth centuries. This was not necessarily an acknowledgment of Rome's unique and supreme authority—which, in fact, the Eastern churches never did acknowledge—but was in the hope of gaining as an ally the one influential bishop who stood outside their quarrels.

Further, in the theological disputes of the time, Rome was always on what turned out to be the winning side. The only apparent and temporary exception to this was when Bishop Liberius, having opposed the efforts of the Emperor Constantius to force Arianism upon the West, was exiled and then, under pressure, turned against Athanasius and begged to be allowed to return to Rome virtually on the emperor's terms. But when he gained this permission and returned, he recanted his recantation, and the church at Rome was once more on the main road of orthodoxy, from which it never again deviated. During the pontificate of his successor, Damasus, a synod at Rome petitioned the emperor that, in case of any future charges against a bishop of Rome, the bishop should have the right of direct appeal so that he might "defend himself before the court of the emperor." Imagine a Hildebrand doing that! Or even a Leo I, less than a century after Damasus. The other documents of Damasus' time similarly picture him as exercising far less than absolute authority, either spiritual or administrative. Yet the prestige of the Roman bishop was increasing, all the more rapidly as the Roman Empire collapsed under the impact of the barbarians from all sides, and as the church at Rome proved itself to be the most stable institution in an otherwise chaotic Italy.

A landmark in the growth of the papacy's actual authority was the edict of Valentinian III, in 445, declaring the bishop of Rome to be the supreme head of the Western church because of the primacy of Peter, the dignity of the city, and "the decree of a holy synod." Just what holy synod had voted this decree, the emperor did not say. It could scarcely have been any other than a local synod of the Roman clergy. Be that as it may, the emperor and the unspecified synod were only putting into words what was already an accomplished fact in the person of the then bishop of Rome. This was Leo I, one of the truly great popes and perhaps the first bishop of Rome who can be called "pope" without reading back into the term an amplitude of meaning derived from the later magnification of the office. It should again be repeated that no question is here raised as to the legitimacy of the title or the theological or exegetical ground for the claim to supreme authority. We are speaking only of the recognition of the claim, and of the historical process by which the *de facto* power and prestige of the bishop of Rome increased.

Meanwhile, during the turbulent years when what was left of the imperial government in the West was in an advanced state of inefficiency and decay, the Roman see acquired vast holdings of property and was burdened with duties of civil administration— and this long before the papacy had anything that could be called "temporal sovereignty." The concentration of such great and varied responsibilities in one office necessarily produced a complication of secular with spiritual concerns. Under the conditions then existing, the papacy rendered valuable services in both areas. One may say, not without reason, that such conditions ought never to have existed—that the church should never have been a party to the policy of compulsory conversion and the violent liquidation of every moral, cultural, and religious influence except its own. But when these things had been done, the papacy undoubtedly exercised a salutary effect on society and on the church in this transition period when it was receiving into its membership a staggering mass of only superficially converted pagans.

MONASTICISM

Monasticism was partly a reaction and a protest against the worldliness of so many skin-deep Christians when the church was in danger of being killed with imperial kindness and of being swamped by the sudden influx of pagans who joined it because it was fashionable, profitable, and safe to be counted among the Christians. But the monastic movement had begun, in a small way, even before this condition arose. Asceticism had been a factor in many religions before Christianity. Many sensitive souls had felt that luxury and ease hindered the pursuit of spiritual or intellectual ends. Socrates was a kind of secular ascetic—though not to a fanatical degree, as the *Symposium* makes clear. John the Baptist, roaming the desert with crude garb and frugal fare, was a typical ascetic figure. The Apostle Paul wrote that "the flesh lusteth against the spirit and the spirit against the flesh, and these are contrary the one to the other" (Gal. 5:17). Jesus told the rich young man to get rid of all his possessions if he would have eternal life. A literal application of these and other passages suggested to some earnest spirits that perfect Christianity required complete poverty and bodily austerity. Furthermore, when Christians were still a despised minority of the pure in a pagan world, they were perforce living in an environment utterly hostile to their principles and practices. Why not get entirely away from a corrupt society the sins of which were—as sins so often are—alternately revolting and tempting? The desert was safer for the soul than the city.

The monastic escape from the world began in Egypt, where a short journey either east or west from the narrow ribbon of fertility would put one into as rigorous a desert as the most ascetic heart could desire. At first these enthusiasts for renunciation of the world went out singly into complete solitude. Then numbers of individual hermit monks located their retreats in calculated proximity to one another, thus forming clusters but not communities, for each was still independent and solitary. St. Anthony, the most famous of the early monks, went through both of these phases. The third phase, destined to be by far the most important, was the organization of the monks into rigidly governed communities with standardized rules. Pachomius, a contemporary of

Constantine, was the pioneer in this type of monasticism. But the solitary life continued to attract many in the East; for example, St. Simeon Stylites, who, a century after Pachomius, lived on the top of an isolated pillar for thirty-five years. Of course a stylite, or pillar-sitter—and there were many—had to have a supporting constituency on the ground to put food into his basket occasionally. Only the community type of monasticism, as invented and developed by Pachomius, took root in the West. There it became one of the most potent institutions of the Middle Ages and left an important heritage to the modern world. Benedict of Nursia, in the sixth century, became the founder of the great monastery of Monte Cassino and set the pattern and basic rule for Western monasticism.

At the gateway to the Middle Ages, when the church was in the throes of readjustment to its changed status and character and was struggling to digest the mass of worldly pagan population it had so suddenly swallowed, monasticism helped to restore the balance by going to extremes in the opposite direction. Later the monks took on some useful practical functions. In this period their greatest value to the church lay in setting an example of complete, self-sacrificing, even if fanatical, devotion to the spiritual life.

More directly influential with the masses of both clergy and laity were these factors that have already been mentioned: the development of a cultus of ritual sacraments, saints, and festivals; the beginnings of a system of discipline including confession, penance, and absolution; and the appearance of such towering characters as Ambrose, the administrator, Jerome, the scholar who produced the Latin (Vulgate) translation of the Bible, and Augustine, the theologian.

It cannot be said that all these influences together prevented a radical change in the general quality of the Christian laity. Such a change was inevitable when an entire population was swept into the church by the combined forces of persuasion, political and social pressure, and downright persecution. Nor can it be said that Christian practice did not adopt some of the features of the popular paganism that it supplanted. But the factors that have been mentioned were effective in restoring to the imperiled church so much of its vitality and virtue that it could presently take up the task of saving Western civilization from barbarism and decay.

X

Beyond the Border

Christianity entered upon a new phase of expansion as the Western half of the Roman Empire tottered toward its fall and approached the dissolution through which it was to pass before its fragments could crystallize into the Holy Roman Empire. This new phase involved the conversion of the barbarians who were gnawing at the edges of the empire and threatening to penetrate to its heart, and of such distant districts as Britain and Ireland, and of the tribes that were in the act of transforming the Roman province of Gaul into the kingdom of France, and, a little later, of the more persistent pagans of central and north Germany, the Low Countries, and the Scandinavian peninsula.

Politically, there was a change, during these centuries from the fifth to the eighth, from centralized governmental control under the empire to a division of sovereign authority among many hands, all of them new to the business of civil government. This was a critical situation for a church that had but lately gained its dominance through the favor and support of that same centralized government that was now disappearing. At the same time there

80

was the transition from a classic culture which, though it had become decadent, still had the maturity that can come only from centuries of continuous intellectual life, to the boisterous adolescence of new peoples who were just becoming literate and had yet to learn the ways of civilized life and to exchange a migratory existence for such a degree of territorial permanence as would entitle them to be called nations rather than tribes.

THE CONVERSION OF THE BARBARIANS

Could the church survive the changing order? It could, and it did. It survived by converting the barbarians. It absorbed them while they were absorbing the material assets of the empire. This achievement was no less remarkable than the early expansion of Christianity in the Graeco-Roman world or the sudden increase of its power and prestige in the fourth century. It was all the more so because during this crucial transition period there was a continuous running fight within the church itself between Arianism and the Athanasian doctrine which—thanks largely to the influence and authority of the popes—was to become the standard of Catholic orthodoxy.

Professor K. S. Latourette calls the period from about the year 500 to 950 the time of the "Great Recession" in the history of Christianity. There was enough decadence and disorder throughout these centuries to furnish some justification for that characterization; yet it was within this period that Christianity conquered the new peoples that were thereafter to dominate the fortunes and the civilizations of Europe. In doing this, it insured its own future.

In those areas that lay beyond the settled borders of the old empire, the conversion process was the resultant of various forces and pressures, political and religious, but it was quite different from what it had been within the empire itself, both East and West, when first imperial favor and then imperial laws had been the determining factor. The barbarian tribes—some so large and powerful that they assumed the proportions of migratory nations seeking a permanent location—cared little for the edicts of an

33619

emperor with whom they were chronically at war. When the wars died down, whether by reason of temporary terms of peace or by the victory of the barbarians, the choice was still theirs as to whether or not they would accept Christianity, if they had not already voluntarily done so, and, if they did, which of the two contending kinds. The decision was still most often made by tribal units and at the will of their political or military leaders, rather than by free individuals, but it was no longer made under any one centralized compulsion. Moreover, there was in it a large element of genuine missionary work aimed at the conversion of individuals to the Christian gospel and their instruction in Christian faith and morals.

Consider the Goths. They had drifted down from some region that cannot be exactly identified, perhaps the Baltic shores, into the area just north of the Danube and reaching east as far as the Black Sea. Some of them got permission to cross the river and settled in the Balkan territory. But they were never satisfied with what they had. They wanted room to expand southward—and needed it, with the Huns pushing them from behind. Here was the original Teutonic demand for *Lebensraum*. Inevitably there was border warfare between Gothic and Roman forces. The Emperor Decius, infamous as instigator of the first general persecution of Christians in the middle of the third century, died fighting the Goths on the lower Danube. A few years later another emperor, Claudius, earned the surname Gothicus by a victory over the invading Goths in what is now Yugoslavia. Another century went by and the fighting went on intermittently. The Emperor Valens was killed in one of these battles (A.D. 378) scarcely more than a hundred miles from Constantinople. The Eastern capital itself had a narrow escape. It was not many years later (in 410) that Rome itself was captured and sacked by the Goths under Alaric. After only one more generation Rome lay completely at the mercy of Attila the Hun, who, having completely ravaged northern Italy, would doubtless have treated Rome even more savagely if he had not been checked by sickness in his army, by his hope of marrying the daughter of the Eastern emperor, and, most important of all, by the impressive persuasions of Pope Leo I, who led an embassy out to meet the invader. Evidently the roof had fallen in for the Western Empire even before its nominal existence ended in 476. The Eastern Empire survived, after a fashion, for another thousand years, until the Ottoman Turks took its capital, having long since taken most of its territory.

Those Goths on both sides of the Danube were, to be sure, dangerous enemies of the Eastern Empire, and of the Western as long as it lasted, but there was also a degree of cultural inter-mingling and much infiltration of the northern tribesmen into the southern population. The old empire had for centuries been receiv-ing into itself all kinds of streams of migration. When it divided, the Greek empire was not Greek nor was the Latin empire either Roman or Italian. Many Goths, as well as barbarians of other strains, took service in the Roman armies. The new peoples who had been hammering at the borders of the empire finally took over partly by conquest but partly also by infiltration.

While all this was going on, Christianity was also filtering into the barbarians. A little before that disastrous campaign in which Emperor Valens lost his life, Ulfilas (or Wulfila) had crossed the Danube to become a missionary among the Goths. Aided by other missionaries of whose names there is no record, he converted them. This was in the half-century after the Council of Nicaea, when it was still uncertain whether the Athanasian or the Arian doctrine would ultimately prevail—and it remained uncertain a good deal longer than that. Athanasius had won the theological battle at Nicaea, but it was still impossible to tell who had won the war. Ulfilas and his fellow missionaries were all Arians, so naturally they converted the Goths to the Arian faith. That this conversion was something more than yielding to social and political pressures is strongly suggested by the fact that Ulfilas translated the Bible into the Gothic language, with the exception of the Books of Kings, which he thought too bellicose to be edifying for a people already too fierce and warlike. Early manuscripts of parts of the Bible of Ulfilas are the oldest extant specimens of any Teutonic lan-guage.

Crowded by the Huns, who were in what is now southern Russia, the Goths moved westward. Then or earlier they divided into two groups, the Ostrogoths and the Visigoths. The prefixes really mean "splendid" and "noble," but it is easier to remember them as "eastern" and "western," and that is what they actually were. Theodoric, greatest of the Ostrogoth leaders, had spent most of his youth in Constantinople as a hostage. He was on good enough terms with the Eastern emperor to be commissioned by him to lead an army into Italy and drive out another barbarian force under Odoacer. In this he was almost too successful to please his imperial master, for after getting control of Italy he established his seat of government at Ravenna, nominally as exarch, or provincial administrator for the emperor, but actually as king of an Ostrogothic kingdom. Through a long reign he used his power in an enlightened and, in general, a Christian manner. Some of the finest Christian monuments of that interesting city date from his time, and the rest from the reign of the Eastern Emperor Justinian, who ascended the throne the year after Theodoric died. Within another century, the Ostrogoths had lost both their tribal identity and their Arianism, but they were still a part of Europe's new Christian population.

The Visigoths, also Christian and Arian by the time of their successful but impermanent foray into Italy under Alaric (410), moved westward in a slow migration through southern Germany, crossed the Rhine into southern Gaul, where they tangled with the Burgundians, and ultimately occupied Spain, taking over control from the Vandals, who had preceded them, and extinguished what little there was left of the Roman regime. The Visigothic kingdom in Spain endured until the Moorish invasion in the eighth century. Before that, however, they had been converted from the Arian to the Athanasian theology. So the Visigoths not only made a large contribution to the racial strain of what was to become the Spanish people, but also became pillars of Catholic orthodoxy. As a symbol of this, it may be noted that the filioque addition to the Nicene Creed (asserting that the Holy Spirit proceeds from the Father *and from the Son*) originated with a council at Toledo, in Spain, A.D. 598—"to seal the triumph of orthodoxy over Arianism," as

Philip Schaff puts it in his monumental work *The Creeds of Christendom*.

THE BAPTISM OF CLOVIS

During all these adventures of the Goths, an even more important population shift was occurring in a higher latitude. The Germanic tribes of Franks, still pagan, were moving westward into the northern half of Gaul. Not many years passed before they got control of all of it. Clovis, king of the Salic Franks, has two titles to fame. He became in effect the first king of France and the founder of the French nation; and he was the first barbarian chief of any importance to become a convert to Athanasian (that is, orthodox or Catholic) Christianity. The consequences of both events were tremendous. The motive of his conversion was partly matrimonial. He had married a Burgundian princess who was herself orthodox, though most of the Burgundians were Arian. The princess was evidently one of those rare individualists who did not necessarily go with the tribe in religion. But Clovis went with her, and his people went with him. When a chief was converted, the conversion of his men usually followed as a matter of course. So when Clovis was baptized on Christmas Day, 496, three thousand of his followers were baptized with him. Doubtless his political position was strengthened by this act. There was already a strong Christian element in Roman Gaul. Irenaeus had spent most of his active life at Lyons in the latter part of the second century, and St. Martin was bishop of Tours in the fourth. About the middle of the fourth century—long before Clovis became master of southern Gaul and before his conversion—a council at Arles had declared bishops derelict in their duty if they did not invoke the imperial laws and the police power to stamp out pagan worship. But Gaul was sufficiently marginal to the empire by that time to render the techniques of compulsion relatively ineffective when Christianity became the only lawful religion, so it may be presumed that most of the Gallic Christians were Christians by conviction. Clovis therefore had a good foundation to build on when he made Gaul (hereafter to be called France) not only Christian but Catholic.

CHRISTIANS IN BRITAIN

Legends tell of Christians in Britain in the first century, possibly the Apostle Paul. He had expressed the wish to evangelize in Spain (Rom. 15:24, 28), and there is a wild conjecture that he may have gone there and then on to Britain. More specific, but no more historical, are the legends of Joseph of Arimathea's going to Britain, planting his staff, which grew into a thorn tree at Glastonbury, and founding an abbey there. These can be classed with the lovely but wholly imaginative Provençal legends of the "three Marys," who were wafted miraculously the length of the Mediterranean in a skiff without oars, landing on the south coast of France near Aigues Mortes with their servant "Sarah the Egyptian" (wherefore half the Gypsies in Europe gather at Les Trois Saintes Maries on the proper day every summer); and of Lazarus going to Marseilles for his last years and his second death (for which reason the cathedral church of Marseilles is St. Lazare and this saint is popular enough in France to have a railway station in Paris named after him); and of Martha, formerly of Bethany, settling and dying at Tarascon on the Rhone just below Avignon; and of Joseph of Arimathea (this is an alternative to the Glastonbury legend) becoming the first king of nearby Les Baux. These pleasant tales tell us little about the beginnings of Christianity in either Gaul or Britain. Legends aside, the historical evidence supports the belief that it did begin quite early in Gaul, not so early in Britain.

The Romans went to Britain with Julius Caesar in the century before Christ. Constantine was born there. His mother, Helena, was a British princess, but she did not become a Christian until the very year of her imperial son's great Edict of Toleration. The Romans came to Britain to conquer and administer, not to colonize. Indeed, they were never colonizers, as the Greeks were. It seems that some Roman civilians, but not many, went to Britain with the army, and some of them who knew the right people received grants of land—something like the Spanish *encomiendas* in Mexico in the days of Cortez and after. They worked these tracts with native slaves and built the handsome villas with mosaic floors that are even now being unearthed from time to time. But the whole

Roman project in Britain was essentially a military occupation. All the "-chesters" in England—Colchester, Dorchester, Winchester, Westchester, and the like, including plain Chester—were originally *castra*, camps of the Roman armies.

Christianity was probably bootlegged into Britain by Roman soldiers, but not early, because Christians did not become soldiers during the first two Christian centuries, though doubtless some soldiers became Christians. In one way or another Christianity certainly did get into Celtic Britain during the Roman occupation. The lack of documentary evidence leaves the field open to conjecture as to when and how. One piece of clear and definite testimony as to the main fact is the statement by St. Patrick, who was born in the southwestern part of England in or near the year 389, that his father was a deacon and his grandfather a presbyter. This points to the presence not merely of scattered Christians but of some church organization in Britain at least as early as the middle of the fourth century. This deduction is confirmed by the record that three British bishops attended a church council at Arles no later than the year 350. Granted that the "bishops" may have had very limited jurisdictions compared with modern dioceses, the fact that there were at least three of them, with sufficient constituency to finance a trip to southern Gaul to attend a council, indicates a substantial beginning of organized Christianity.

By the end of the fourth century the Romans were beginning to withdraw their forces from Britain. The Irish (then called Scots) were harrying the western coast. The northern Scots (then called Picts) were overrunning the wall that had been built across the island to keep them out. The occupation of northern Gaul by the Teutonic tribe of Franks made communication with Britain difficult. To complete the catalogue of troubles, the forerunners of the Danish and Saxon invaders were beginning to come across the North Sea, and presently they came in force.

ST. PATRICK AND IRELAND

All these unfriendly factors that tended to make the situation untenable for the Romans also made it a difficult field for the Christians. The Picts and Scots were solidly pagan. The menacing and presently invading Saxons and Jutes were pagan. All but a very few of the Celtic natives of Britain were pagan, and so were most of the Romans. Through all the turbulent years before the greater part of Celtic Britain became Saxon England, it must have seemed that the Christian mission was a feeble plant in an inhospitable climate. Yet that frail shoot of Christianity showed itself to be surprisingly rugged. For one thing, it had Patrick.*

The story of St. Patrick is fantastically implausible, but its main facts are well-enough authenticated. In brief, this young third-generation British Christian while still in his teens was captured by Irish marauders and taken into slavery in Ireland, escaped after six years, somehow got shipping to France and made his way to the monastery of Lerins on a tiny island off the Mediterranean shore (almost opposite Cannes), where he spent several years; at the age of about forty-three was consecrated as a missionary bishop by Bishop Germanus of Auxerre in central France; and then went back to the scene of his early slavery in Ireland to take the gospel to his former masters. In the remaining twenty-nine years of his life all he did was to convert Ireland—no less.

Such a sweeping statement must, of course, be taken with a reasonable degree of allowance. Patrick did not go to all parts of Ireland. He worked chiefly in the northeastern part of the island. And he did not convert all the people there. Ireland at that time had no unified government, but was ruled by many independent chiefs. Patrick converted enough of these chiefs, and through them their subordinates and subjects, so that Ireland became a Christian region with many organized dioceses and many monasteries. The Irish pattern of church organization stressed the monastic rather than the diocesan structure, and in general the priors of the monasteries were more powerful than the bishops.

Ireland in turn became the base for the evangelization of Britain. Columba was the most conspicuous figure in this movement. As we have seen, there were Christian churches in Britain before Patrick's day, and there were Irish missionaries to Britain

---

* It also had Pelagius, a British-born Christian who became famous for his theological controversy with St. Augustine and as the originator of the Pelagian "heresy." He was an older contemporary of Patrick.

before Columba, but the founding of the monastery of Iona, a century after Patrick's time, gave a new and vital impulse to the whole enterprise. Though the location of Iona, on an island in the Hebrides, was peripheral, it became the radiating center for the influence that soon led to a considerable development of Celtic Christianity in Britain.

Still more surprisingly, Celtic monks from Ireland and Britain became missionaries to the Continent. They established monasteries in Germany and Switzerland and even in northern Italy which became centers of evangelization and of devout learning. Columbanus is the great name in this connection, though he was only one among many, and St. Gall and Bobbio were two of their most famous monasteries. Since Celtic Christianity had grown thus vigorous before the bishops of Rome had gained general recognition of their unique status as popes, this Celtic influence on the Continent and the independent spirit of the Irish and British monks became a somewhat disturbing factor. As we shall presently see, one of the assignments of Boniface, the great apostle to Germany, was to bring these Celts and their converts into line.

THE GREAT MISSIONARY MONKS

The Saxons and Angles* came in the fifth and sixth centuries as conquerors of a Britain that already had something more than a sprinkling of Christians. Unlike the Romans, these Teutonic invaders came not only to conquer but to make the land their home. Pagan though they were, the word no doubt had got around, even to barbarians on the Baltic and marauders on the North Sea, that the new religion was being accepted by the most powerful chiefs and the best people not only of the old empire on the Mediterranean but of the new nations that were taking over its assets. In Britain, too, it could be seen that Christianity rather than druidism was the religion of the future. In 597 Pope Gregory I sent the

* It seems that not very many Angles came, but their name got attached to the island they did not conquer, as that of Amerigo Vespucci did to the continent he did not discover. History is sometimes more whimsical than just in its nomenclature.

monk Augustine—not to be confused with the theologian of the same name who lived two hundred years earlier—to convert the English. Perhaps he did not know to what extent they had already been converted, but he did know that they did not give what he considered proper allegiance to the See of Rome. This presently became particularly manifest in that they did not give their monks the kind of tonsure that was applied to the Continental monks, and that they did not observe Easter on the date approved by Rome. One must not belittle the issue because these matters may seem trivial. The real question was not the style of an ecclesiastical haircut or a date on the calendar, but the organizational and administrative unity of the Catholic Church and the authority of its pontiff.

English Christianity took a fresh start with this second Augustine. He became the first archbishop of Canterbury (601). He made a beginning of the diocesan system which still prevails. His work prepared the way for the conference at Whitby (664) at which the political leaders made the fateful decision that the rule of Rome was to be followed whenever it differed from the British or Celtic practice. Henceforth, the church in England, in spite of its rather independent origin, was firmly integrated into the Catholic Church. So it may be truly said that the Church of England—in the sense of the Catholic Church *in* England—began with Augustine.

Central and northern Germany still remained pagan. This region had been definitely outside of even the widest boundaries of the Roman Empire. Its peoples had not attacked the frontiers or fraternized across the borders as had the Goths and Burgundians. Neither orthodox nor Arian Christianity had reached them, though there were some exceptions, especially along the Rhine. Trier (or Treves) was founded by Augustus, and it had a bishop in the fourth century. Cologne was originally Colonia Agrippinensis, a Roman colony. But Germany in general was little known, in spite of the book about it by Tacitus, and little affected by the changes of the fourth and fifth centuries. This was also true of the Low Countries, around the mouth of the Rhine.

The evangelization of these regions was primarily the work—

by this time the reader will expect it—of British missionaries. The first of the great two was Willibrord, a native of Northumbria; he made Utrecht the center of his operations. The second, Winfrid, better known as Boniface, born in Devonshire, was commissioned by Pope Gregory II in 729 to evangelize Germany. His primary task was to convert the pagan population, and in this he had great success. Besides that, it was his function to bring the British and Irish missionary monks and their converts into proper relations with the See of Rome, and to establish dioceses and appoint bishops as might be required. This Boniface was undoubtedly one of the great missionaries of all time, and his versatility matched his devotion to the cause. He could chop down a sacred tree while the shuddering multitude watched to see him struck dead by fire from heaven, and then win them to Christ by his eloquence when the supposedly offended god failed to protect his tree. He could diplomatically engage the assistance of local Germanic chiefs and of the Frankish rulers to put the pressure on reluctant converts or on ecclesiastics of too independent temper, and he could so organize the districts in which he exercised his powers as to leave behind him a Germany that, if not yet completely converted, had at least a great body of professed Christians and a church structure that bound them firmly to the central authority at Rome.

Boniface became archbishop of Mainz and would have ended his splendid career there in peace if final qualms about the failure of his early efforts in Frisia had not drawn him back to that still-pagan field. There he sealed his faith with martyrdom. If that was in the year 754, as is generally supposed, the young Frankish prince Charles, who was destined to become the Emperor Charlemagne and founder of the Holy Roman Empire, was twelve years old at the time.

XI

The Holy Roman Empire

For several centuries after the fall of Rome, the political and social structure of Europe was such a mass of confusion that it defies representation in any simple pattern. As always in eras of general instability and disorder, there were periods of peace and even of reasonably good government in limited areas. Life went on at all levels; there was seedtime and harvest, marrying and giving in marriage; and probably most of the people of that time would be surprised to learn that the whole age in which they lived could be described by later historians as "one vast welter of fighting and political anarchy." Yet viewed from afar and in a perspective that takes in the whole map of Europe through those centuries, the description is true enough as a generalization. The shifts in population and sovereignty were too rapid, the struggles among conflicting interests too fierce and lawless, to permit the total picture to be other than one of confusion. Any simplification of it for the modern reader is an oversimplification. With this warning, we proceed to oversimplify.

Out of that welter emerged three institutions that gave to the whole some coherent structure and provided some intelligible pattern in what would otherwise appear to be chaos. These were: the imperial church, the Holy Roman Empire, and the feudal system.

"After the fall of Rome," we said. But when and how did Rome fall? The first term in the title of Gibbon's famous work was more appropriate than the second. After the division of the empire and the removal of the seat of its western part from the city of Rome, there was a long decline—an evaporation of authority, a sinking of its vitality, the gradual fading and ultimate disappearance of its apparatus of government. Though moribund, it still drew a labored breath after the raid on Rome by Alaric the Goth (410). The invasion of Italy by Attila the Hun (455) left the Western empire virtually unconscious. It died in a coma a few years later, though already it had practically ceased to exist. When the insignificant Romulus Augustulus was deposed (476), there was no longer even a titular emperor. The ghost of the Western empire—feeble even for a ghost—was the shadowy claim of the Eastern emperor at Constantinople to the allegiance of the barbarian chiefs who exercised independent military control in Italy, Gaul, Spain, and North Africa. The only part of that claim that ever had any historical reality was the Eastern emperor's exarchate at Ravenna.

Justinian, the most memorable and competent of the emperors of the East, had great plans for asserting his imperial authority throughout the West and thus becoming, as Constantine had been, the ruler of the whole Roman Empire, with his seat at Constantinople. He got so far as to take Italy from the Goths and North Africa from the Vandals, thanks to the generalship of Belisarius and Narses, to get control of the Mediterranean islands, and even to occupy a corner of Spain. Ravenna again became a subordinate seat of Eastern government in the West. A monument of this brief period is the splendid mosaic portraits of Justinian, his disreputable consort, Theodora, and some members of their court, occupying one full side wall of the chancel of the Church of San Vitale in Ravenna. Justinian died in 565—more than a century after the ignominious exit of Romulus Augustulus—and the dream of restoring the total empire died with him. His conquests fell away.

As for Italy, most of it was taken over by the Lombards, a late-arriving Teutonic tribe which Justinian had permitted to settle in the northern part of his dominions and which started on a vigorous campaign to the south as soon as he was dead. All that was left of Byzantine rule in the West was the shrunken exarchate of Ravenna, a strip of the eastern Italian coast below that city, and a bit of southern Italy. Almost two hundred years went by before the Lombards took Ravenna (751). They took it only to lose it almost immediately to a new arrival on the scene, and this turned out to be quite an important event. To find out who took it from the Lombards, and what he did with it, and what came of all this, we must go back to the Franks.

In the preceding chapter we told how Clovis the Frank made himself master of most of Gaul while he was still a pagan, laid the foundations of modern France, and became an orthodox Christian in 496. His successors in the Merovingian dynasty committed the unpardonable political sin of allowing their top assistants to gain more power than they themselves had. The office of "mayor of the palace"—at first chief steward or major-domo, then prime minister—was hereditary. It got into the possession of a very vigorous family whose encroachments on the functions of royalty left in the hands of the kings less actual power than the president of the Soviet Union now has. The second of this Carlovingian or Carolingian line was the great Charles Martel, who, still not a king but only "mayor of the palace," saved central Europe from a Moslem invasion by stopping the Moors in the Battle of Tours (732). The third was Pippin the Short, who put the surviving Merovingians in a monastery, assumed the kingly title, and was crowned by the missionary Boniface. Pippin extended his power even to northern and central Italy. His father's policy toward the Lombards in that region had been one of peaceful coexistence, but Pippin's was more aggressive. Pope Stephen II visited him, dubbed him Patrician of Rome (on no authority whatever), and re-crowned him as king of France. A year or two later Pippin revisited Italy at the pope's invitation, took the exarchate of Ravenna away from the king of the Lombards, and gave it to the pope.

What Pippin actually did was to give him the keys of the city and a formal deed of gift for them, and these together were taken to Rome and laid on the tomb of St. Peter.

THE TEMPORAL SOVEREIGNTY OF THE PAPACY

This was the beginning of the temporal sovereignty of the papacy. The year was probably 756. The questions are: Just what did the pope and his successors get from Pippin, and how valid was the title? After the Lombards had captured Ravenna (five years before the "donation") there was no exarch, because the Eastern emperor never authorized the king of the Lombards to act as his representative. Since there was no exarch there was no exarchate. The Lombard king simply took a piece of territory by the sword and his only certificate of title was the fact of military conquest. All that Pippin could take from him, and consequently all that he could transfer to the pope, was the sovereign rule over the seized territory. But what territory? Of course it included the city of Ravenna and its vicinity. The fact that the city had long been the seat of the emperor's lieutenant, or exarch, for the administration of as much of Italy as he could dominate, is irrelevant in this connection, because Pippin, never having been exarch, could not transfer the exarch's authority (whatever it was). No sort of legality or "legitimacy" attached to any of these transfers. The famous Donation of Pippin was simply the act of transferring to the pope his title, such as it was, to the conquered territory—Ravenna and an adjacent district called the Pentopolis. But it did give the pope the new status of sovereign over something, and that claim to papal sovereignty was soon to attach itself, on flimsy but sufficient grounds, to a larger and more important area, to Rome and the extensive States of the Church in central Italy. As to Ravenna, it soon broke away and became an independent state, then was under the sway of Venice for a long time, and did not again become a part of the papal dominion until Julius II, the "Pope in armor," sent his own army against it early in the sixteenth century.

If the papal claim to sovereignty over Rome and the great Papal State which later occupied a large part of central Italy rested solely on the Donation of Pippin, it would have a very shaky title. But if its legal basis is compared with that of the other European sovereignties, it seems about as good as any. Non-Catholics may think it is a terrible distortion of Christianity for the head of any church to be the sovereign of a territorial state, but when the question is the legality of his title as compared with other royal titles, there is little to be said against it. One can, of course, comment cynically on the exchange of favors between Pippin and the pope, but the Donation of Pippin actually had little more to do with the pope's acquisition of sovereignty than the deposition of Romulus Augustulus had to do with the fall of the Roman Empire. Both were episodes that symbolized a state of affairs that had already come about, or was in the process of coming about, without regard to them.

The greatening of the papal power in relation to secular affairs was not confined to the acquisition of a territory over which the popes could thereafter exercise *de jure* as well as *de facto* sovereignty. It involved also the assumption of authority to take a decisive part in the determination of other sovereignties. Perhaps the earliest experiment in the latter direction was in connection with the crowning of Pippin the Short. Pippin was technically a usurper putting himself and his family in the place of the Merovingians, whose title to the crown of the Frankish kingdom was as legitimate as any title could be under the circumstances. Conditions being as they were, Pippin was scarcely to be blamed for that. But Pope Stephen II went farther than merely crowning him, and so sanctioning the usurpation. He anointed Pippin and his queen and their two sons with holy oil, setting them apart as the chosen of God, and formally forbade the Franks ever to choose a king from any family other than the Carlovingian under penalty of excommunication. It was not exactly an innovation, therefore, when another pope, Leo III, a generation later decided that the Western Empire should be revived and that one of Pippin's already anointed boys, then the most powerful king in Europe, should be its emperor.

THE REIGN OF CHARLEMAGNE

This most powerful king, who had been anointed in boyhood, was, of course, Charlemagne. He had inherited half of his father's kingdom and took the other half when his brother died at a young age. He had enlarged that kingdom by thirty years of wars, in the course of which he conquered the Saxons in the north, the peoples of what later became Hungary in the east, a strip of the eastern Adriatic coast to the southeast, Italy to a line below Rome to the south, and a belt across northern Spain to the southwest, as well as Corsica and the Balearic Islands. Though still just the Frankish kingdom, it was quite an empire in extent. It did not fall too far short of matching the extent of the western part of the old Roman Empire, and it had a good deal more square mileage than the diminished Eastern Empire could boast.

Pope Leo III, not one of the strongest who have occupied the Roman see, was in trouble with the turbulent nobility of Rome and their still more turbulent retainers. In fact, they had compelled him to seek safety in flight from the city. He called upon Charlemagne for help, and Charlemagne came. He had already got the preceding pope to crown his second son as "king of Italy" almost twenty years earlier. The pope was restored to Rome under the protection of Frankish troops. Very soon thereafter, at a mass in old St. Peter's on Christmas Day in the year 800, the pope crowned Charlemagne as emperor, after first swearing fealty to him. Here begins the Holy Roman Empire.

On the face of it, this was another exchange of favors like that between Pippin and Stephen II, but it was more than that. The empire in the East was moribund, and the empire in the West was dead, but the *idea* of empire still lived. Charlemagne's reported assertion that the coronation took him by surprise, and that he would not have gone to church that day if he had known it was going to happen, need not be taken too seriously. There is evidence that he was no more reluctant than most other candidates who insist on being "drafted" for public office. Perhaps he felt that this mild disclaimer would throw the whole responsibility on the pope and make it appear that he had not deliberately encroached upon the empty claim of Constantinople to be still the capital of an undivided empire. Two things made his assumption of the imperial dignity seem reasonable. The first, and chief, was that he already controlled most of the territory that had formerly constituted the Western Empire (the main exceptions being Spain and North Africa, then held by the Moors, and southern Italy and Sicily) and some that had been outside of its boundaries. The second was that a woman sat on the throne at Constantinople, the Empress Irene, who had recently blinded her son to prevent his accession to the throne. Though she had recently restored image worship in the Eastern church, and thus partly healed its rift with Rome, she was an odious character in Western eyes. There was no unfavorable reaction to the step that re-established the Western Empire entirely independent of Constantinople. Charlemagne negotiated for the recognition of his new empire by the Eastern ruler, and got it twelve years later.

We shall not at this point follow the fortunes of the new Holy Roman Empire farther than to say that it dissolved in the weaker hands of Charlemagne's sons and had to be reconstituted by their more vigorous successors. But the initial step had been taken that led to bridging the gap between the period of the new barbarian kingdoms and the medieval unity—insofar as unity was attained—of the Holy Roman Empire.

Charlemagne was a great character in history, but an even greater one in legend. When a man turns out to be the kind of person about whom legends accumulate, that is itself a solid historical fact about him, though the legends may be a tissue of fancies. The two great cycles of medieval romances were the Charlemagne cycle and the Arthurian cycle. The stories that arose in later generations about Charlemagne and his paladins (knights) were concerned largely with their fights against the Saracens. They originated during the period of the Crusades, when fighting Moslems was deemed the ideal occupation for a Christian knight. Popular imagination therefore ascribed to Charlemagne a round

of heroic exploits in defense of the faith against the "infidels." *
The truth is that Charlemagne's principal campaigns were not
against the Moslems. The *Chanson de Roland* blew up the record
of a small rear-guard engagement with a tribe of Basques near a
pass in the Pyrenees into the Battle of Roncevalles, which was
represented as an epic struggle of Christians against Moors ending
with the heroic death of both Roland, the greatest of Charlemagne's knights (celebrated later in the Italian epics, Pulci's
Morgante, Boiardo's *Orlando Innamorato*, and Ariosto's *Orlando
Furioso*), and Archbishop Turpin of Rheims, a muscular prelate
whose legendary exploits on the battlefield alternated with the
performance of his priestly functions. As a matter of history, the
expedition that ended at Roncevalles got no farther into Spain than
Pamplona. Legend also credits Charlemagne with a share in the
discovery of the body of St. James, who, as St. James of Compostela, was to become the patron saint of Spain and the object of
the "Cult of Santiago." The finding and identification of the body
were no less miraculous than its transportation in the first century
from Jerusalem to the northwest corner of Spain, or the vision in
which the son of Zebedee appeared to Charlemagne in the guise of
a "fair and comely lord" and promised him a crown in heaven if he
would seek the lost tomb in Galicia. The accepted date of the
discovery is 813, but even legend does not credit the finding to the
emperor.

Charlemagne's actual importance was not as a crusader against
the Moslems. His functions were to push out the boundaries of the
Frankish kingdom until it had absorbed the territories of most of
the other peoples who, along with the Franks, had been the invading "barbarian tribes" two or three centuries earlier; and to turn
that enlarged kingdom of the Franks into an empire which, though
itself presently dissolved, served as a link in the chain to carry

* In 1924 the writer of this chapter found in Palermo, Sicily, a marionette
theater that had been operated for a hundred years by four generations of
the same family, and in which nothing was given but plays based on the
Charlemagne cycle. The repertoire contained three hundred plays, one for
each day of the year, allowing for a few holidays, all dealing with
Charlemagne's fights with the Moors.

over the old imperial concept of a unified western Europe to the time when it could be embodied in a Holy Roman Empire more stable and comprehensive than his. Charlemagne's principal contacts with the Moslems were of an entirely unwarlike sort. He exchanged embassies and gifts with Haroun al Raschid, the fabulous caliph of Baghdad, who designated him as "protector of the Christians" in his dominions.

THE RISE OF ISLAM

The Moslems were, however, a conspicuous feature in the history of this period. They had appeared as a new rival on the scene before Christianity had completed the conquest of Europe. A century before Charlemagne's time the followers of Mohammed had burst upon the stage of history as a terrifying surprise. The Arab prophet had fled from Mecca and taken over the rule of Medina in 622. That is the year one in the Moslem calendar. It may be helpful to note that at this crucial date the monk Augustine was still archbishop of Canterbury. Mohammed died ten years later. While the Saxons were settling England and had not yet been Christianized, the Moslems were spreading through the Middle East and sweeping across North Africa. With a unique success in giving religious sanction to military conquest and in turning conquered peoples into ardent propagandists of the faith of their conquerors, within a century after the prophet's death Islam had conquered and converted Arabia, Egypt, Syria, Persia, North Africa, and Spain, and had advanced its armies almost to the middle of France.* Charles Martel, Charlemagne's grandfather, had

* The religion of Mohammed's followers is Islam. The adherents of the religion are called Moslems. The terms "Mohammedan" and "Mohammedism" are odious to Moslems because of the seeming implication that they regard Mohammed as a divine being. Moslems insist that they do not worship Mohammed as Christians worship Christ. Mohammed was, they say, a man like other men, sometimes mistaken, sometimes sinful, but God's final and greatest prophet and the recipient of direct revelations from God through the angel Gabriel. He is therefore to be revered and obeyed, but not worshiped. "There is no God but Allah." How Christians can believe that God is one and yet believe what they do believe about Christ is a perennial puzzle to Moslems.

stopped them at Tours in 732. This was just three years after the pope had commissioned Boniface to convert the Germans. Thus new and unsettled was the state of Europe when the great Moslem menace came.

Rather quickly the Moorish Moslems were forced back across the Pyrenees, and more slowly into the southern half of Spain. They held Cordova, and made it the seat of a high Islamic culture, until it was taken by a Christian king of Castile in 1236. Granada, the last stronghold of the Moors in Spain, held out until 1492. Through a great part of that period the Moslem powers con- stituted a menace and a challenge to Christian Europe on three sides. For more than two centuries the Crusades furnished an outlet for the energies of the Christian peoples, a field for knightly exploits, an opportunity for giving a pious coloration to deeds of violence and pillage, and a method of combining meritorious pil- grimages to sacred places with profitable adventure. The Crusades were, in the aggregate, only an episode in this long Moslem threat. From the seventh century to the seventeenth (there was a Turkish siege of Vienna in 1683), European Christianity knew that it had an enemy, sometimes only potential, sometimes actual, in the powerful religio-political system of Islam.

It has been customary for Christians to regard with a sense of moral superiority the slogan "the Koran or the sword," which is supposed to represent the ruthless technique of the Moslem ad- vance. This attitude requires correction for two reasons: first, historical research has shown that the expansion of Islam, though paralleled and accelerated by military action, did not rest wholly or even chiefly on that basis; second, a frank recognition of the known facts about the expansion of Christianity itself during and after the fourth century requires the admission that it rested quite as much on compulsion as on conversion.

Charlemagne's line played out within a century, and his Holy Roman Empire became virtually nonexistent. It was revived by a line of those Saxons who, even after Charlemagne had conquered them and incorporated them into his kingdom, retained their pride and potency. The reconstituted Holy Roman Empire at first had Saxon emperors. So it moved on into the Middle Ages as one of the fundamental institutions that held the world together through that turbulent period. The disintegration of the old imperial unity had been overcome in part by the integration of central Europe in the new empire. But the new empire never had the full extent or authority of the old. When it had detached itself from the Frankish line of Charlemagne and had become Saxon (though it did not remain so), it lost, and never again included, France as an integral part of it.

The development of the papacy as one of the determinative medieval institutions became so much more notable a little later that we had better leave it to the next chapter. During the latter half of the ninth century, while the empire was in a state of suspended animation, the papacy in the person of Nicholas I took some decisive steps toward its later claim to be the universal arbiter, "judging all and judged by none." Though this theory once affirmed was never retracted, the papacy sank to a shamefully low level, both morally and politically, in the tenth century and did not begin its rise to a higher status in power and character until near the end of the eleventh. If there is any period that deserves the now generally discredited term "the Dark Ages," this would be it. The humiliating details need not be stressed. It was while temporal sovereignty was still a new possession of the popes that the spurious "Donation of Constantine" was inserted into the collection of documents known as "the Decretals of Isidore" which was put together in France in the ninth century. It was probably written about the time of the Donation of Pippin. The purpose, obviously, was to lend the sanction of antiquity to the newly acquired temporal power of the popes.

THE FEUDAL SYSTEM

The third of the three medieval institutions mentioned at the beginning of this chapter was the feudal system. This was a pattern of organization that arose gradually, determined for centuries the relations between individuals and classes, and faded slowly, leaving behind it a residue of class consciousness and legal rights and duties which persisted even into modern times.

The feudal system was at once a system of land tenure, civil government, social stratification, military organization, and the administration of justice. It profoundly affected the fortunes and operations of the church because the church was so intricately involved in all these secular interests.

Some recent historians think that "feudalism" is an overworked word and that there was nothing very distinctive about the institution it denotes. The view here presented is that, though most of its elements had appeared in other societies, the combination of them in a single system was a unique characteristic of the Middle Ages. Certainly there was nothing unprecedented about a stratification of society into upper, middle, and lower classes with subdivisions of each. Such a "pecking order" is found even in some primitive communities. So usual is the gradation of ecclesiastical offices that the word "hierarchy," which should mean rule by priests, more often designates an orderly arrangement of offices, persons, or things according to the scale of their importance. The feudal system was not unique in being "hierarchical" in this sense. Its distinguishing feature was the application of this pattern to every aspect of life and the recognition of certain rights and loyalties as the ties that bound together the various orders of society. This introduced some delicate problems in the area of church-state relations.

About the middle of the ninth century the sons of Louis the Pious (the one son of Charlemagne who survived him) issued an edict that "each free man shall choose a lord." Personal loyalty to one's lord would be a stronger bond than loyalty to the state, since the tribes had as yet scarcely become nations, or to the remote head of the state. By becoming the vassal of a lord, the freeman got protection that he sorely needed and assumed obligations for service. The lord might be the vassal of a greater lord, or of the king, and the vassal might have subvassals under him. If the freeman were a landowner, the title passed to his lord, and the vassal (a tenant in this respect) received it back for occupancy and use. In case of the conquest of new lands—as in the Norman conquest of England—the king could give his nobles large allotments, which they, in turn, would subdivide among their vassals.

So in the process of time it came about that central and western Europe were pretty well covered with this network of feudal tenures, reaching up to the kings, who theoretically owned everything, and down to the peasants, who tilled the soil but owned nothing. One essential of the military aspect of feudalism was knighthood and the institution of chivalry.

This structure of society necessarily involved the church, because the church had become a great landowner. Bishops and abbots could be feudal lords, as many of them were. Endowments of dioceses and abbeys were in the form of land. While some of the monks sometimes worked part of the land held by their institutions, the cathedral clergy certainly did not work theirs, but had it cultivated by feudal tenants. Moreover, the ecclesiastical feudal lord owed fealty to his feudal superior, the king or the emperor. This ambiguous position of the great landowning ecclesiastics, as owing allegiance on the one hand to the church and the pope, and on the other to the civil authority under which they held their land by feudal tenure, was the source of the hot controversy about the right of "investiture" which came to a head when the papacy began to rise to the summit of its power in the high Middle Ages.

XII

East and West

Here we will consider the Great Schism between the Eastern and Western churches, the expansion of Christianity among new peoples in both East and West, and the Crusades, which set up a new relation between East and West.

The three major divisions of Christianity in the twentieth century are Roman Catholicism, Eastern Orthodoxy, and Protestantism—stretching the third term to include certain communions in Europe and America that are classed as Protestant by everyone except themselves. Of these three, the least known in the West is Eastern Orthodoxy. For the present purpose we allow their particular use of "Orthodox," as we do of "Catholic" in a limited sense, without compromising the claim of the "Orthodox" to be catholic and the "Catholic" to be orthodox, or of other communions to be both.

What ultimately became the Great Schism between East and West was the long-delayed result of a gradual growing apart in culture, government, religion, and church organization. One could go even farther back to note some fundamental differences between East and West—with the Adriatic as the dividing line—but for simplicity it may be said that the rift began when the Emperor Diocletian decided that the empire needed two emperors. Things were never the same after that. From time to time this dual empire had a single ruler; and when it had, his capital was Constantinople, not Rome. Even when there was a Western emperor his seat was no longer Rome, but Milan or Ravenna. After 476 there was no Western emperor until Charlemagne. The papacy developed in a political vacuum—a turbulent vacuum, to be sure, but one in which the succession of barbarian, Byzantine, and Saracen conquerors possessed no such moral or civil authority as was exercised by the bishops of Rome. The very factors that built up the supremacy of Rome in the West made it inevitable that this supremacy would not be recognized in the East.

In the West, the pope was more powerful than the government. In the East, the government was more powerful than any or all of the metropolitans and patriarchs. In the West, the church had asserted its moral authority even in the teeth of strong emperors, as in the case of Ambrose and Theodosius. In the East, the church was so habitually subservient to the state that even a stout and splendid spirit like Chrysostom (see Chapter VIII) could win only martyrdom by his courage.

There were differences of culture and of language. Greek had been the language of the whole church, even at Rome, until the middle of the third century. Paul wrote his Epistle to the Romans in Greek. Clement of Rome, listed as the third bishop of Rome, wrote in Greek. Irenaeus, bishop of Lyons in Gaul in the second century, wrote in Greek. But Tertullian, in North Africa in the third century, wrote Latin said to be as good as that of Tacitus. After that the Western Romans forgot their Greek and the barbarians never learned it. The older classic culture survived longer in the East. Greek was the common tongue there, though, strangely enough, Latin remained the official language of government at Constantinople until the time of Justinian in the sixth century. Western culture was regarded as inferior, and it was.

The West tended toward ecclesiastical unity under the bishop of Rome. In the East, four rival patriarchs struggled for precedence, which none attained. The concept of divided authority, even of a divided church, was not unfamiliar in Eastern experience. From the Eastern point of view, the bishop of Rome was simply one of the five patriarchs, the head of one of several churches that had been founded by apostles and, as it happened, the only one in the West. If appeal was made to him in some Eastern disputes, it was not as to a supreme judge but as to an arbiter who stood outside the quarrel.

The East had been the birthplace of Athanasian orthodoxy. The Council of Nicaea was ninety-five per cent Greek, but Rome became the most competent and consistent defender of the creed it framed. Most of the barbarians—Visigoths, Ostrogoths, Vandals, Burgundians—had been converted to Arian Christianity, but under steady pressure from Rome they became Athanasian. In the East even the ecclesiastical high command had been deeply infected with Arianism. When that passed, other diverse doctrines arose which, successively labeled as heresies but commanding large regional followings, became occasions for division. Some of these will be mentioned presently when we come to speak of the various Eastern churches. Meanwhile, it may be noted that the existence of these theological variants tended to emphasize the contrast between East and West.

POINTS OF CONFLICT

When the West, beginning with Spain, accepted the filioque clause (the Holy Spirit proceeds from the Father *and from the Son*) as a clincher to the anti-Arian formula of Nicaea, the East refused to accept it because it was no part of the creed that the council had adopted. It is still a point of contention between the two churches. Even more heat was generated by the controversy over the use of images. Emperor Leo III forbade this practice in 723. It is significant that this decision came from an emperor, not from the church itself. The West adhered to the use of images. The issue was hotly debated. It took a hundred years for the image-using faction in the East to prevail. Meanwhile, the Eastern and Western churches were not in communion.

Soon after this matter had been settled, a bitter quarrel arose between Photius, who had become patriarch of Constantinople under rather shady circumstances, and Pope Nicholas I. The gist of it was that Nicholas would not recognize the validity of Photius' title, which was dubious in any case, unless Photius would acknowledge him as supreme head of the whole church, which Photius would not do. A somewhat similar issue arose more than a century later between Pope Leo IX and the Constantinople patriarch Cerularius. Though Leo had been appointed by the then emperor, Henry III, he was firmly committed not only to a policy of reform in the church (it badly needed it), but also to the affirmation of the papacy's independence of the civil power and of his own primacy over the whole church. When the patriarch of Constantinople, following precedent, refused to concede the latter point, the pope's legates laid on the altar in the great church of St. Sophia a document excommunicating the patriarch and consigning him to the hottest fires of hell. This was really the end. The Great Schism was an accomplished fact. The year was 1054. There were, indeed, later consultations and even a protocol for reunion (at the Council of Florence, 1439), but only when Constantinople was in such imminent danger of capture by the Turks that the motto of its patriarch could be "Any port in a storm." Nothing came of this. The Eastern churches would not go along.

While all this was going on, the church in the East was being so fragmented by doctrinal disputes that it was no longer a church, but, rather, a complex of churches. As stated earlier (Chapter VIII), the Council of Chalcedon (451) had rejected the Monophysite doctrine concerning the relation of the human and divine elements in the nature of Christ. This was a victory for Constantinople over Alexandria. These were two of the five patriarchates. The other two in the East were Antioch and Jerusalem. Rome was the fifth, and, in the Eastern view, it was co-ordinate with the others. Cyril, the former eminent patriarch of Alexandria, was believed to have taught the Monophysite doctrine which the council condemned. Moreover, the council, under the influence of Constantinople, deposed the then incumbent patriarch of Alexandria. In a natural reaction, Alexandria and all the rest of Christian Egypt went Monophysite. So also did the church in Nubia, which later disappeared, and the church in Ethiopia. Thus detached from the rest of the Christian East, Egypt offered only halfhearted resistance to conquest by the Arab Moslems in 642. The abiding result was the Coptic Church, which today includes most of the Christians in Egypt and Ethiopia and is entirely independent of the other Eastern churches. The council had created the patriarchate of Jerusalem and elected a patriarch, but the church in Palestine so bitterly resented the whole action of the council that the new patriarch had to go back and get a military escort to force a way for him into the city against the violent popular opposition. Syria also turned Monophysite, angered because the council had cut into the territory of the patriarchate of Antioch for the benefit of others.

In addition to these specific grievances, there was a general resentment in the Middle East against the attempted domination of Eastern Christianity by the Greeks. Such domination seemed all the less justifiable because the territory of the Greek Empire at Constantinople was steadily shrinking. Long before the Great Schism reached its climax, the Eastern Empire had shriveled to little more than the vicinity of Constantinople, Greece, the western end of Asia Minor, and the heel and toe of the Italian boot. The Greek church being subservient to the emperor, and the emperor progressively losing his grip on his territories, there was nothing to hold Eastern Christianity together.

In fact, the same thing that had happened in the West was now happening in the East—an empire was being dissolved into a complex of independent nations made up of new peoples who had pushed in from the north and east. In the West, the old imperial organization simply vanished for some centuries, but the church held the pieces together by an authority centralized at Rome and ultimately by a common creed. In the East, the name and form of empire persisted but even while its capital was becoming increasingly important as a commercial center, its political vitality ebbed until it was scarcely more than one of the nations into which its former domain had been divided; and the church, having in itself no unity of either creed or administration, had no power to integrate the fragments of the erstwhile empire into a new social order.

Besides Monophysitism, there was the opposite heresy of Nestorianism. (See Chapter VIII.) This also had to do with the nature of Christ. The Council of Ephesus (431) had condemned this heresy, but it had a large following in Syria. Those who held it were so vigorously persecuted by those who did not that many of them fled to Persia. The strong Nestorian church that developed there sent missionaries to China in the seventh century. Chinese Christianity flourished for a time and even had its own metropolitan. When it died out, or was killed, the Nestorians started it again. The mother of Kublai Khan was a Nestorian Christian, but her conquering son, after giving the various religions a hearing, favored the Lamaist variation of Buddhism.

SLAVIC CONVERSION

Though the Byzantine Empire had shattering losses and the Eastern church suffered fragmentation, Christianity slowly won acceptance by tribes whose very existence was not known to Constantine or even to Justinian. Slavic tribes moved in from the east —progenitors of the Bulgarians, Serbians, and Croatians. The Balkans became pagan again and had to be reconverted to Christianity. It might have been done sooner if the bishops of Rome and the patriarchs of Constantinople had not competed for their allegiance. "Czar" Boris of Bulgaria was baptized in 863, and took his subjects with him as a matter of course. A considerable native Christian culture developed, including literature in the idiom now called "Church Slavonic." Bulgaria served as a base for the conversion of other Slavic peoples.

Russia was still far from consolidation into a nation when Prince Vladimir, reigning at Kiev, formally accepted Christianity in its Greek form in 987. Constantinople supplied a metropolitan, but the Scriptures and liturgy were Slavonian. The native element made its way slowly. The great Mongol invasion of the thirteenth century so confused the situation that the metropolitan moved his seat to Moscow. When the patriarch of Constantinople, in a panic over the Turkish menace at the gates of his city, consented to terms of union with Rome (1439), the Russian grand prince at Moscow was so incensed that he broke ecclesiastical relations with Constantinople. The direct result was the complete independence of the Russian church in 1448—independence, that is, of everything except the political powers in Russia.

The Serbians, somewhat slow to respond, had been sufficiently converted to make Byzantine Christianity the state religion late in the twelfth century and became an ecclesiastical dependency of Constantinople. When the Fourth Crusade captured the Eastern capital and threatened to bring them under the jurisdiction of Rome, they escaped that outcome by establishing an independent national church.

In short, Eastern Christianity took the form of an aggregation of national churches—a pattern that anticipated the general pattern of the Protestant state churches during and after the Reformation period. The function of patriarchs and metropolitans never developed into the type of ecclesiastical autocracy that the bishop of Rome acquired in the Western church. The synod remained the supreme authority in each of the Eastern churches. Those that did not become Monophysite or Nestorian called themselves "Orthodox," and that term became the name of the Eastern churches as a group. "Orthodoxy" came to designate also the common features of their liturgy and cultus.

CHRISTIAN EXPANSION IN THE NORTH

The hundred years from 950 to 1050 were a century of extraordinary Christian expansion in the north and northwest. The surprising thing may seem to be that some parts of Europe now regarded as most solidly and soberly Christian had remained pagan so long. The details must be omitted, though many of them would make interesting stories. If the reader will let his imagination, or his eye, play over the map of Europe, even this bare outline may take on some depth and color, especially if it is remembered that Christianity had been in Europe nearly a thousand years before it reached the remoter parts of the Continent or even some of its central parts. The area that was to become Hungary was taken by pagan Magyars from the east about the year 890. Converted in the eleventh century by influences from Constantinople, it nevertheless allied itself with the Western church. Bohemia and Poland were converted around the year 1000. The Slavic peoples beyond the Elbe—Pomeranians, Lithuanians, Prussians (of old East Prussia), Estonians, and Letts—were being Christianized in the twelfth and thirteenth centuries, and the Finns and Lapps even later. Scandinavia was still stoutly pagan when its adventurous population began to boil over in an expansion movement that demonstrated its dynamic quality.

Milton was perhaps thinking of what we commonly call the "barbarian invasion," the earlier southward flow of the Germanic tribes from the southern side of the Baltic, when he spoke of Satan's host of fallen angels as

> *A multitude like which the populous North*
> *Poured never from her frozen loins, to pass*
> *Rhene and the Danaw, when her barbarous sons*
> *Came like a deluge on the South, and spread*
> *Beneath Gibraltar to the Libyan sands.*

But with a little modification of geographical details these lines could well enough describe the Scandinavian expeditions and migrations. Certainly the North seems to have been superfluously populous, and her "frozen loins" marvelously fruitful.

The Swedes descended into central Russia in the ninth century and established a temporary, but not brief, mastery at Novgorod and Kiev. In history, the Swedes in Russia are known as the Varangians. The western Scandinavians—Norse, Northmen, Normans, and Danes—were a seafaring people who matched the ancient Phoenicians in their skill and courage in navigation. They left their mark on every coast they could reach, and they reached far. Raiding and then settling the most accessible coast of France, they made it Normandy. From Normandy they conquered England. Before that they had found Iceland and established settlements in Greenland and reached the coast of North America. Turning southward they entered the Mediterranean, temporarily occupied the lower Rhone valley in France and set up a line of kings in Sicily.

The conversion of the Norwegian people to Christianity is

credited to their favorite hero, King Olaf Tryggvesson, who had himself been baptized by a hermit monk on the Scilly Islands, fifty miles off Land's End at the southwest tip of England. Huge, handsome, and in every way the perfect viking, Olaf used every instrument of persuasion and compulsion to make his people Christian when they had chosen him king. He had just about done this when he was killed in battle, at the age of thirty-six, in the year 1000. Sweden's conversion came a little later and less spectacularly. It was the work of English missionaries in the eleventh century. Sweden got a good start with a serious kind of Christianity, for its first archbishop was a Cistercian monk, a member of the order that was leading a great monastic reform. He established his see at Uppsala, which is still the seat of the primate of Sweden.

THE CRUSADES

The Crusades linked the East and West together in an unprecedented way, and also created fresh antipathies between them. They began ostensibly to lend aid to the Eastern empire in carrying out a common purpose; they developed into an exploitation of the East by Western forces; they ended in a complete fiasco on both counts. The First Crusade (1096) had for its announced objective the recovery of the tomb of Christ and the other sacred places from the profane hands of the "infidels"—that is, the Saracens—and it attained that end with surprising speed. The Seventh (and last) Crusade was followed by the loss (in 1291) of every foot of territory that the Christians had won from the Saracens and with all the sacred places back under non-Christian control, just as they were before the First Crusade started, and as they are now. The enduring results of the Crusades were all by-products, and they were not unimportant. But first let us sketch the course of the events.

There had been many pilgrimages to the shrines in Palestine by Europeans in the ninth and tenth centuries and many more in the eleventh. Some high nobles had made the journey. The father of William the Conqueror was one who did. It was a difficult and dangerous trip at best. So long as Arab Moslems held Syria and Palestine, some decent consideration was given to the pilgrims.

When the Turks displaced the Arabs, the conditions became much worse. The Turks, moreover, continued the momentum of their westward drive and threatened the integrity of the Eastern empire. When the Eastern emperor suffered a serious defeat and lost a great part of Asia Minor to the Turks, he called on the West for help. The Western emperor, seeing a chance to enhance his own power and prestige, was not reluctant. But Pope Urban II also discerned an opportunity to exhibit and enlarge *his* authority. At a council held at Clermont, in France, the pope made what must have been one of the greatest speeches of all time, judged by contemporary reports and by its long-range effects. He announced a crusade to rescue the sacred places. His eloquence aroused his hearers to a fury of enthusiasm—knights, nobles, and clergy alike. Everyone who could find a piece of red cloth tore it into strips and made a cross to pin on his breast in token of a vow to join the crusade. This sudden burst of zeal was only the firing mechanism for a still-greater explosion, a chain reaction of crusading enthusiasm that swept across Europe. Of the many monks who went preaching the crusade, Peter the Hermit was one whose energy and eloquence gained for him the undeserved credit for having initiated the whole enterprise.

Before the real crusade could get under way—for even in those days of simple armament a military expedition did take some planning and preparation—an irresponsible rabble of men, women, and children set out on foot for the East with neither weapons nor provisions. The whole thing seemed to them so miraculous that they thought they could go out, like the seventy, without staff, scrip, or wallet. Panhandling and pillaging as they went, most of them did reach Constantinople. They got a cold reception there, where military reinforcements were expected rather than an army of beggars, but a hot reception from the Turks, who massacred most of them.

Back in Europe many fighting men and armed civilians who could not conveniently go to Palestine to kill Turks thought that the next best thing, and perhaps equally meritorious, was to stay at home and kill Jews. Especially in the cities along the Rhine there were horrible massacres of Jews. In the vocabulary of the time, Moslems and Jews were classed together as "infidels," so it seemed fastidious to spare the one while warring upon the other. This was one of the by-products of the crusades—a fresh impetus to anti-Semitism.

When the First Crusade got on the road in 1096, it was a powerful military force, ill organized but effective. The Eastern emperor, recognizing its potential and more than a little apprehensive about it, made the leaders swear that they would hold under his sovereignty any lands that they might conquer. This oath the crusaders immediately ignored. Within three years from the time of their starting they had captured the city of Jerusalem and murdered in cold blood almost all its civilian inhabitants. Godfrey of Bouillon was made protector of the Holy Sepulcher, but the next year (1100) his brother Baldwin took over as king of the Kingdom of Jerusalem, which included a wide area besides Palestine. The West also took over ecclesiastically with the appointment of a full complement of Roman bishops and archbishops and a patriarch and the founding of several monasteries filled with Western monks. It was shortly before the taking of Jerusalem that one Peter Bartholomew, reportedly led by a vision and an audible communication from God, discovered the Holy Lance at Antioch and, according to the chroniclers, proved its genuineness by passing unscathed through the "ordeal by fire."

The Second Crusade, fifty years after the first, was stimulated by the Cistercian reform. St. Bernard was a leader in both. The Moslem forces, whose previous disunion had been their weakness, had reunited and recaptured Edessa. The immediate aim of the new crusade was to take Damascus. It failed.

The great Saladin, Sultan of Egypt, became the leader of all the Moslem forces and recaptured Jerusalem in 1187, thus ending a little less than a century of Christian occupancy. The Third Crusade was designed to win back Jerusalem. In its personnel it was the greatest of all the crusades, and in its results the most disastrous. King Henry II of England took the cross but died before the crusade started. The three kings who went were his son and successor, Richard I (the "Lion-hearted"), Philip Augustus of France, and Frederick Barbarossa, Emperor of the Holy Roman Empire.

Nothing was accomplished except the siege and recapture of Acre, after which the gallant Richard executed 2,700 prisoners whose ransom money was slow in being delivered. Frederick Barbarossa was drowned in a little stream in Asia Minor. On the return journey overland, Richard was captured by Frederick's successor, Henry VI, and held for a ransom equal to three times the English government's annual income. Raising that exorbitant sum forced the invention of new forms of taxation and taught later English kings how to get money from their people. The crusade was a complete failure. It succeeded only in proving that the forces of Christian Europe would not unite for a common cause.

The Fourth Crusade (1202-04) was backed by Innocent III, who proclaimed it at the Fourth Lateran Council. The crusaders never got to Palestine, but they took Constantinople from the Greeks and set up a "Latin Empire" which lasted until 1261. This was only carrying to its logical conclusion the policy the crusading royalty and nobility had followed all along, so far as opportunity permitted—to carve out for themselves domains and principalities in the East. It did not turn out to be a good way to heal the schism between the Eastern and Western churches.

The tragic "children's crusade" occurred between the Fourth and the Fifth. About twenty thousand children, chiefly German, were the victims of this ill-fated youth movement. The Fifth Crusade was that of the Emperor Frederick II, who was under excommunication when he went. He got Jerusalem by treaty, and lost it by the defection of his own nobles. Probably every crusade except this one had at least some shred of genuine religious motivation. The Sixth (1249) certainly had, and perhaps more than any other, for it was led by the sincerely pious Louis IX of France, "Saint Louis." He captured a minor Egyptian port and a little land in Palestine, but not Jerusalem. The Seventh and last (1270), with Louis IX again the chief figure, attacked Tunis unsuccessfully. Whatever its main aim was, it missed it, and Louis died of the plague at Tunis. The last foot of Christian territory in Palestine was lost in 1291.

Were the crusades in the long run an asset or a liability to the Christian cause? Did they "show the authority of the church" and increase the authority of the popes even more than did their victory in the "investiture" controversy (see Chapter XIII) as some historians say? Or was the popes' prestige weakened by the costly failure of a tremendous enterprise that they had so consistently backed? Or do the crusades simply illustrate the power of a religious appeal to crystallize men's impulses and justify their actions when secular interests furnish their real motivation? No definitive answer can be given to these questions. Certainly the slogan "God wills it" stirred the fighting forces of Europe to a high pitch of enthusiasm. Certainly, also, the summons to the crusades marshaled the chivalry of Europe on a congenial way that promised glory and profit. The business of knights was to seek adventure, and here was the prospect of adventure in its most appealing guise. Pilgrimages were recognized as the coin by which one could gain absolution from sins, and here was the superpilgrimage of all time. Nobles wanted domains to rule and soldiers wanted loot, and both were to be expected in the opulent East. Yet without a common religious ideology the fire of crusading fervor never could have been lighted. The crusades illustrate, as well as any episodes in history, the mixture of motives in the most dramatic events.

This chapter has been peppered with dates more than most. They need not be remembered, but it is well to note them insofar as they may serve to show how this mighty East-West transaction, spreading over two centuries, was related in time to the final stages of the Christian conquest of Europe, the ultimate rupture between the Eastern and Western churches, the ascent of the papacy to the peak of its power, and the religious and intellectual movements to be considered in subsequent chapters.*

* If any reader is curious to know how the crusades looked to people of that time, he may refer to the following contemporary accounts, translated into excellent English but preserving the flavor of the originals:

A History of Deeds Done beyond the Sea, by William, Archbishop of Tyre, translated by E. A. Babcock and A. C. Krey, 2 vols., Columbia University Press, 1943. William (1130-1185) was born in Jerusalem, lived there nearly all his life, and died just before Saladin's recapture of Jerusalem precipitated the Third Crusade. He drew his data about the First Crusade from earlier chroniclers, but was an eyewitness of the Second. Besides being archbishop of Tyre, he was chancellor of the Latin Kingdom of Jerusalem for the last ten years of his life. His history became so standard that chroniclers of the later crusades described their accounts as being continuations of his.

The Crusade of Richard Lion-Heart, by Amboise, translated from the Old French by M. J. Hubert, Columbia University Press, 1941. The author, unknown except by name, was probably a Norman jongleur, or professional minstrel, who wrote in England after the Third Crusade, which he describes. His record is in verse, in a style between that of the *chanson de geste* and the prose chroniclers—pretty pedestrian poetry for the most part, but vivid and frank. He was an eyewitness of the events, except the siege of Acre. He ends with a bare mention of Richard's imprisonment in Austria, his ransom, and his return to England.

XIII

The Two Swords

The two centuries of the crusades were approximately the period in which the papacy was rising to the dangerous summit of its worldly power and was beginning to experience the ebbing of its political authority though not of its claims to exercise it. In an earlier section (Chapter XI), we spoke of the acquisition of temporal power by the popes. This, of course, meant only that the popes became the rulers of a specific territory which became simply one of the Italian states. Before the Donation of Pippin (756) the pope was the proprietor of vast estates. In the absence of competent civil authorities, he had the responsibility for carrying on the functions of government over a considerable area.* After the Donation, he was one of the sovereign powers of Europe. This was a step in the evolution of the papal power, but it was only in-

* The situation was something like that on one of the large Mexican haciendas during the Diaz regime. I had a friend who was manager of an estate covering some hundreds of square miles. He had his own police force and his own jail and held his own court, because there were no others. The peons were, in every practical sense, his subjects. Without a scintilla of legal right to do so, he ruled, because he represented the owner.—W. E. G.

cidentally related to the development of the kind of power which was most significant and of which we are now to speak. What the papacy aimed at was not simply to *be* a temporal power by reason of sovereignty over a little Italian state, but to exercise a universal sovereignty over all sovereigns by reason of the spiritual office of the pope, who was to be the master and arbiter of all other temporal authorities.

The development of that ideal, the partial achievement of it, and some of the reactions against it are what we must now consider. Lest this should seem to the modern reader a threshing over of old straw and a discussion of dead issues, there should perhaps be inserted here a reminder that all the popes of the last six centuries have worn the triple tiara. According to present-day Roman Catholic authorities, its three crowns signify "universal episcopate, supremacy of jurisdiction, and universal supremacy." In the coronation of all popes—including Pius XII, on March 12, 1939—the tiara is placed on the candidate's head with the words: "Receive the tiara adorned with three crowns and know that thou art Father of princes and kings, Ruler of the world, Vicar of our Savior Jesus Christ." If this phraseology had not been sanctified by long usage, it would not have been coined in this generation to express the relation of the pope to the political and social order; but it would not have been created in the first place if it had not meant then what it says—"Ruler of the world."

Going back to the time of Charlemagne—say the year of his coronation as emperor in 800—we see the heads of church and state working together harmoniously. In a letter to Pope Leo III, who had crowned him, Charlemagne likened himself and the pope to Moses and Aaron. Aaron might be the priest, but Moses was God's chosen leader of the people and did not hold his commission subject to Aaron's approval. We are not told how the pope liked that analogy, but in any case he was in no position to protest. It was a genuine collaboration between the secular and spiritual powers that Charlemagne had in mind, but his whole course of action showed that he was more impressed with the secular ruler's religious responsibilities than with any secular functions to be discharged by the head of the church. That situation was to be re-

versed as weaker emperors and stronger popes succeeded Charlemagne and Leo.

The course of the dramatic struggle for supremacy between
the rulers of the church on one side and the rulers of the state
on the other can best be indicated by telling the story of four
popes. The "great contention" between ecclesiastical and secular powers, or the doctrine of the "two swords," has infinite
ramifications, but its main lines will be clear if one knows the
claims and the fortunes of these four: Nicholas I, Gregory VII,
Innocent III, and Boniface VIII.

NICHOLAS I AND EXCOMMUNICATION

Nicholas I (858-867) exercised his office at a time when Charlemagne's Holy Roman Empire, first divided among his sons and
then discredited by their weaker successors, seemed on the verge of
dissolution. The feudal system was rising to supply the lack of centralized authorities. In its earliest stage the local lords and petty
nobles were an arrogantly undisciplined crew with little of that
allegiance to their superiors that later characterized the system.
Theoretically the pope was absolute ruler of the church, but the
practice did not conform to the theory. Bishops were often the
creatures of the secular rulers of their dioceses. Some archbishops,
being themselves the lords of vast feudal domains, assumed the
prerogatives of minor sovereigns over their estates and little popes
in their archdioceses, and were not readily amenable to Rome.
Nicholas, a man of strong personality and keen conscience, dealt
vigorously with the issues that were presented. He saw the assertion of the papal power as the only way out of this confusion. It
was not on his own initiative but after he had been called in as
arbiter that he demoted Photius from the Patriarchate of Constantinople. His intervention alienated the Byzantine church but
strengthened his prestige in the West. When a group of bishops
had compliantly sanctioned the divorcement of his wife by the
king of Lorraine, and the pope's legates had been bribed to ratify
the sanction, Nicholas boldly asserted his authority over all of
them, the king included. He won his case by the weapon of ex-

communication. In this episode he proved two things: that a king can be disciplined for what the pope considers a breach of morality, and that the decision of bishops anywhere can be reversed by the pope. A third case, involving Hincmar, Archbishop of Rheims and perhaps the most powerful ecclesiastic in France, proved that the pope can overrule an archbishop. Though the issue did not arise as to the relative authority of religious and secular rulers in civil affairs, Nicholas's whole course of action tended to build up the prestige of the papacy as supreme in any field in which it chose to assert its authority. He appealed—doubtless in entirely good faith—to the pseudo-Isidorean decretals, which were forged about this time, to prove that the newly acquired papal power had an ancient origin.

During the two centuries after Nicholas I, the Holy Roman Empire began to get on its feet again under the Saxon emperors, but the papacy passed through a period—notably the tenth century —in which it was in every respect at a lower ebb than ever before or since. It became for a time a plaything of the most corrupt families of the Roman nobility. It would serve no good purpose to recite the old scandals, some of which were probably not true. The historical fact is that the conditions were so bad that not even the most outrageous tales of corruption and immorality seemed to lack verisimilitude. Such a state inevitably weakened the whole structure of the church. What it needed was reformation in head and members. In the monk Hildebrand it got a head who gave it just that and then went on to assert the superiority of the religious to the secular power in unprecedented terms.

GREGORY VII, THE COLLEGE OF CARDINALS, AND CANOSSA

Gregory VII (1073-1085) was one of those physically insignificant men whose moral and spiritual stature towers over their more muscular contemporaries. Even when a mere monk, he was the chief adviser of two popes in regard to temporal affairs and internal reforms. He straightened out the papal finances, recovered church property that had been seized by Roman nobles, put teeth into the generally ignored law of priestly celibacy, reformed some notoriously corrupt monasteries, went far toward stopping appointment to ecclesiastical offices by secular lords and rulers, and, most important of all, set up the college of cardinals (1059) as the body charged with the election of popes instead of leaving it to the king of Germany. It is hard to tell what might have happened not only to the papacy but to the whole structure of the church if it had not been for this doughty little monk.

When at last he came to the papal office himself, he was ready to go beyond the mere reform of the church in morals and discipline and to lay down some new principles governing the relations between the secular and spiritual powers on the highest level. Two basic ideas determined his attitudes, as defined in the following declarations, which are quoted verbatim (in translation) from his encyclicals and decrees. These principles were: first, the pope is absolute master of the church; second, the church is absolute master of the state. Here are a few of his most significant declarations:

The pope alone can depose bishops or reinstate those whom archbishops or others may have deposed.

The pope's legates take precedence over all bishops and, though they themselves may be of lower rank, can pass sentence of deposition upon them.

All princes should kiss the feet of the pope, and of him alone.

It is lawful for the pope to depose all secular rulers (*imperatores*).

The pope can annul the decrees of any authority, spiritual or secular, but none can annul his decrees.

The pope can be judged by no human authority, but by God alone.

The Roman church has never erred and will never err.

The pope has power to absolve subjects from their allegiance to unrighteous rulers.

Comment upon these propositions would be superfluous. Here is the prospectus for a thoroughgoing theocracy. Since the new college of cardinals was hereafter to elect the popes, and since the popes were to appoint the cardinals, it was in effect a closed circle of absolute authority, a self-perpetuating theocratic autocracy.

The famous episode at Canossa, when the pope made Emperor Henry IV stand in the snow for three days before permitting him to confess his sin and receive absolution, put this theory to the test. The pope won what proved to be a rather costly victory. The trouble and the "sin" grew out of the "investiture" controversy. It was a complicated situation. Ecclesiastics were practically the only literate members of society. The great ecclesiastics were also the lords of great feudal domains—in effect, princes of the realm. They were administrators, judges, councilors, secretaries, ambassadors. No others had the necessary education—the church had seen to that. As lords of great feudal estates, these bishops and archbishops also controlled a great part of the military forces upon which the rulers had to depend to defend their realms against invasion or to suppress insurrection. It seemed to the secular rulers that they should have something to say about the choice of the men who were to exercise these secular functions. But these same men were also the high clergy of the church. Could the head of the church permit its most important clergy to be selected by laymen? That is what the investiture controversy was about.

Emperor Henry IV was determined to choose his own clerical princes. Gregory VII was determined that, whether princes or not, clergy should be selected and inducted into office by the spiritual power. When Henry insisted, he was excommunicated. When he was excommunicated, his subjects feared to obey him under penalty of damnation. Being thus shorn of his power, Henry capitulated. He stood in the snow, yielded the point at issue, confessed his sin, and at the pope's leisure received absolution and the lifting of his excommunication.

It was, as we have said, a costly victory for the papacy. Hitherto the empire and the papacy had collaborated in friendly fashion for the discharge of a shared responsibility for the temporal and spiritual welfare of Europe. Thereafter each was on guard against encroachments by the other. To be sure there were periods of collaboration. If there were heretics to be pursued, and perhaps burned, the secular power was willing enough. It was no friend of heresy. It went along with the theory that every citizen of Christendom must conform to Christendom's one authorized religion. Heresy was treason and must be treated as such. But always the secular authorities were on guard against the pretensions of the church to a superior right to dominate the whole social and political order.

INNOCENT III AND PAPAL DOMINANCE

Innocent III (1198-1216) came on the scene a century later. It was not possible to go much farther than Gregory VII had already gone in affirming the dominance of the ecclesiastical over the secular power, but it was possible to implement that general affirmation by specific projects to bring kings into subjection to the papacy. Innocent was only thirty-seven years old and was not yet even a priest when he was elected to the papacy, but he was a priest at heart, experienced in the techniques of papal administration, the nephew of Pope Clement III, and deeply learned in theology. He was quickly put through the orders before he was crowned as pope. From the start he had no doubt as to the extent of his commission, which was to rule the world. To Philip Augustus, King of France, he wrote:

> To princes power is given on earth, but to priests it is attributed also to heaven; to the former only over bodies, to the latter also over souls. Whence it follows that by so much as the soul is superior to the body, the priesthood is superior to the kingship. Single rulers have single provinces, and single kings single kingdoms; but Peter, as in the plenitude so in the extent of his power, is pre-eminent over all, since he is the Vicar of Him whose is the earth and the fullness thereof, the whole wide world and all that dwell therein.

This was not merely a pious and uncontroversial observation that the soul is more important than the body and that therefore the spiritual outranks the temporal in dignity. It was intended to serve notice that the ruler of the souls of men claimed the right also to control their temporal affairs whenever and insofar as it seemed to him desirable.

The "sun and moon" analogy which Innocent III employed gives an even clearer picture of his theory of church-state relations. In the same year in which he assumed his high office he wrote:

> As the Creator of the universe set two great lights in the firmament of heaven, the greater to rule the day and the lesser to rule the night, so also for the firmament of the universal Church, which is spoken of as heaven, he appointed two great deputies, the greater to bear rule over souls (these being, as it were, days), the lesser to bear rule over bodies (these being, as it were, nights). These dignities are the pontifical authority and the royal power. Furthermore, the moon derives her light from the sun, and is in truth inferior to the sun in both size and quality. In the same way the royal power derives its dignity from the pontifical authority.

It should be noted—and critics of the papacy should be careful to observe this—that, even in thus boldly asserting the superiority of the pontifical to the imperial power, Innocent was thinking primarily of the "firmament of the universal Church" and of the care of souls. It was of the essence of his religious conviction that souls could not be saved unless they were "ruled" by the church. In order to rule over souls, the church itself must be free from rule by the secular authorities. The church's vast temporal possessions— the feudal domains of its bishops and archbishops, the vast estates of its monasteries, and the great part of central Italy over which the pope himself held regal power—were all considered essential instruments for ruling over souls. Therefore the church must be free from any kind of secular control over its temporalities as well as its spiritualities. Since church and state could not both be free from each other's control in this field of overlapping interests, it followed that the more important should dominate the less important; the church should dominate the state. There was logic in this. If the presuppositions are granted, the conclusion is inevitable.

Putting this theory into practice, Innocent III took occasion to require Peter of Aragon to transfer to him the title to his kingdom and receive it back as a fief of Rome. The feudal system was then fully developed, and the most effective way of registering a claim to superior authority over anyone was to have him accept the status of a vassal. The feudal lord thus acquired legal title to the property concerned (in this case, the Kingdom of Aragon), and the vassal (in this case, the king) became merely a tenant holding his property and status at the will of his overlord (the pope) and subject to the performance of the specified feudal duties. Similarly the prince of Bulgaria became a vassal of the pope, to strengthen himself against his rivals and the Eastern emperor. Many other princes with smaller territories followed the same procedure. The feudal system had, in fact, been built up by weak proprietors or petty princes seeking the protection of the more powerful. The pope now seemed to be actually the most powerful, and many weak rulers sought shelter under his protection at the price of declaring their allegiance to him as their feudal lord. Excommunication and interdict were powerful weapons in bringing the reluctant to heel, and Innocent employed this weapon at least fifty times.

Most conspicuous in the whole list was the intimidation of King John of England, who was forced by the interdict to surrender his kingdom to the pope as its feudal lord and receive it back as a fief for which he would render loyal service. That affair got rather complicated. King John was so weakened at home by this transaction that his barons were able to extract from him the Magna Charta, and then the pope protested vehemently against that rudimentary charter of popular liberties.

The Fourth Crusade occurred within the pontificate of Innocent III. This was the crusade that captured Constantinople and established a Latin empire and Roman Catholic dioceses in the East. The pope had been active in promoting the crusade. He protested mildly against its subversion of the Eastern Empire, but waived his objection when it led to the expansion of his own ecclesiastical dominion.

It is agreed by all historians that, when both claims and actual accomplishments are taken into account, the pontificate of Innocent III marks the very apex of the papal power in secular and political affairs. His claims for the papacy were summarized in a letter to the patriarch of Constantinople: "The Lord left to Peter the governance not of the Church only but of the whole world." Never, either before or after his time, did any pope come so near to exercising such governance.

BONIFACE VIII AND SECULAR RESISTANCE

If this was the ultimate in the direction of claiming the rule of the whole world, there remained the possibility of emphasizing and reiterating that claim and also of falling much farther short of making it good. Boniface VIII (1284-1303) did both. Nearly a century had gone by since the great days of Innocent III. That century was the thirteenth, extolled by some able Catholic historians as "the greatest of centuries." Later we shall note some phases of the greatness of that century. It was not, however, a time in which secular rulers were disposed to subordinate themselves to the demands of a universal papal monarchy. The crusades, always promoted by the popes, had fizzled out. The weapon of excommunication, used too often, had lost some of its terrors, and counterweapons had been devised. When the king of France was excommunicated for taxing the clergy and church property, his answer was a currency-control act forbidding the sending of money out of the country, and so cutting off the French revenues of the papacy. The case had to be settled by compromise. The spirit of nationalism was rapidly rising. Stronger kings, better organized national governments, populations with a newborn sense of patriotic pride in the independence of their countries—all these things made it impossible to impose upon Europe the type of papal rule that Innocent had affirmed in general terms and Boniface reaffirmed with picturesque detail.

The earliest of the declarations was the famous bull *Clericis Laicos*. The gist of this was the assertion that secular authorities had no right to tax the clergy or the property of the church. The property in question was not, of course, merely such buildings used for religious services as are now exempt from taxation in the

United States; it was the vast feudal domains held by and for the church. The secular case in the investiture controversy had been weak because it really did involve encroachment upon the right of the church to select its own higher clergy, but the church's case was weak when it claimed that its vast holdings of land— amounting to perhaps one-third or more of a country's area— should bear no part of the government's fiscal burden but should transmit their revenues to Rome.

The bull *Unam Sanctam*, with its figure of the "two swords," is often cited as a parallel to Innocent III's "sun and moon" analogy, and so indeed it is. Its essential paragraph is worth quoting:

> We are taught by the Gospels that there are two swords, the spiritual and the temporal, both in the power of the same person [Peter and his successors, of whom Boniface was speaking in the lines immediately preceding]. . . . Each of these swords, the spiritual and the material, is under the control of the church. The material sword is to be used for the church, the spiritual by the church; the latter to be wielded by the priest, the former by the hands of kings and soldiers but always at the will and by the permission of the priest. . . . Furthermore, we define, assert, declare and pronounce that it is necessary for every human creature to be subject to the Roman pontiff in order to be saved.

In another, somewhat less familiar, bull, *Apostolica Sede*, dated between the two that have been mentioned, Boniface spoke of the "Apostolic See to which every living soul is bound to be subject and through which princes rule and potentates administer justice and kings reign." It was the Apostolic See which had "transferred the Roman imperium to the Germans in the person of Charles the Great," so that "whatever of honor, dignity or status the Roman imperium has, it has by the grace, favor and free gift of the Apostolic See."

If this seems to be carrying the assertion of the emperor's subservience to the pope to the extreme of absurdity, one should note how completely consistent it is with the terms of the so-called "Donation of Constantine." Clumsy ninth-century forgery as it was later found to be, doubtless Gregory VII, Innocent III, and Boniface VIII sincerely believed it to be genuine. In that document

Constantine was represented as transferring to Pope Sylvester and his successors not only the Lateran palace and Rome and all Italy but also "all the regions of the West"—meaning everything west of the Adriatic—together with all the imperial insignia that symbolized sovereignty over them, thus making the popes *de jure* emperors of the Western Empire. That they might also be emperors *de facto*, Constantine says he intends to move his own seat of empire to Constantinople for the specific purpose of leaving to the pope undisputed and unmistakable sovereignty over the West. If that grant of complete and sole dominion were regarded as valid, Innocent III and Boniface VIII must have felt that they were nobly generous in allowing the emperors and kings of western Europe to continue to exist even as lesser luminaries and as subservient wielders of the temporal sword instead of ordering them off as trespassers on their premises.

There was a shocking disparity between the extravagant claims put forth by Boniface VIII and his complete failure to get acceptance for them, the humiliation he suffered at the end of his career, and the servile estate of his successors during the next century. His two great bulls, *Clericis Laicos* and *Unam Sanctam*, were both launched against the king of France, Philip the Fair. Neither produced the desired result. The latter brought violent resistance. The quarrel had already led to the calling of representatives of the French nation—clergy, nobles, and commons—to the first States General, and this assembly supported the king against the pope. When the pope struck back with *Unam Sanctam*, the assembly charged him with heresy and crimes and called for a general council of the church to bring him to trial. Physical violence and the arrest of the pope by Philip's partisans in Rome forestalled his response by an edict of excommunication and probably hastened the pope's death while the quarrel was still at its height.

It was no disgrace to Boniface that he went down fighting. He was a better man than Philip by any modern standard. What counted most was that he was not fighting Philip the Fair. He was fighting the up-surging force of a national consciousness which was ready to side with its king as against any clerical claimant to world dominion in temporal affairs. There is much truth in the explanation by Roman Catholic historians that "the objective of the papacy in the Middle Ages was the salvation of souls and the permeation of all human institutions with Christian principles." But the actual course of papal policy was determined by the conviction that the only way to attain these worthy objectives was by complete domination of church over state and absolute authority of pope over church—in short, by putting into the hands of the pope, in Innocent's words, "the governance of the whole world."

XIV

Monks and Friars

No institution was more characteristic of the middle period of Christian history than monasticism. To be sure it began at least as early as the third century, and it continues even to this day to be an indispensable element in some of the most important streams of Christian life, the Roman Catholic and the Eastern Orthodox. Nevertheless, it was in the Middle Ages that its influence was most widespread and most determinative.

A basic difference between monks and friars is suggested by the derivation of the words, though here, as in so many other cases, the etymologies must not be applied too rigidly. "Monk" comes from a Greek word meaning solitary. "Friar" goes back through the old French to the Latin *frater*, brother. By definition, therefore, monks were men who sought their own salvation in solitude, while friars were a band of brothers who were also taught to think of themselves as brothers to all mankind.

Monasticism began when certain devout men withdrew into desert places to live the ascetic life in complete solitude. Such, though not the first, were St. Anthony of Egypt and St. Simeon Stylites. The basic impulse in this, as in later forms of monasticism,

132

was twofold: first, to buffet the body in order to save the soul; second, to escape the temptations and distractions of this evil world by withdrawing from it. The first of these naturally included the repudiation of all possessions and the denial of every appetite of the flesh. Especially it included celibacy and chastity. The second involved separation not only from sinful pagan society but from communities of ordinary Christians and from the church as a worldly institution.

As early as the end of the second century, the church had freed itself from the taint of the Gnostic heresy, which affirmed a dualism between the world of spirit, which was the realm of God and was therefore good, and the world of matter, which was inherently evil. Its theology held that God, as creator of both spirit and flesh, was master of both, and that such jurisdiction as the Devil exercised over the flesh—and he did have it to a terrifying degree—had been granted to him by God for the fulfillment of his own purposes. So it became incumbent upon Christian men to fight against the Devil's employment of the flesh and the things of this world for *his* purposes. The metaphysical dualism was excluded, but the moral dualism remained.

The issue became more acute as the increasing popularity of Christianity brought into the church great numbers whose motivation was doubtful and whose way of life was not radically changed by their professed commitment. It was not merely that the body of the faithful was diluted by the inclusion of an increasing number of merely nominal Christians. What was even more significant in this connection was that the church itself, now becoming a property-owning institution with its hierarchy of ecclesiastical dignitaries and its status in the secular world, seemed to have lost that reckless ecstasy which was believed to have characterized it in its beginnings. The less the difference between the church and the world, the more those earnest souls felt the need of a special group which, not separating from the church as the Montanists had done, should exhibit within the church the pattern of the completely Christian life. This required withdrawal from the society of ordinary Christians and sometimes from the sacraments of the church and the jurisdiction of its higher clergy. But the church had the wisdom to keep within its fold, and on its honor roll, those who fled to the desert or immured themselves in monasteries to escape its worldliness and its compromise.

The period of the anchorites, or individual isolated monks, did not last long. Soon there were aggregations of such monks, still independent but having their hermitages not far from one another; then groups that, without formal organization, put themselves to some extent under the direction of some experienced hermit such as St. Anthony; then monks definitely forming a community and living together under a set of rules, such as those formulated by St. Basil in the fourth century. (These last were "cenobites," community monks, as distinguished from "anchorites," hermits.) The Egyptian Pachomius, a little after Anthony and a little before Basil, but not so well remembered as either, except by historians, seems to have been the real inventor of the plan of having a community of monks living together under a rule and a director. By Basil's time there were thousands of anchorite and cenobite monks in Egypt and the Middle East. Monasticism had developed far in the East before it was transplanted to the West. It is Western monasticism that concerns us most.

THE BENEDICTINE RULE

There were monasteries (and also a few hermit monks) in Gaul as early as the fourth century. St. Patrick dotted Ireland with them in the fifth century and gave them the active functions of preaching and teaching, which monks and monasteries had never had before. But monasticism in western Europe did not begin to settle into a standardized pattern until Benedict of Nursia, having tried the hermit life not very satisfactorily, enlisted a company of monks, established what grew into the great monastery of Monte Cassino, and drew up the rule that, universally known as the Benedictine Rule, became the accepted guide to the duties of the monastic life thereafter. The so-called Augustinian Rule was constructed several centuries later out of materials gleaned from some of the letters of St. Augustine, who never actually formulated a rule, and was adopted by several important orders. For the first five hundred years after St. Benedict's time, however (he died about 547), to be a monk was to be a Benedictine.

The Benedictine Rule has been called, with perhaps some pardonable exaggeration, "the most important document of the Middle Ages." It was about contemporary with Justinian's codification of Roman law, and also with the closing of the schools of philosophy at Athens, which was the last step in the extinction of pre-Christian classic culture. One of Justinian's laws made monastic vows irrevocable, legally binding and enforcible by the civil magistrates. The Rule provided that the monks were to be strictly cloistered and that they were to occupy their time in praying, reading, studying, and doing manual labor to produce food for the monastery. It did not anticipate that some of them would become administrators in church and state, chroniclers, schoolteachers, missionaries, even artists, nor could the founder foretell that the monks, though individually sworn to poverty, were to become collectively the possessors of vast wealth.

Half a century after Benedict's death, the Lombards raided and burned Monte Cassino. The monks sought refuge at Rome, where they were received and protected by Gregory I, who himself became a Benedictine, if he was not one already. Shortly after that, Gregory selected the Benedictine monk Augustine for that mission to England (see Chapter X) which turned out to be one of the most successful and important missionary efforts in the whole history of Christianity, for it led to the establishment of the See of Canterbury and the reduction of the British Isles to submission to Rome.

The ascetic program of monasticism became the church's ideal of the completely Christian life, and so it still is for some great parts of the church. Other kinds of Christian life may be good, even excellent, certainly necessary—as marriage is honorable but virginity superior—but the monastic life was viewed as the best. This presupposed a double standard for Christian living. The normal requirements of Christian ethics were enough for ordinary Christians and even for the "secular" clergy, that is, those of the clergy who lived in contact with the world. (Clerical celibacy, by the way, was not the rule when monasticism was getting its start and gaining its prestige.) Above this was the higher level of ascetic monasticism. This came to be regarded as requiring a "vocation," a special calling by God. Monks and nuns were "the religious." Jesus had said to the rich young man, "If thou wilt be perfect, go and sell that thou hast and give to the poor." He did not give that instruction to all his followers, because he did not expect them all to be perfect.

Some of the monasteries rendered services of inestimable value to their own time and to subsequent ages. They kept learning alive by preserving and copying manuscripts and by establishing libraries. They fed the hungry, gave refuge to the poor, and set an example of industry and dignified manual labor by their performance of it. They furnished islands of security and tranquillity in a turbulent time. Not all of them did these things, but many did, and they did them through long centuries when there were no other institutions to perform these services.

Abuses crept in, in spite of these meritorious qualities, and even because of some of them. As the quality of Christian life had been diluted when thousands crowded into the church for other than worthy religious reasons, so the quality of the monastic life suffered from the influx of monks who joined the orders for purely selfish purposes. One may well ask: What selfish reason could possibly move one to take the vows of "poverty, chastity, and obedience" and submit to the rigorous monastic regime? The answer is not hard to find. The regime was not always as rigorous as the Rule required. The individual monk might have no property but his monastery might be rich, and this gave him a degree of economic security to be found nowhere else. It was like owning an undivided interest in a great estate. A monk was exempt from military service in any feudal army. The manual labor on the lands of rich monasteries was often done by hired workers or serfs while the monks took their ease. Though theoretically cloistered, many monks were permitted to roam at large, ostensibly on errands for their monasteries but actually in pursuit of their own pleasure or profit. Some monks became abbots, and some abbots became persons of power and prestige. Practically anything was better than any lot to which an ordinary member of the lower social class could look forward. "Poverty, chastity, and obedience"—with such alleviations of all three as might be arranged by a not too scrupulous monk—seemed a small price to pay for the advantages to be gained. One need not quote the derogatory data that have been assembled by the later avowed critics of the system. It is sufficient to consider the reports of the official "visitations" to many monasteries to document the statement that the general level of the monastic life sank far below its Rule and its profession. Not all monks became as immoral as Boccaccio represented them or as uncouth and illiterate as Erasmus pictured them, but monasticism was sadly in need of reform long before either of these voiced their criticism.

The most effective criticisms and reforms came from the inside. They can be remembered as the three C's—Cluniac, Carthusian, and Cistercian. The first serious reform began when William the Pious, Duke of Aquitaine, founded the monastery of Cluny, in France, about seventy-five miles west of Geneva, in 910. It was to be an independent self-governing institution—as all Benedictine monasteries were supposed to be—subject to no control by any lord or bishop but under the direct patronage of the pope. The aim was to set a good example of what a good monastery should be, and it did, chiefly because it had a series of able and conscientious abbots. So influential did its example prove that many other monasteries put themselves under the direction of Cluny. Its abbot appointed their abbots, and the Cluniac reform developed into a chain of monasteries under centralized control and gave rise to what was virtually a Cluniac "order," though still within the Benedictine system. Benedict's idea was that every monastery should be an autonomous unit.

THE CARTHUSIAN ORDER

Equally earnest, though never quite as extensive or influential, was the reform that came when St. Bruno established in 1084 La Grande Chartreuse, the mother monastery of the Carthusian order. Its monks were strictly cloistered, each with his separate cell and his separate garden to cultivate. It always remained relatively small, but it had imitators in other countries. In England the name is "Charterhouse." The Carthusians maintained a high type of monastic life.*

The great Hildebrand, himself probably a Benedictine, was an ardent reformer of ecclesiastical abuses and clerical laxities for many years before he became Pope Gregory VII and achieved his costly triumph for the papacy by humiliating Emperor Henry IV at Canossa. He was contemporary with the Carthusian reform and his influence was one of the factors that gave it such success as it had.

THE CISTERCIAN REFORM

Most fruitful of all the monastic reforms was the Cistercian. It stemmed from the founding of a monastery at Citeaux, about fifty miles north of Cluny, in 1098 by a Benedictine monk named Robert from the abbey of Montier, who seems to have been one of those little men who start something great and then drop out of sight. The Cluniac movement, then almost two centuries old, had lost its reforming zeal and itself needed reforming. The Cistercians went back to the Rule of St. Benedict and applied it more strictly than had been the custom of the Benedictines. They gave themselves to a regime of plain living, "apostolic poverty," prayer and contemplation, and the cultivation of the soil. Though scholarship and teaching were not among their main objectives, the shining light of their order was St. Bernard (1090-1153), who became

* Later their chief industry became the manufacture of the famous liqueur known as Chartreuse. When the monks were evicted from their ancient seat in the nineteenth century they set up their distillery in Spain, where they continued to produce the "Liqueur des Pères Chartreuses," which they claimed was the only authentic chartreuse because they alone had the secret formula. A lay concern at the old location began to market a "Liqueur de Grande Chartreuse" which they held to be the only genuine article because it included among its ingredients some herbs found only in that rather magically picturesque region thirty miles north of Grenoble. A judgment between these conflicting claims is beyond the authors' jurisdiction.

eminent and influential above any of his contemporaries, popes included, as theologian, mystic, guide to the devotional life, ecclesiastical statesman, and defender of Catholic orthodoxy by the persecution of all variants. Bernard founded what became the famous abbey of Clairvaux and remained its abbot for life, declining all other preferment, though he could have had almost anything. Within a generation from the founding of Citeaux its abbot had rule over some dozens of affiliated monasteries, and after less than two centuries their number was reported as 671. The Cistercians were the latest and greatest of the "three C's."

Admirable as were these efforts toward monastic reform, and effective within their limits, the total situation undoubtedly remained very bad. It became worse through the centuries from the twelfth to the fifteenth. The monks became too numerous and the monasteries too rich. It was impossible to maintain either moral or ecclesiastical discipline. Too many monks had no authentic "vocation." Too many monasteries were haunts of either idleness or vice, and sometimes of both. When Henry VIII confiscated the property of the monasteries in England, his own motives may have been no higher than theirs, but he had a point when he said that they had become an incubus upon the English people. They really had. The Catholic Reformation in the sixteenth century brought a great change for the better, not only by the founding of new orders but by sweeping away the abuses which had so largely discredited the old ones. We shall come to that later.

THE DOMINICAN AND FRANCISCAN FRIARS

Back at the beginning of the thirteenth century a new movement began which, though monastic in a general way, was different in some of its basic principles. This was the founding of the mendicant orders of friars—Dominican and Franciscan. The members of these orders were not monks but friars. They were ascetics, but not cloistered. They were religious "knights of the open road." Vowed to "poverty, chastity, and obedience" like the monks, they were not to be immured in monasteries but were to range the streets and highways, begging a minimum of subsistence from any who would put food into their beggars' bags and preaching the gospel to all who would listen.

Dominic, a Spaniard and a theologically educated priest, had contacts with the Albigensian heretics in southern France, who were later to be massacred in the crusade that Innocent III instigated against them. Dominic thought they might be converted if they were approached by Catholic missionaries as devoted as they were. The crusade against them began before he really got started, but he had already formed the idea of an ascetic order of preachers whose main business would be to defend the orthodox faith against all deviants. The order received papal recognition in 1216, grew rapidly in numbers, and spread into most of the countries of Europe. Preaching and scholarship were its principal fields of activity. Since these do not go well with mendicancy, the practice of begging for bread did not long continue to be a conspicuous feature. Many learned Dominicans became teachers in the newly founded universities. The beggar's bag evolved into the academic "hood" which we now see draped around the shoulders of new-fledged Ph.D.'s at university commencements and lending its poly-chromatic splendor to otherwise colorless faculty processions on such occasions. Albertus Magnus and Thomas Aquinas, the greatest theologians of their time, were Dominicans. So also were the mystics Eckhart and Tauler. So too was the inquisitor general Torquemada, who instigated the burning of many heretics and had much to do with the expulsion of the Jews from Spain in the reign of Ferdinand and Isabella; and Savonarola, who about that same time was burned for heresy in Florence. Dominic's "Order of Preachers," closely organized with a "master-general" and with provinces and monasteries and appropriate heads for each, was a very potent society.

No disrespect to St. Dominic, but to turn from his austere countenance and rigid mind to the winsome figure and lyric voice of St. Francis is like moving directly from a November night to a May morning. World-renouncing piety as a monastic ideal had always been regarded as meritorious; Francis made it gay and beautiful. His heart was that of a saint, but also of a troubadour.

His gospel could be sung as well as preached. An inheritor of wealth, which he cheerfully renounced, he carried the practice of ascetic poverty to the farthest possible extreme. When, as he put it, he "espoused Lady Poverty," it was no forced marriage, but a union entered upon with a lover's enthusiasm. Total commitment to God was his basic motive; a childlike faith in the infinite goodness of God was the substance of his theology; identification of himself in bonds of brotherhood with all living things, but especially with the weak, the despised, the loathsomely afflicted, and the desperately sinful, was the principle of his behavior. Francis has been almost everybody's favorite saint from then until now. Some of his most appreciative biographies have been written by Protestants.

Francis did not set out to found an order. He set out to do what seemed to him the most natural thing for one to do who loved God and man with complete devotion—that is, to serve them both with absolute disregard for his own comfort or safety. Others had done this before him, and still more after him, inspired by his example. What was unique about Francis was the blithe and debonair spirit in which he did it. Drawn by the magnetism of his personality, a few followers gathered about him and imitated his way of life. Though they came to be called a "mendicant" order, the plan was to depend primarily on working, not on begging. The followers were to wear the coarsest of ordinary peasant garb and were to do any menial work that came to hand but to accept only food for it, not money. As they went among the poor rendering these helpful services, they were to preach, though Francis himself and his companions were all laymen. This raised a question. Were they ignoring the authority of the church by preaching without its authority? The last thing Francis wanted to do was to rebel against the church and its constituted authorities. When the number of followers reached twelve, he said: "This begins to look like a 'movement,' even though we have no organization. We ought to get the Pope's sanction before we let it go any farther." So they went down from Assisi in the Umbrian hills to Rome and saw the pope, and came back with his blessing. (Written authority for a formal organization came ten years later from another pope.)

The papacy was then at the height of its worldly power and splendor. The pope who sanctioned this movement and authorized it to become an order was the mighty Innocent III, who himself lived in a palace, had the status and pomp of an earthly sovereign, and claimed authority over all the other sovereigns in the world. How could such a pope bring himself to sanction a movement that preached and practiced "evangelical poverty"? The answer is very simple. Francis didn't preach it; he only practiced it. His espousal of poverty grew out of a reversal of the values of poverty and wealth. He had discovered that for himself poverty, not wealth, was to be desired. Poverty was not a Christian duty; it was a blessed privilege for those who had discovered where the true values of life lay. He did not go about seeking converts to his way of life or criticizing the rich for having property. Somebody had to have it. For him, poverty was freedom and joy, and it enabled him to get closer to the poor people to whom he preached the gospel of love. Others did not have to join his company, but any who did would have to adopt his way. The wise pope could see at once that there was nothing subversive about this. The church could always find room for reformers who only reformed themselves and their own comrades and would not try to reform the whole church.

Francis' program was indeed too demanding even for most of those who undertook it. The rule was eased, somewhat against his will. The extent of the tension is a matter of dispute. Certainly there was a rift later between those who followed the easier rule and the "Observants," who imitated Francis' strict adherence to poverty; and certainly Francis was gently eased out of the leadership of the order some years before his death, though he died at the age of forty-four.

The order was a great success under the new regime. It modestly took the name of "Friars Minor." A second order was established for women, the Clares; then a Third Order (usually known by that name) for lay men and women. All three grew great and popular—the most numerous and the most popular of all the orders. Because it was popular on account of its good works, wealthy citizens began to leave money to the order in their wills.

That raised a question: Could lands and buildings be owned by an order composed of friars whose vow was to own nothing? The legal problem was solved (in the affirmative) largely by the ingenuity of Bartolo Sassoferrato, an eminent thirteenth-century jurisconsult, and the point of conscience was settled by following the example of the earlier monasteries, which had solved the same problem in the same way but with less hesitation. So the order acquired substantial buildings and ample lands—quite in contrast with the branch-and-bark shelters behind the Portiuncula at Assisi and the caves on Mount Subasio that had been the only homes of the original band—but never an inordinate amount of wealth. Though scholarship and statecraft had no place in the program that Francis envisaged, the order produced at least four popes and a roster of eminent scholars and theologians, among whom were Roger Bacon, Bonaventura, Alexander Hales, Duns Scotus, and William of Occam. Franciscans became no more strangers to the professorial chairs of universities than were the Dominicans. There was always a certain rivalry, not to say antipathy, between the two, and some of the theological controversies of the scholastics can be better understood if one will note who was a Dominican and who was a Franciscan.

XV

Rites and Customs

The supernatural was not something remote or speculative to the medieval man. The world of his thought, and of his experience, as he understood it, was permeated by the supernatural. It was not merely that ultimate reality is spiritual, that God is the Creator and Sustainer of all things, and that Christ exerts a saving power for those who will accept it, as modern Christians generally believe. It was not merely that the supernatural has sometimes "broken through," as some modern Protestant theologians say, into the realm of history and human experience. It was more than that. For the medieval man, the supernatural was constantly breaking through. The air was full of supernatural beings—angels and devils. Miraculous interventions were so much a feature of the expected order of things that any reported miracle was regarded as prima facie credible. Evidence seemed superfluous. Priests had supernatural powers by which they could perform the miracle of the mass and give absolution from sins. The pope had supernatural authority as the Vicar of Christ. Every sacrament was a supernatural event. Relics, talismans, the sign of the cross, gave supernatural protection from bodily injury. Appeals to the saints
144

brought supernatural aid in every kind of emergency. The devil and his associated demons, exercising a supernatural but malign power, made direct attacks on the faithful or teamed up with the ill-disposed to produce the phenomena of witchcraft. One cannot understand the spirit of the Middle Ages without realizing how completely this idea of continuous supernatural and miraculous intervention dominated the thinking of the period. The rites and customs that are to be briefly described derived their motive and meaning from this fact. They were the techniques by which favorable interventions of supernatural power could be secured and unfavorable ones averted.

All this is included in the definition of the "age of faith." "Faith" had come to mean *the* faith, that is, the Catholic Christian faith and all its accompanying lore. The word *infidelis*, which had originally meant "untrustworthy," came to mean "infidel," or one not holding the Christian faith, and was especially applied to Jews and Moslems. All other traditions had been either eliminated or absorbed into the Christian tradition, and everybody held it. Not to hold it made one a social and political as well as a religious outcast and was a very dangerous position which few cared or dared to occupy. In this respect there was an "integrated society" in spite of wide differences in fortune, piety, morals, and culture.

The basic doctrines of Christian theology had been given definitive formulation by the great councils of the fourth and fifth centuries. Even the important Council of Trent in the sixteenth century did little more in this field than to reaffirm what had been done by the councils of Nicaea, Chalcedon, and Constantinople. But theology is chiefly for theologians. Then, as now, the laity knew little about it. It may be the foundation of a religion but, like any other foundation, it is not the most conspicuous part of the total structure. Much more evident to the observer are the rites and customs and the states of mind that these express.

THE SACRAMENTS

The concept of sacraments is an essential in almost all forms of Christianity, more highly developed in Roman Catholicism, both medieval and modern, than in most others. Peter Lombard, who died in 1160, was the first influential writer to fix the number of sacraments definitely at seven. When the list was completed the seven were: baptism, confirmation, the Eucharist, penance, extreme unction, marriage, and ordination. The first five were necessary for all Christians. Marriage was optional. Ordination was only for priests.

The practice of baptizing infants was introduced long before the beginning of the Middle Ages, if it did not exist from the start. The postponement of baptism until near the hour of death (as in Constantine's case), so as to guarantee the forgiveness of all sins, was frowned upon by the church and was early abandoned in favor of baptism at the earliest possible moment of infancy, to eliminate the curse of original sin. Confirmation naturally followed from infant baptism to give opportunity for the candidate's conscious participation and commitment. The Eucharist, or Holy Communion, was of such central importance as sometimes to be called "the Sacrament." The doctrine of transubstantiation was first rather clearly stated by the monk Radbertus in the ninth century, and the word was coined in the twelfth. It meant that the real *substance* of the bread and wine was changed into the substance of the body and blood of Christ while their *qualities* (or "accidents"), as known to the senses, remained unchanged. Ever since Plato and Aristotle there has been philosophical argument about the nature of the "substance" or "essence" of existing reality in general and of particular things. It is, indeed, one of the fundamental problems of philosophy. One way of looking at it was to say that every material object as known consists of an inner "substance," which constitutes its reality or essence, and certain "qualities" which alone can be known by the senses. The "substance," as that which "stands under" the qualities and holds them together so that they form a knowable object, cannot itself be observed by the senses. It was therefore conceivable that, by pure miracle, one "substance" could be substituted for another while the sensible qualities remained as they had been. Belief that such a "transubstantiation" has actually occurred is an act of pure faith, for it can be neither proved nor disproved by observation, since, by definition, it is only the unchanged "qualities" of the bread and wine that can be observed.

With this sharper definition of the doctrine and with greater emphases on the concept of the Mass as a continuation of the sacrifice on Calvary—that is, the continued offering of the flesh of the victim that had been slain once for all—came the more extensive use of the Mass as a means of conferring spiritual benefits upon any to whom they were directed by the officiating priest, and as a meritorious offering to God having a definite value whether or not any communicants received the elements. Three results of this view were: infrequent communion; the giving of only the bread to the laity, since the entire substance of the body and blood was declared to be present in the smallest particle of either the bread or wine when duly consecrated, and the reservation of the consecrated bread and wine for worship in the "adoration of the Host."

The church had early undertaken to guard the sanctity of marriage, and some sharp quarrels grew out of the efforts of bishops and popes to check the loose practices of prominent persons who wanted to put away their wives and take others for political or personal reasons. Marriage was not generally recognized as a sacrament, however, before the eleventh century. This clinched the claim of the church to have sole jurisdiction over marriage and its laws. Simultaneously, the earlier practice of clerical celibacy, which had been general but with many exceptions, was more strictly insisted upon. Gregory VII found great numbers of married priests, and many more living in concubinage. Remedying this situation was the object of one of his most urgent reforms. This was a reform that had to be many times repeated. One need not regard as history all the bawdy tales that were told about the scandalous relations of priests and monks with women, but there was too much acknowledged illegitimacy in clerical circles, both high and low, to permit brushing off all these stories as mere libels.

The sacrament of penance, with which absolution was associated, became one of the most important of all the sacraments in its effect upon the life of the people and upon the control exercised by the church. With it came the practice of private confession.

The medieval man had a vivid sense of sin and its dangerous consequences. He also knew what to do about it. The church not only kept him reminded of his sins but provided the means of getting them forgiven and so escaping the eternal penalties at the cost of some temporal sacrifice or inconvenience. The first step was confession. In earlier days, confession of sin had been public, before the whole church, after which the local bishop would declare forgiveness and receive the penitent back into communion. The publicity of the confession was regarded as a sufficient penance. Private confession to the priest and the assignment of a definite penance was an established custom by the eleventh century, but it had become the usual practice centuries earlier. Secrecy of the confessional was a reversal of the earlier mode, in which publicity had been of the essence. Techniques of inquiry by the priest were developed and manuals of penance for the guidance of confessors (*i.e.*, priests receiving confessions) were written by experts. There were collections of such rules in Ireland as early as the sixth century containing some rules that were ascribed to St. Patrick. More formal manuals appeared in the seventh century and later. They were very detailed, describing hypothetical sins of every variety and degree and assigning appropriate penances for each. Assigned penances as the condition of absolution might be fasting or abstinence from meat for a specified period, pilgrimages to holy places, benevolent gifts, or other meritorious acts. Scanning these books, or penitentials, gives a vivid impression of an earnest effort to impose moral discipline on a somewhat crude population, both lay and clerical, that badly needed it. It was something of a turning point when, about the twelfth century, the priest began to say, "I absolve thee," instead of declaring that God had forgiven the penitent. This was more than a merely verbal change, for it reflected a closer control by the priesthood.

This system could not have developed as it did without the accompanying concept of purgatory as a post-mortem state in which unabsolved sins might be burned away if they were not serious enough to precipitate the sinner immediately into hell. It was an essential feature of the disciplinary system. Purgatorial penalties, like such earthly penances as fasting, were under control of the church and could be shortened or remitted on terms prescribed by the church. Letters of indulgence, issued by authorized dignitaries of the church, could provide remission of both temporal and purgatorial penalties. Indulgences could be purchased for cash. In this case the commutation of penalties to the person for a money payment was viewed as comparable to the acceptance of a fine in lieu of imprisonment by a criminal court. In theory, true penitence was essential to the remission of penalties whether by an indulgence or by confession and absolution. Limited indulgences were granted automatically and without price for the performance of certain pious acts, such as visits to shrines. Plenary indulgences came in with the Crusades, since taking the cross as a crusader was deemed so meritorious as to counterbalance any sins that could be purged by even the longest period in purgatory.

The practice of selling indulgences lent itself easily to abuses which the church later had reason to regret and to reform. When, as sometimes happened, the main object in pushing the sale was to collect money, the requirement of true penitence as a condition of the validity of the indulgence naturally dropped into the background or was entirely omitted. To most modern readers the abuses are better known than the system itself, for they became the immediate stimulus that touched off the Protestant Reformation. We shall need to say more of them later. The abuses were no part of the original intention when the plan was being developed and were not a conspicuous feature of the medieval period with which we are now concerned. Indulgences at that time were simply one part of the total system in which it was understood that forgiveness of sins and ultimate salvation were to be gained by "good works" performed under the direction and with the sanction of the priesthood.

THE CULT OF THE SAINTS

No feature of medieval religion was more conspicuous or more characteristic than the cult of the saints. The earliest saints were the martyrs of pagan Roman times. Every martyr was *ipso facto* a saint. Then certain persons who had exhibited extraordinary virtues and performed conspicuous services for the church were given local or diocesan recognition as saints after their death. Some became saints by acclamation, so to speak. The first formal canonizations in the name of the whole church were in the tenth century. The present process, by which four attested miracles are required for canonization, was established by Urban VIII in 1634. From a very early time it was believed that beneficent miracles were performed by the saints or, especially, by divine power operating through their relics. The saints became intercessors or advocates at the throne of grace on behalf of their devotees. By their "heroic virtues" and their services beyond the call of duty, the saints had accumulated stores of merit in excess of what was needed for their own salvation. This surplus constituted a "bank of merit" at the disposal of the church. Devotion to the saints gave access to these stores of merit. The saints were also a very present help in frustrating the attacks of the demons, those "indefatigable malignant spirits" that swarmed in earth and air. For those who could understand it, a careful distinction was drawn between the adoration (latria) that was due only to God and the devotion (dulia) that could be rendered to the saints. The Virgin Mary, standing in a sense in the category of the saints, since she was a human rather than a divine being, yet rose uniquely to a level far above the others and was entitled to a special kind of higher devotion (hyperdulia).

The element of the miraculous in the cult of the saints included the miracles that they themselves were said to have performed while alive and the miracles ascribed to their relics after they were dead. Legends of the saints multiplied and accumulated. They were the favorite reading of that rather small minority of lay people who could read, the most popular stories for oral telling, and the substance of many sermons. The great collection of stories of the saints by Jacopo da Voragine, popularly known as *The Golden Legend*, was the best seller of the Middle Ages. It was translated into many languages and circulated in hundreds of manuscript copies for two centuries before the invention of printing, and its English version was the text of one of William Caxton's earliest publications in the fifteenth century. Every saint had a special "day" in the calendar. By Jacopo's time there were far more saints than days in the year, so that he had to choose among them when he arranged the stories in the order of the saints' days from January 1 to December 31. By his time the miracles ascribed to the saints had expanded even beyond the limits of the uncritical credulity of the day, so he does not guarantee the historicity of all that he records but often introduces a tall tale with such a phrase as "Some said," or "It was reported," or "Many believed." The masses were more credulous. If not all the miracles alleged to have been wrought by the saints and their relics were held to be veritable events, they were thought of as at least the kinds of things that might easily have happened. The miraculous was regarded as no more improbable than the natural; it simply didn't happen quite so often.

RELICS AND ART

A similar credulity prevailed as to the identification of relics. Responsible leaders of the church sometimes had to intervene to give warning against the mania for collecting relics of saints and against the fraudulent traffic in fake relics. Yet the church itself saw a great spiritual value in relics. Many of the most important were lavishly enshrined, and in time it became mandatory that the stone table of every altar should contain a relic of some saint in a cavity (the "sepulchre") under its front edge. Most churches of any importance had bones or parts of the body or other relics of one or more saints and exposed them periodically for the veneration of the faithful. Whatever one may think of this practice, at least it was generally carried out with dignity and decent restraint. That cannot be said of the exploitation of the popular mania for relics by unscrupulous individuals. Relics were produced, not by the hundreds but by the tens of thousands, with authentications that would have convinced no one who was not prepared to believe any fanciful tale without evidence. The stories of their discovery were as miraculous as the operations of the relics themselves. They were peddled, traded, exchanged, stolen. The successful theft of a relic was regarded as no crime because the desire to have it was such a holy impulse. There was great rivalry among monasteries for the possession of the most and the best relics. The legend of Helena's finding the true cross dates from the fifth century, more than a hundred years after the alleged discovery. The Holy Spear which pierced the side of Christ (now in St. Peter's at Rome) was found at Antioch during the First Crusade in 1098, and its genuineness was established by an ordeal by fire. The seamless coat somehow got to Treves, in Germany, and the Sancta Scala (the steps by which Jesus climbed up to Pilate's judgment hall) to Rome. Mary's house at Nazareth was said to have been transported to Dalmatia by angels in 1291, across the Adriatic three years later, and in 1295 to Loretto in eastern Italy, where it is now, with miracles all along the way. There were twigs of Moses' burning bush and samples of the manna. Halle had a collection of forty-two bodies of saints and 8,932 fragments of the bodies of others. The Church of St. Ursula at Cologne had the bones of the eleven thousand virgins who were slaughtered by the pagan Huns. The discovery of the body and severed head of the Apostle James in Spain early in the ninth century is a shining example of the employment of relics in the grand style. A document three hundred years later than the discovery mentions the fact that a letter (unfortunately already lost) had been found with the body authenticating it as that of the apostle and telling of his mission to Spain. On that evidence he became St. James of Compostela, the patron saint of Spain.

The age of faith was also the age of cathedral building and of the glorious Gothic. Not representation but symbolism was the dominant principle of medieval art. Its sculpture, painting, stained glass, and mosaic, crude and unrealistic as representations of the objective, were splendidly symbolic of spiritual truth and Christian lore, and they were often superb in composition and color. They had the beautiful naïveté and sincerity of the "primitive." The highest achievements were in architecture, an art in which excellence in form and symbolism cannot be corrupted by lack of either skill or interest in representation. A Gothic cathedral was at once a supreme expression of the dignity of an episcopal see, the civic pride of a community, the humility of the anonymous geniuses who made the plans, the religious devotion of those who did the heavy work, the patience that carried on the construction sometimes for centuries, the liturgical worship that it was designed to house, and the feeling for beauty and symbolism that welded into a unit the work of many minds and hands. The mass and height of the cathedral dominated its environment as religion dominated the lives of those who built it. The lift of its pointed arches summoned the worshiper to a mood of aspiration. In its vast and lofty spaces, man felt the smallness of himself in the presence of the infinite. In the intricacy of its aisles, transepts, and chapels—for one cannot see the whole of any Gothic interior from any one point of view—he sensed the mystery of all that he could believe and worship but not understand. There were many crudities in the life and popular religion of the Middle Ages, but remember that they built Chartres and Saint-Michel, Cologne and Notre Dame.

THE CULT OF THE VIRGIN

Simultaneously with the growth of the cult of the saints was the development of the cult of the Virgin Mary. Her perpetual virginity became a Catholic doctrine, though not a formal dogma, in the fourth century. It required a careful reinterpretation of certain passages of scripture (Mark 3:31; 6:3; John 2:12) which mention the brothers of Jesus. The title "Mother of God" became common later in the same century, and the rejection of it by Nestorius was accounted a heresy. The phrase was at first intended as a way of affirming that Jesus was God; later its use was to honor Mary. Augustine held that she was "born in original sin," but later declared that out of respect for the Lord no question ought to be raised about his mother's inheritance of this common curse. Anselm, the great theologian of the eleventh century, said that she was "born with original sin." The Immaculate Conception—that is, Mary's birth without the taint of original sin—was a controversial question in the early Middle Ages, was generally denied by the Dominicans, later was declared to be a "pious opinion" which only the Dominicans were permitted to discuss, and became a dogma of the Roman Catholic Church in 1854. The Assumption of the Virgin—that is, the removal of her body from earth to heaven shortly after her death—was first mentioned in certain books of the fourth and fifth centuries which were condemned by the pope as apocryphal, but had become a pious opinion by the end of the sixth century or a little later. It did not become a dogma of the Catholic Church until 1950.

While these specific doctrines were slowly developing and were gaining general acceptance long before they became the law of the Catholic Church, the Virgin was constantly being given a more important place in the Catholic cultus. Soon after the Council of Ephesus (431) she began to be considered as a mediator between man and Christ. The greater the exaltation of Christ as King of Heaven, the greater the apparent need for mediators who, once human but now sitting in heavenly places, could understand the needs of frail humanity and present their case before the throne of grace. Prayer to the Virgin Mary and repetition of the Ave Maria became common about 1050 and had become general by the thirteenth century. At that time the Angelus was introduced, a bell to which all who heard should respond with a triple Ave Maria. From 950 to 1350 there was much religious poetry in rhymed Latin (with meter based on accent, not on quantity as in classical Latin), and much of it consisted of hymns in honor of the Virgin.

The institution of chivalry encouraged the cult of the Virgin. Devotion to a lady came natural to knights whose vows included loyalty to feudal superiors and the church and to the lady of their choice. In the other sex there was the parallel phenomenon of nuns becoming the "spouse of Christ," even with the ring. The erotic imagery in such cases should not be grossly interpreted.

The College de gai Savoir, the oldest literary society in Europe, founded at Toulouse in 1324 and still existing, continued the tradition of the troubadours, who had passed out of the picture by that time, and gave it a religious turn. There had been no Provençal poetry in honor of the Virgin Mary before the thirteenth century. It began after 1250, stimulated by "the ardent preaching of the Orders, especially the Dominicans, the great promoters [zélateurs] of the Marian cult," * in spite of their skepticism about the Immaculate Conception. The College de gai Savoir—also called the College des Jeux fleureaux, and the Gai Consistoire—gave (and still gives) floral prizes annually for poetry on assigned themes, the golden amaranth, the silver violet, and the like. The volume containing the winning poems for the first one hundred and sixty years shows a very large proportion either wholly or partly in praise of the Virgin. This theme is seldom absent even when it is not the main topic. Poets with the troubadour heritage felt the compulsion to sing of love. Making adaptations from the earlier *chansons d'amour*, they could apply to religious uses the romantic clichés with which they were already familiar. The religious feeling of these verses is, in general, better than their poetry.

Going on pilgrimages to holy places was a favorite occupation which had the double advantage of winning religious merit and enabling the pilgrims to see the world and enjoy themselves, though the risks and hardships of travel were not slight. The most meritorious of all pilgrimages was to the holy places in Palestine. Thousands had made that arduous journey in the century before the First Crusade, and others made it during and after the crusades. Aside from these Biblical scenes, the principal places of pilgrimage were the shrines of the saints. Those who remember the *Canterbury Tales*—as who does not?—will not need to be reminded of that company's destination or told that pilgrims did not always go in the mood of solemn piety. It may be recalled that Chaucer's "Wife of Bath" boasted that she had three times made the pilgrimage to Jerusalem.

WITCHCRAFT AND INFIDELS

If the saints were ever-present supernatural forces in the medieval world, so also were the demons. That was the reason it seemed so necessary to have protecting saints, guardian angels, and talismans and relics with magical beneficent powers. Belief in

* Alfred Jeanroy, *La Poesie lyrique des Troubadours*, 2 vols., Paris & Toulouse, 1934, p. 310.

witchcraft grew naturally out of the conviction that men were at all times beset and bedeviled by evil spirits, except when they were defended by equally miraculous spiritual forces. Witches were malevolent persons who had made terms with the Devil to borrow his power for the injury of others and to gain pleasure or profit for themselves. The Inquisition attacked witchcraft in 1256. If any doubted the reality or the demonic origin of the reported phenomena, their doubts could be put to rest by the decree of Innocent VIII in 1484 affirming both. The book *Malleus Malificarum* (1489), by two Dominicans, was not only an incredibly detailed description of the nature, powers, and behavior of demons but also a legal manual for the guidance of judges in the trial and punishment of witches. It is a conservative estimate to say that more than 300,000 women were put to death for witchcraft (generally by burning) between 1484 and 1782. Witches were burned in Protestant countries also. Witchcraft trials continued in England until 1712, in Scotland until 1722. Why point the finger of scorn specifically at Salem, which hanged twenty-one witches in a mad period of six months and then repented in sackcloth and ashes?

Trial by ordeal came to be frowned upon by the church. It had been a custom, though never very general, to require a person accused of crime or heresy to plunge his hand in boiling water or walk through fire if there was lack of evidence in the case, on the theory that God would miraculously protect the innocent. Instead of this, Innocent IV in 1252 gave his sanction to the use of torture to elicit testimony or confession from suspected heretics, and this became the standard practice of the Inquisition.

The influence of the church was generally on the side of peace among Christians. It made praiseworthy efforts to mollify the rigors of war and to limit hostilities to two or three days of the week. War against heretics and infidels was a different matter. St. Thomas Aquinas wrote: "It is not injuries to themselves but injuries done to God that the knights avenge." St. Bernard said: "The Son of God delights to receive the blood of his enemies; he is glorified in the death of pagans."

XVI

Scholars and Mystics

If the intellectuals—those who wrote books and even those who could read them—were a small minority of the medieval people, their influence on their own and later times warrants some attention to the character of their thinking. By the time of Charlemagne a cloud of ignorance and illiteracy had settled over Europe. That many-sided ruler initiated schools which brought about what is sometimes called the Carolingian Renaissance, but the term gives an exaggerated impression of the extent of the revival. Alcuin, an English ecclesiastic, was the chief director of this movement, but the schools were palace schools, promoted by the emperor and some of his nobles, rather than church schools. Their light faded before the end of the ninth century and left a few monasteries as the only centers of what could even loosely be called learning.

In the eleventh century there was an intellectual awakening which culminated in the thirteenth. This had two phases: the founding of the universities and the development of scholastic philosophy and theology. The two were related, because the universities were the homes of scholasticism. With these we must think of the mystics, some of whom were scholars, too, but whose

157

approach to what they considered the highest truth was by another route.

There were schools connected more or less directly with some of the cathedrals in the eleventh century and they flourished still more in the twelfth. Scholars gathered to teach at such places. They were supported by the fees of their students. Students came from all over Europe to hear the lectures of eminent teachers. Since Latin was the common language of scholarship, there was no linguistic barrier. At each center where a university arose there was already something to organize before any university was formed. The first kind of organization was that of a guild of teachers. The students often organized themselves into "nations." The degrees of "master" or "doctor"—which for a long time meant the same thing—were certificates of competence to teach, or a kind of teacher's license.

Paris set a pattern of university organization. A body of rules was adopted by the teachers in 1208. Three years later they were recognized as a corporation by Innocent III. The cathedral school of Notre Dame and some private teachers united to form four "faculties," one preparatory, teaching the "liberal arts," and three for professional studies in theology, canon law, and medicine. The liberal arts included the *trivium* (grammar, rhetoric, and logic) and the *quadrivium* (astronomy, arithmetic, geometry, and music). On completion of the liberal arts the student received the bachelor's or baccalaureate degree (meaning "laurel-crowned) and could then be admitted to the higher studies of the university proper. Universities were under the patronage of the church—except the one Frederick II founded at Naples in 1225—so their primary interest was in theology and its accompanying philosophy. A few had other specialties, for example, medicine at Salerno and law at Bologna. University students were regarded as "clerics," though not priests. The present double meaning of the word "clerical" arose from the fact that few except university clerics could write well enough to do clerical work. It also accounts for the seating plan in the college chapels of the English universities, with all the seats sideways to the altar, as in the chancel of a church. The status of university students as clerics removed them from the jurisdiction of the secular courts and made them amenable only to the ecclesiastical courts—a fertile source of friction between "town" and "gown."

ANSELM

In touching some of the high spots in medieval theology and philosophy and mentioning a few of the great names, we can begin with Anselm (*c*. 1033-1109), who lived and died before there were any universities. He was called from a monastery in Normandy to become archbishop of Canterbury. In philosophy he was what is called, in this context, a "realist." This means that he regarded classes of objects as more real than individual things. "Horse," as a type or category, is more real than any particular horse. Old Dobbin or Charlie gets such reality as he has—but only a kind of secondary or derivative reality—from participation in the greater reality of the genus Equus. "Horse," in turn, is less real than the more inclusive class "quadruped," and so on. The similarity of this to Plato's doctrine of "ideas" or archetypal patterns being more real than objective things gives assurance that Anselm's theory was not as foolish as it may sound at first hearing. Anyway it set off one of the greatest controversies of the period. Anselm held, further, that the doctrines of the Christian faith, even such as the Trinity, the Incarnation, and the resurrection of Christ, can be proved by reason. For example, why should there be a God-man? (This is the title of his best-known book, *Cur Deus Homo*.) God's justice requires full satisfaction for sin; man's sin is greater than man himself can atone for; but atonement must be made by *man*, not by a being of some other order; so the need can be met only by a being who is both man and God. Thus, in his view, the incarnation and the substitutionary atonement are rationalized and demonstrated. Anselm also used the famous "ontological argument" to prove the existence of God. He wrestled mightily with the problem of reconciling predestination and free will, but did not solve it. (Who has?)

ABELARD

Abelard (1079-1142), a younger contemporary of Anselm, was the *enfant terrible* of the scholastic era. Romantic interest in his love affair with Héloïse has diverted attention to some extent from his philosophy. Abelard was precocious, brilliant, probably vain. He studied under William of Champeaux and Roscelin, and must have realized that he had a better brain than either of them. At twenty-two he was a popular teacher near Paris. At thirty-six, as a canon of Notre Dame, he was by far the most popular lecturer in the community of masters and students that was to develop into the University of Paris. His was a critical mind that demanded evidence before belief. In his *Sic et Non* (*Yes and No*) he paralleled contradictory passages from scripture and the Fathers, thus raising doubts about the reliability of authority. The scholastics always knew the conclusions they had to reach before they started; their problem was to find proofs of what was already accepted on authority as the truth. Not so Abelard. He said: "The function of dialectic [*i.e.*, rational argument] is to *discover* truth." That was a radical idea. Just as radical and rational was his theory of the atonement as an act of pure grace not requiring any compensatory payment on man's part. God forgives sin as a loving parent does his penitent child's misdeeds, and does not exact an equivalent for it. Christ's death shows God's love and so awakens love in man, thus changing him and making him forgivable. This later came to be called the "moral theory" of the atonement. Abelard was brought to trial for heresy, at the instigation of Bernard of Clairvaux, and his teaching was condemned, but he was permitted to die quietly in retirement. He was indeed a dangerous man, for his doctrine not only tended to discredit ecclesiastical authority as the court of last appeal in matters of theological truth, but it struck a blow, perhaps unintended, at the church's whole disciplinary system by making penance and priestly absolution seem superfluous. Some who were influenced by Abelard carried his reasoning and his individualistic attitudes farther than he did and landed in more extreme positions.

THOMAS AQUINAS

Thomas Aquinas (1225-1274) was born of a noble family near Monte Cassino, between Naples and Rome. It will be a help in defining the age in which he lived to remember that he was born four years after the death of St. Dominic and the year before the death of St. Francis. The two great mendicant orders were then in the first flush of their vigorous youth. His life occupied almost exactly the middle half of that "greatest of centuries," the thirteenth, and was one of the things that made it great. It was wholly between the pontificates of Innocent III and Boniface VIII, the pope who exercised the greatest earthly power and the one who made the greatest claims to power. Thomas was a cousin, in a not very remote degree, of the Emperor Frederick Barbarossa. His father planned for him a great career, but Thomas had other ideas. After studying at Monte Cassino as a boy, he joined the Dominicans before he was a man, and continued his studies at Paris with Albertus Magnus. (The "Magnus" attached to his name attests the esteem of his contemporaries and successors. Yet we mention him only in passing, for no more need be said of him here than that he was the principal preceptor of Thomas till Thomas overshadowed his teacher as Abelard had his.) Thomas lectured at various universities. Lacking the precocity and the brilliance of an Abelard, his indefatigable industry enabled him to produce, during his twenty-five years, an enormous mass of the most solid and closely reasoned theological writing.

It was the special function of Thomas to make the transition from Plato to Aristotle as a philosophical instrument for Christian apologetics, and to draw a clear line between the doctrines that could be proved by the natural reason and those that must be accepted from the proper authorities on faith. Earlier theology had owed much to Platonism. The "realist" philosophy, as already suggested, had found some support in Plato's doctrine of "ideas" as the locus of reality. Aristotle, less known at the time, had seemed to be on the side of the "nominalists," who held that reality was found only in specific objects that could be observed. Actually that was not good Aristotelianism, though Aristotle had been the first great advocate and practitioner of scientific observation as the starting point of knowledge. Thomas rose above the sterile controversy between these two schools of thought. He fought his battles of the mind on different ground. Neoplatonism, with its pantheistic tendency, had been a dangerous rival of Christianity with the thinkers of the early Christian centuries, but the spirituality of its view of the world continued to be an inspiration even to those who rejected it as a system of thought, as of course all Christians must.

Thomas differed from Plato on the nature of being, the nature of man, and the nature of knowledge. *Being* is not static, as in Plato's "ideas," and cannot be separated from becoming. Here he was both Aristotelian and existentialist. *Man* is not a soul inhabiting a body but a soul-and-body unit. Plato (like some theologians) spoke of the immortality of the soul; Thomas (like Paul) spoke of the immortality of man. *Knowledge* is not, as with Plato, the apprehension of a pure "intelligible essence" of reality in archetypal ideas; it is, as with Aristotle, based on apprehension of the material world through observation by the senses. The complete man is not, as with Plato, a being who merely thinks; he is a being who also knows and acts. Matter is not, as with Plato, an element alien to mind, existing within the realm of potential reality but in itself unintelligible and having no definable relation to the causative activity of "ideas." In all these ways Thomas was Aristotelian rather than Platonic. But he differed from Aristotle, too, especially in his concept of the nature of being, and most especially on the nature of man's being. For Aristotle, the reality of any object is its entelechy, the end for which it exists or that into which it can develop, but he could suggest no adequate entelechy for man. Thomas could, and did.

Thomas Aquinas used the Aristotelian logic in proceeding from observation to knowledge, in breaking up his arguments into propositions, enumerating reasons, and stating and answering objections. He did not use the Aristotelian syllogism, and some of his "reasons" are only unsupported affirmations. For example, in his famous proofs of the existence of God one argument is "from the gradation to be found in things." Whatever quality exists anywhere "more or less," he says, must exist somewhere in the absolute degree because, as Aristotle says, "the maximum in any genus is the cause of all in that genus." His illustration is that since we find various degrees of heat in objects, we know that they must all be derived from fire, which is absolute heat. Similarly, since we observe power in various degrees, we know that absolute power must exist somewhere, and that can be only in God. Therefore, God exists.

Central to the system of Thomas was his distinction between natural and revealed theology. This was his solution of the problem of the· relation between reason and revelation. To put it briefly, reason should go as far as it can, and revelation go on from there. Neither contradicts anything that the other affirms. But how far can reason go? It can, he said, go so far as to discover and demonstrate the existence of God, his unity and creative power, and his dealings with the world and man in the natural course of things. It can also discover its own limitations and man's need of something which it cannot supply. All this is natural theology. He treats of this in one of his two greatest works, *Summa contra Gentiles*, which (except Book IV) is addressed to philosophic doubters and presupposes nothing. But natural theology cannot discover the character of God or prove the distinctive and saving doctrines of the Christian religion, which must be learned from revelation. These are treated in the other, and still greater, of the two great books, the *Summa Theologiae*, which includes also a comprehensive discussion of Christian ethics. There is rather common consent that this is the greatest theological work ever written. Even those who would criticize some of its details are generally agreed that in its monumental qualities and the firmly woven texture of its argument it looms above its field. Since it was designed for the instruction of readers who are already believers, it presupposes the truth of the Catholic dogmas and the authority of the sources from which they had been derived. On the use of authorities, Thomas writes:

> Sacred theology properly uses the authority of the canonical
> Scriptures as a necessary demonstration, and the authority of

the doctors of the Church as one that may properly be used, yet merely as probable. For our faith rests on the revelation made to the apostles and prophets, who wrote the canonical books, and not on the revelations (if any such there are) made to other doctors.

To the basic problems of the scholastics: Is revelation reasonable? Is it consistent with reason? Can its content be proved by reason? these were Thomas's answers: It is reasonable to believe that there has been a revelation. The revealed truths are consistent with all the truths discovered or discoverable by reason. Reason cannot discover the truths which are the special content of revelation. Transubstantiation, for example—already approved by the Fourth Lateran Council in 1215—can be explained by the distinction between substance and qualities, but cannot be proved. Nor can it be proved, as Anselm had tried to prove, that the death of Christ was the necessary way, or even that it was the best way, for man's redemption. It must simply be accepted on faith as the way God chose.

St. Thomas Aquinas was not popular in his own time, but his prestige increased rapidly. He was canonized in 1323 by John XXII, one of the Avignon popes, and his philosophy was made official for the Roman Catholic Church by Leo XIII in 1879.

NOMINALISM VERSUS REALISM

The clash between the scholastic "realists" and "nominalists" continued in spite of the refusal of St. Thomas to side with either. The position of the realists has already been indicated. They regarded only classes of objects as real, and the more inclusive the class the greater its degree of reality. They expressed this thought in the slogan "The most general being is the most real being." Most of the orthodox scholastic theologians were realists. One advantage of this was that it enabled them to think of the church as a whole, or the church in the mind of God or as a mystical entity, as being more real than any or all of the individuals and institutions that made up its visible structure. Realism clearly lent its support to centralized religious authority, for those in high place who exercised such authority did not profess to be the voice of the aggregate of the church's members but of the *real* church and so of God, who was the most real being of all. Conversely it stood against every form of individualism. The word "heresy," let it be remembered, literally means "one's own opinion," as distinguished from an established opinion sanctioned by legitimate authority. No wonder then that such an individualist as Abelard refused to align himself with the realists.

The opposing camp was that of the "nominalists," who called themselves that from the word "name." It had reference, as did the word "real" in this connection, to a conception of the nature of classes of things, not to the nature of the things that are the object of observation. They held that reality is to be found in individual persons and things, and that the words used to denote classes of objects are nothing more than names that can be conveniently applied to all or any of the things that have enough similarity to warrant grouping them together. The word "horse"—to revert to the previous illustration—has no metaphysical significance. It is simply a convenient term to use if one wants to mention an animal with the general characteristics which it designates but does not care whether it is black or white, Charlie or Dobbin. Actually there is no such thing as "horse in general"; there are only particular horses. Each one is individually real; but "horse" is just a name for the resemblance between them, to be used when for the moment one pleases to disregard their incidental differences. The quarrel, remote and speculative as it may seem, had profound consequences. It was never settled by a clear-cut victory of either side, but for a long time the scales tipped toward the realist side. This was because nominalism inclined toward what was deemed heresy and especially toward a degree of freedom of thought and individualism inconsistent with that submission to authority which was essential to the "medieval synthesis."

Although Duns Scotus (1265-1308) may be classed as a moderate realist, he had a keen sense of the reality of particular things and of the necessity of considering their individuality. This aspect of his thought tended toward nominalism. He was a Scottish Franciscan. His admirers called him "the subtle doctor"; his detractors later derived from his name the word "dunce," which originally meant not a stupid person but one too subtle for his own good.

Full-blown nominalism came with William of Occam (1280-1349), an English Franciscan of the Strict Observant branch who taught at Oxford. William's clash with the papacy, then established at Avignon, was embittered by his advocacy of poverty not as simply an optional practice (as St. Francis had taught) but as necessary for all Christians and especially for all the clergy. He was tried for heresy, was imprisoned, escaped, and spent his last years in Munich. The head and front of his offense, aside from the poverty question, was his repudiation of all authorities in philosophy and his corresponding demand for complete freedom of thought in that field. In attempting (unsuccessfully) to avoid the charge of heresy, he set up the defense that there are two kinds of truth, theological and philosophical. A proposition could be true in philosophy and false in theology, or vice versa. He was willing to accept the whole body of Catholic doctrine on the authority of the church; it was contrary to reason, yet was theologically true because the church said so and the church was master in the field of theology. In philosophy, however, the mind must be free, even to the point of denying what the church affirmed.

This double standard of truth was a way of trying to get freedom for philosophical thought at a time when it was impossible to get freedom in theology and dangerous to demand it. But it was a weak and futile evasion of the real issue. The church was not to be taken in by any such flimsy excuse for denial of its doctrines. It was, for one thing, in complete antithesis to St. Thomas's much more rational explanation of the relation between reason and faith, and Thomas was being canonized while William was teaching his dangerous doctrine. It was indeed a dangerous doctrine, for it would inevitably lead to doubt concerning any "truth" that was contrary to reason and had only the support of authority. Its tendency was to undermine respect for authority even while William professed his submission to it. Back of that "double truth" evasion lay a much more genuine philosophical issue. The denial of "absolutes" into which his nominalism led him opened the way for all kinds of relativism in philosophy, religion, and ethics. Since the absolutes he repudiated were at that time defended by the sanctions of prison, torture, and fire, it may be said that he was, like Abelard, a pioneer in the cause of liberty.

The continuing issue is between authority, which must always use some form of power to enforce its absolutes, and the free operation of individual intelligence. It is scarcely surprising that William of Occam is even now the *bête noire* of the neomedievalists who regard St. Thomas as the ultimate in Christian philosophy and who yearn for a return to the "medieval synthesis."

THE MYSTICS

To turn from the scholastic theologians to the mystics is to enter a different spiritual atmosphere, though there were some who could breathe the airs of both worlds. The mystics were those who sought an immediate knowledge of God by the soul's direct vision, as one knows the physical world not by argument or on authority but by observation and experience. Their key word was "immediate," meaning, not "sudden," but "without intervening media." They thought Christianity was self-evidencing to those who persistently sought communion with God through contemplation, prayer, and works of charity and benevolence. For the most part they resolved the tension between the authority of the church and the liberty of the individual by humbly accepting the doctrines and discipline of the church, yet finding their own spiritual satisfaction chiefly in independent and unmediated communion with God. William of Champeaux, after Abelard had worsted him in debate, retired to the monastery of St. Victor, where he and his associates, known as the Victorines, became the forerunners of the great mystics of the thirteenth century and later. Bernard of Clairvaux, tough-minded enemy and even persecutor of heretics, was a mystic in his own religious life.

The mystics' emphasis upon direct communion with God, rising in its climax to an ecstatic sense of complete union with God and absorption into him, could sometimes expose them to the charge of pantheistic heresy, or even to the danger of it. Meister Eckhart (1260-1327), earliest of the great German Dominican mystics, believed it possible to receive direct communications from God, and claimed to have them. Such messages must, of course, take precedence over anything that might seem to conflict with them. He continually asserted that he was doctrinally orthodox, but John XXII (the same pope who canonized St. Thomas) declared heretical seventeen statements found in his writings. The last of this series of German mystics, known collectively as the "Friends of God," was Tauler (died 1461), who also was a Dominican. He was so little the theologian that he was doubtless honestly surprised at being even suspected of heresy. His religion was simply to believe and do what he thought God told him and to be faithful to the church whenever orders from higher up did not prevent it. Catherine of Siena (1347-1380), of the Third Order of St. Dominic, engaged much in solitary prayer and meditation. Besides being a contemplative, she was a practical mystic, like the somewhat later Joan of Arc. Toward the end of her short life the times were ripening for the return of the popes from Avignon to Rome. It was Catherine's campaign of prayer and publicity that, as much as any other one factor, brought about the decision to return.

A line of Flemish mystics began with Jan Ruysbroeck (1293-1381), whose leading characteristic was an immediate sense of the love of God. His work was carried on by his younger contemporary Gerhard Groote and by Thomas à Kempis, who was born about the time Ruysbroeck died. It is still uncertain whether Groote or Thomas à Kempis was the author of *The Imitation of Christ*, but it became and remains one of the most popular and serviceable devotional books ever written. Out of this movement came also the anonymous *Theologia Germanica*, to whose influence on his life Luther paid high tribute, and the society known as the Brothers of the Common Life.

The mystical strain was a continuing factor in Catholic life, with notable representatives in Spain and France in the sixteenth century. Our immediate concern is with the middle and latter part of the Middle Ages. The scholastics and the mystics of whom we have been speaking in this chapter were always few in number compared with the total mass of the church's members, which was virtually the entire population. But their impact upon the religious life and thought of their own and later times was tremendous. Though their forms of reasoning and argument are antiquated, their influence continues even to this day.

XVII

Rifts in the Unity

If it should seem to some that the authors of this book are devoting too much space to the medieval period in the story of Christianity, let it be remembered that this is the period most readers know least about; that more than half of the entire history of Christianity lies between the years 500 and 1500; that patterns were established then that still dominate more than two-thirds of the Christian world, while the acceptance of some of these patterns and rejection of others goes far toward defining the attitudes of the other third; and that this is the period in which the history of Christianity is most closely linked with the history of political change and all forms of intellectual and cultural activity.

The medieval unity was never as solid as has often been supposed. On the political side the Holy Roman Empire, while something more than a shadow and a name, was a good deal less than an empire. The feudal system, beautifully systematic as a diagram of reciprocal rights, duties, and loyalties, was in practice a jumble of inconsistencies and became more so as cities developed. Many of these were "free cities," and every city was a focus of incipient revolt against feudal lordships. The system never did get a good

169

hold in Italy. The rise of scores of autonomous and virtually sovereign states made the political map of Europe far more intricate than it is today. As to religion, there was only one body of ortho- dox doctrine west of the Adriatic, and one church defending its monopoly by police methods and by the threatened terrors of hell, but there were persistent as well as sporadic heresies, and there were revolts—or "reforms," depending on how one views them— that won formidable followings and called for fierce, but not always completely successful, measures for their repression. And there was a schism in the papacy itself which, for nearly half a century, divided the loyalty of Christendom between two or three rival popes. These are some of the kinds of "rifts" that we must now consider.

THE GREAT SCHISM

Boniface VIII (see Chapter XIII) had overshot his mark. His extravagant claims to dominion over all temporal powers—claims such as no pope of the present century would think of making— set up a tension that only awaited a weak pope and a suitable political situation to bring disaster. Boniface, for all his lofty language about the royal "moons" deriving all their light from his pontifical "sun," was a weak pope. He emerged frustrated and humiliated from a contention with Philip IV of France (Philip the Fair). Following his almost immediate death and that of his suc- cessor—an admirable Dominican whose reign was cut short after eight months, probably by poison—Philip took matters into his own hands and engineered the election of a French pope, Clement V, who transferred the seat of the papacy from Rome to the pleasant city of Avignon on the Rhone about thirty miles above its entrance into the Mediterranean. There it remained, under the thumb of France, for sixty-eight years (1309-1377). This is known as the Babylonian Captivity of the church. Avignon did not belong to France but to the counts of Provence. The papacy bought it from them in 1341 and kept title to it until revolutionary France took it in 1791.

The seven Avignon popes were all French. At least four of

them were excellent men, and the other three were by no means as bad as the reputation of the Avignon papacy. The first one, the pope who made the move, is described by Catholic writers as "a man of grave moral faults," but, in general, papal Avignon was not the sink of iniquity sometimes depicted. The worst that can be truthfully said is that its court was worldly, luxurious, self-indulgent, with little interest in spiritual matters and little capacity for them. Though not an open scandal, this was no help toward regaining the moral authority and international prestige that were compromised by subservience to French influence. The completeness of this loss of prestige was evident when John XXII, the second Avignon pope—he who canonized St. Thomas, imprisoned William of Occam, and burned some Franciscan Observants—revived the old pretensions to universal dominion by claiming that it was the pope's right to administer the affairs of the empire during a vacancy due to a deadlock between rival candidates for the imperial crown. The German electors not only rejected this idea but passed a resolution, which the Reichstag confirmed, declaring that the pope had nothing whatever to do with the choice of an emperor or with his induction into office. Only a few years earlier, but within the Avignon period, Dante had written his *De Monarchia*, taking the same side that the Germans were now taking in the state-versus-church struggle. Marsilius of Padua in his *Defensor Pacis* went even farther than Dante and the Germans in demoting the popes from their political supremacy. He would not allow papal supremacy even over the church. All power on earth comes from the people, he said—power in the state from all citizens, power in the church from all Christians. A general council, with lay representation, is the only authentic voice of the church, as the New Testament is its only authority. John XXII excommunicated Marsilius, but could not silence him or stop the reading of his book. The wide acceptance of such revolutionary ideas indicated a serious rift in the medieval unity. One symbol of this was the existence of the two warring parties, Guelphs and Ghibellines, which, though many other issues came to be involved, basically represented acceptance or rejection of the high claims of the papacy to supremacy over the emperors.

During the Avignon period, when many of the former sources of papal income were dried up, it became necessary to find new revenues and to reorganize the financial system of the Holy See. Along with a wide extension of the pope's appointing power came a claim to the first year's income (*annates*) from all papal appointees, and also the income of all vacant benefices, many of which were left long vacant by inadvertence or design. There was extensive development in the collection of fees for all kinds of papal documents, favors, dispensations, indulgences, and the like. The papacy's financial problem was satisfactorily solved, but these methods did nothing to increase its popularity. Some resentments began building up that later reached the boiling point. It was at this time also that the brilliant adventurer Cola di Rienzi, taking advantage of the turmoil of conflicting interests of the great families in Rome, attempted a revival of the old Roman Republic. Its life and his were both brief. The old forms had no vitality, and Rienzi was murdered (1354).

Gregory XI moved the seat of the papacy back to Rome in 1377 and died the next year. It was unfortunate that the election of a new pope came so soon. The cardinals, mostly French, wanted a French pope and a return to their pleasant life in Avignon. However, holding their conclave in Rome and under strong local pressure, they chose an Italian, Urban VI, whose anti-French attitudes immediately provoked the cardinals who had elected him. After four months they met again, voided the election on the ground that they had been subjected to violence and duress (a disputed question ever since), and elected a Swiss cardinal as Clement VII. (He is to be distinguished from the Renaissance Clement VII, who was a member of the Medici family.) This rival pope and his cardinals moved back to Avignon. Urban VI sat tight, appointed some more cardinals, and remained in Rome. Now there were two popes, or two claimants to the office, each with his own loyal constituency: for the pope at Rome, northern and central Italy, most of Germany, England, and Scandinavia; for the pope at Avignon, France, Spain, southern Italy, Scotland, and part of Germany.

This was schism on a scale unprecedented since the separation between East and West. It proved to be less enduring, but it produced much confusion during the forty years that it lasted. For a time there were three popes. The "antipope" Clement VII held his place at Avignon for twenty-six years and was succeeded by the Spaniard Pedro de Luna, as Benedict XIII, one of the most remarkable personalities ever to hold or claim the papal office. The shift of loyalties was steadily to the side of Rome. Benedict lost France and was forced to leave Avignon. He took up residence first at Perpignon, then in Spain, where his constantly shrinking support forced him to withdraw to a rocky promontory near Valencia. Having only a castle and a harbor, he kept up the pretense of power by maintaining a tiny navy, so that he came to be called "Pope of the Sea." It would have been ruinous to grant his claim to the tiara, yet it was too plausible to ignore. After all, there was a reasonable doubt as to whether there *had* been duress in the election of 1378, and his claim would be good if there had been. The Council of Constance induced two of the three popes to abdicate, and the Emperor Sigismund—after he had finished burning John Huss—journeyed to Perpignon to persuade Benedict to abdicate also and clear the way for a new election. Benedict was willing on one condition. If the election of all three popes had been of doubtful validity, as the council said, then all the cardinals they had appointed must be equally doubtful. Benedict had been a cardinal, and he was now the only surviving cardinal who had been appointed before the schism. Consequently he was the only cardinal of undisputed legitimacy. So, said Benedict, I will abdicate as pope, go into conclave with myself, as the only authentic cardinal, and elect myself pope. This may have been a logical argument, but obviously it was no help toward settling the schism. After that there was nothing to do but ignore him and wait for his death—and he lived into his nineties, apparently out of sheer determination to outlive the opposition as he had already outwitted it.

The settlement of the schism was the work of the reforming councils of Pisa, Constance, and Florence. The emergency brought into prominence the theory of "conciliar supremacy"—that is, that the supreme voice of the church was that of a general council, not that of a pope. Though this theory seemed to triumph in these councils, the victory was brief. The schism was ended when the council at Florence deposed Benedict XIII, having already disposed of the other two claimants, and when a member of the great Colonna family of Rome was elected as Martin V by a conclave composed of twenty-three cardinals and thirty delegates to the council. This was a really revolutionary procedure. Moreover, the council had rather positively asserted the superiority of its authority over that of a pope. Martin did not directly challenge this claim, and he was willing to benefit by the council's bold action in clearing the field of the rival popes. But the next year he issued a formal declaration that there can be "no appeal from the pope in matters of faith." Three years passed after Martin's election before he could restore turbulent Rome to such condition that he could again set up the seat of the papacy there. When he did, he took the reins in strong hands. By the time he laid them down eleven years later, there was no doubt in anyone's mind as to the supremacy of the pope over the church in matters of both faith and discipline. The Great Schism was ended and the church had emerged with its structure of authority unchanged from a revolutionary movement that might have transformed it from a spiritual autocracy to a constitutional monarchy. The two-sword theory was never disavowed, but there were no more efforts to put it seriously into practice.

OPPOSITION LEADERS

Even back in the period from Gregory VII to Innocent III, when the papacy had been in the heyday of its power, there had been subversive movements. Perhaps the most violent was that of Peter of Bruys, early in the twelfth century. It is not unfair to say that he was a fanatical revolutionist rather than a reformer. He rebelled against all ecclesiastical authority, would have no liturgical worship or ceremonial acts, denied the validity of infant baptism, and held that the church should own no buildings or other property. He had a special aversion to the use of the cross as a symbol, and went through the countryside preaching his negative gospel, publicly burning crosses, and winning a considerable number of followers, who came to be called Petrobrusians. He was himself burned, probably by a mob, sometime before 1130.

Like this Peter, but a little less extreme, was Henry of Lausanne, who was a kind of latter-day Donatist in holding that the sacraments were valid only if the ministering priest were morally pure and lived an ascetic life. He preached through western and southern France from 1101 until 1145. His followers were called Henricians. The movement grew important enough to draw vigorous attack from Bernard. The wonder is that Henry remained alive and active as long as he did, and that he died a natural death. The apparatus for the suppression of heresy had not yet been perfected. Peter and Henry were leaders of what was largely a proletarian revolt against the wealthy and luxurious clergy who controlled institutional Christianity, but they also had some intellectual motivation. They represented the fanatical fringe of the movement of thought initiated by Abelard.

Arnold of Brescia, a more picturesque character than either of those just mentioned, and for a time more dangerous to the existing order, agreed with them in attacking the worldliness and wealth of the clergy. Like St. Francis, he exalted poverty, but unlike Francis he insisted that all the clergy should practice it. The pope should have no temporal power, he said, and the bishops should engage in no political activity. Bernard had him condemned in 1140 by the same council at Sens that condemned Abelard. Arnold got to Rome and cast in his lot with a revolutionary movement which had set up a temporary republic and banished the pope. The republic collapsed. Arnold later returned to Rome to attempt its revival. He was hanged in 1155 at the insistence of Pope Hadrian IV, who refused to crown Frederick Barbarossa until he had agreed to execute Arnold. He was no heretic in doctrine, but was a foe to clerical authority, wealth, and temporal power. It will be noted that all three of these revolutionary movements came in the half-century immediately following Gregory VII and his humiliation of Emperor Henry IV at Canossa, and also that all three were anti-clerical more than they were doctrinally heretical. Presently there came a movement that was very definitely both and on a much larger scale.

THE ALBIGENSIAN HERESY

The lovely region of the Midi in southern France—from Toulouse through Carcasonne to Narbonne—was the scene of the most formidable development of the Albigensians. This was a real heresy, and no doubt about it. The roots of this heresy were deep. It went back to the Paulicians of the seventh century or earlier and their claim to teach "simple Christianity," and had in it a strain of that Manichaeism to which Augustine had been devoted before his conversion. There had been an outcropping of this tradition in the tenth century in Bulgaria, where its adherents were called Bogomiles, and when they moved westward they were sometimes called Bulgars. The collective name for all of them, then and later, was Cathari, or "the pure ones." The core of their doctrine was metaphysical dualism—that Good and Evil were two independent powers. These, equally eternal and almost equally potent, were engaged in endless conflict for the souls of men. Spirit and matter were the manifestations of these two. Around this basic concept was woven a tissue of doctrines and practices strangely at variance with the common Christian tradition. Yet they practiced a strict morality which, for the special class they called the "perfecti," was intensified into a monastic austerity. In the large communities which they developed in southern France, northern Spain, and northern Italy, they were a peaceful, prosperous, and virtuous people. What made them doubly dangerous was that they gave no allegiance whatever to the hierarchy centered at Rome but had set up a rival ecclesiastical system, held their own councils, and even, as some said, had their own pope.

The Third Lateran Council voted a crusade against the Albigensians in 1179, but nothing was done about it until Innocent III took up the fight thirty years later. The French king collaborated. Simon de Montfort (father of the man of the same name who was later to become "Father of the English Parliament") and other nobles from the north of France responded to the call and brought their forces. It was a war against an unarmed and unresisting enemy. The process was wholesale slaughter in which many of the orthodox were slain along with their heretical neighbors. It was during this operation that a papal legate is said to have uttered the famous words: "Kill them all; God will know his own." When it was over, the Albigensians as an organized body were extinct, though some scattered and went underground. Since they had professed to draw their teachings directly from the Bible, a council at Toulouse condemned all vernacular translations of the Bible and forbade the laity to possess copies of it even in Latin, except the Psalms and such passages as were found in the breviary.

One nineteenth-century historian said that the Albigensians would have won Europe away from the papacy and the Catholic Church if it had not been for St. Francis and the Franciscans. This seems a gross exaggeration of what undoubtedly was a serious sub-versive movement that was all the more dangerous because some of its propaganda was carried on by undercover men. One char-acter in Italy, famed for his piety and good words, was well on the way toward canonization as a Catholic saint when it was discov-ered that he had secretly been an Albigensian.

THE INQUISITIONS

The Roman Inquisition began under Gregory IX (1227-1241). The crusade against the Albigensians had swept away any linger-ing qualms about the burning of heretics. Hitherto the search for and punishment of heretics had been chiefly left to the diocesan authorities with occasional aid from provincial councils and a few monastic leaders of wide influence and with assistance from the civil rulers. Now the heresy hunt was organized. Dominicans were generally chosen as inquisitors. The rules of procedure, laid down in a bull of Innocent IV, 1252, included: secret proceedings, concealment of the identity of informants and witnesses, the use of torture to extort confessions, and the confiscation of the victim's property, which was shared between the church and the civil power that carried out the death sentence. The Spanish Inquisition, much later (1480), was aimed at Jews and Moslems, who, after professing conversion, were deemed to have lapsed, and afterward against Protestants.

The saintly Thomas Aquinas wrote: "Heresy is a sin worthy of death, falsification of the faith worse than false coining, and deserving not merely exclusion from the church but also from the world."

An Anglican historian has written:

> Nothing that took place in the persecution of the Christians under the Roman Emperors can compare in severity and cruelty and inhumanity, or as to the number of victims involved, with what was achieved by the tribunals of the Inquisition for the suppression of heretics.*

Though the liquidation of heretics was regarded as a solemn duty, it was not carried out constantly or consistently. If this aspect of medieval Christianity must not be concealed or excused, neither should it be exaggerated. Ecclesiastics who were also feudal lords or virtual sovereigns had other complicated interests which often diverted their attention from this function or prevented the performance of it. Italy in the twelfth and thirteenth centuries swarmed with individual heretics—none with any great following though some with a good deal of local popularity—whom nobody took the trouble to check.

THE WALDENSIANS

More important in the long run than the heretical and schismatic movements that have been mentioned were the evangelical reformers, whose voices began to be heard in the Middle Ages. The earliest in this category was Peter Waldo, a silk merchant of Lyons who conceived the startling idea that the religion of Christ consisted of faith in him, the practice and preaching of the gospel as anyone can understand it by reading the New Testament, and living a good life. He had a translation of the New Testament made into the vernacular, and he and his associates went forth to preach repentance, the simple Christian life, and a Sermon-on-the-Mount gospel. Not yet in rebellion against the church, he applied

* A. V. G. Allen, *Christian Institutions*, New York, Scribner, 1897, pp. 223-24.

to the Third Lateran Council for permission to preach, but this was refused. It was not that he was a heretic but that he and his colleagues were "ignorant laymen." Besides, the council was already anxious about the Albigensians and was in no mood to encourage any free-lance evangelistic efforts. Waldo and his men ignored the refusal and continued their work. Five years later he was excommunicated for "disobedience." A group called the Humiliati in Lombardy joined the Waldensians. Their work spread, in Germany, Austria, northern Italy, and northern Spain. It was successfully repressed everywhere except in the Cottian Alps, west of Turin in the northwestern corner of Italy. There the Waldensians continued in spite of recurrent persecution. After the Reformation they threw in their lot with the Protestant forces, but were still exposed periodically to fierce persecution. Milton's famous sonnet "Avenge, O Lord, thy slaughtered saints" had reference to a campaign against them in the seventeenth century. Now more vigorous than ever, and essentially Presbyterian, they are the oldest member of the Protestant family.

JOHN WYCLIF AND THE LOLLARDS

John Wyclif is commonly hailed as the "morning star of the Reformation." The period of his life was that of the Avignon papacy and the beginning of the Great Schism. He was a professor at Oxford and, by royal appointment, rector of Lutterworth, a town not many miles north of Oxford. The papacy, apparently tied to France, was at the lowest ebb of its international prestige. The rising spirit of English nationalism made it easy for anyone who challenged it to find defenders. Wyclif first came to prominence not as a reformer needing defenders but as himself a defender of England's position in a quarrel with the pope. The Statute of Provisors (1351) had been England's answer to a new papal claim to the right to make all appointments to church offices. The statute reserved English posts to appointment by English authorities. Ensuing controversies led to appeals to Rome. The Statute of Praemunire forbade such appeals. Wyclif was a mem-

ber of a royal commission that went to Bruges to seek some adjust-
ment of these conflicting claims with the pope's representatives.
His rather too simple scheme of things regarded God as the feudal
lord over all, nobles and clergy as his feudal tenants—the clergy
for spiritual things, kings and nobles for temporal, with the proviso
that the civil powers could take over the property of the church
if the clergy did not use it properly for spiritual ends. This was
pleasing to the powerful John of Gaunt and the other nobles who
viewed the vast possessions of the church with covetous eyes.
Much of this property was not, in fact, being put to any spiritually beneficial use—but who were they to be the judge? The
higher clergy, the pope, and the rich orders of poor monks
were indignant. Wyclif was forced to appear before the bishop
of London to answer charges. A series of condemnatory bulls
came from Gregory XI, who, just then moving the papacy
back from Avignon to Rome and already confronted by a rival
pope, was in no position to do anything but issue bulls. Popular
English opinion and John of Gaunt were on Wyclif's side.

Meanwhile, the strictly religious side of Wyclif's teaching had
developed. It rested on a conviction that the Bible was the only
valid authority. The voice of the church is the voice of the whole
company of the faithful, not of the clergy or the pope. The
worldly power exercised by the clergy and even the existence of
the religious orders are anti-Christian because not authorized by
the New Testament. It was therefore important to get the Bible
into the hands of the common people in a language that they could
read. Wyclif promoted and supervised a translation of the Latin
Vulgate into English and probaby did the New Testament himself. It was circulated as widely as it could be in manuscript copies.
Printing, of course, had not yet been invented. Peripatetic preachers—"poor preachers," they were called—carried about copies of
this first English Bible and preached Wyclif's doctrines, which
included not only the simple gospel but attacks on the priesthood,
episcopacy, and transubstantiation. Wyclif's strength was his scholarship and intellectual power, his courage, his personal piety, his
appeal to the New Testament, and his English patriotism, which

won him popularity and powerful support. He died in peace after a fairly long life. Thirty years later the Council of Constance ordered Wyclif's bones dug up and burned and the ashes scattered on the Avon. So it was said:

> The Avon to the Severn runs,
>   The Severn to the sea;
> So Wyclif's words shall spread abroad
>   Wide as its waters be.

Wyclif's words spread in England, too. His followers, called "Lollards," formed a Protestant underground which helped to prepare the way for the Reformation in England. It is impossible to estimate the strength of this group even approximately. Historians, guided chiefly by their own sympathies or antipathies, have guessed their influence as all the way from "negligible" to "important." Our guess would be "considerable but not decisive." Probably Wyclif's greatest influence on the Reformation was as a memory, as a name that became a watchword for Protestants, and as a translator of the Bible into English.

JOHN HUSS

The work of John Huss in Bohemia was similar to that of Wyclif. It has been well established that the reform in Bohemia had its own initiating impulse, independent of Wyclif, but undoubtedly Wyclif's career encouraged it. Huss, also, was an intellectual, a professor in the University of Prague and for a time its rector. He was a priest and the most popular preacher in Bohemia. His sentiments, evangelical to some and heretical to others, led to a summons to appear before the Council of Constance. To induce him to come, and thus put himself in the power of his known enemies, the Emperor Sigismund gave him a safe-conduct guaranteeing his personal security. Nevertheless, the council condemned him as a heretic and turned him over to the emperor to have him burned. The shocking bad faith of this procedure has made the episode famous. The teaching of Huss and his colleagues did not die out with the fire of his martyrdom. The reform in

Bohemia continued into and through the Reformation period and merged with the Protestant movement.

The fifteenth century was a time of brilliant confusion and contrasting colors. It began with the Great Schism and ended with the Renaissance at or near its height. The monastic orders were suffering such decay and corruption as never before or after. The moral authority of the church was at low ebb. There was a breakdown of its discipline over both clergy and laity. Yet never was papal Rome so indisputably the cultural capital of the world. We turn now to that fascinating and controversial theme, the Renaissance.

XVIII

Renaissance and Religion

Something began to happen in Europe about the beginning of the fifteenth century that, whether one is disposed to approve or to deplore it, produced a profound change in men's ways of thinking, in the values they cherished, in their artistic and cultural activities, and in their attitudes toward religion. This total change has been called the Renaissance. Its earliest and most brilliant manifestations were in Italy. As a period of European history it may be conveniently dated as from about 1400 to 1525.

These dates are arbitrary and perhaps too narrow. The Renaissance cannot be stretched back far enough to include Dante and Giotto, who were thirteenth-century medievalists, but it ought to include Petrarch and Boccaccio of the fourteenth. It might be extended to include the whole career of Michelangelo, who lived and worked until 1564 but with the consciousness in his later years that he had outlived his own era. It moved like a wave across Europe, its crest arriving at successively later dates as it went north and west into Germany, France, the Netherlands, and England. Shakespeare and Bacon were men of the English high Renaissance early in the seventeenth century. The term should not be taken too

183

seriously as denoting a historical period. It was a state of mind rather than the interval between any two dates. Making it a label for a period is relatively recent usage. But this is not surprising. Caesar did not call his writings "ancient history," and Thomas Aquinas did not realize that he was living in the "Middle Ages." Every era is "modern" to those who live in it and every period thinks it is an "age of transition." This one really was.

The word "renaissance" means "rebirth"; or, by analogy, an awakening from a long, deep sleep. Jakob Burckhardt used the phrase "the discovery of the world and of man" as the title of one part of his great book on the Renaissance and it expresses his view of the movement as a whole. John Addington Symonds called it "the attainment of self-conscious freedom by the human spirit." Whether these terms represent true evaluations, whether it was in reality a cultural advance or a recession, is a debatable question. There are those who consider it a great decadence—the passing of the "age of faith," the dissolution of the "medieval unity," the fragmentation of what had been an "integrated society," an anarchistic revolt against legitimate spiritual authority and moral and intellectual absolutes. The authors do not take this view. In any case, we must ask ourselves what, if anything, was reborn or woke from sleep, and what were the consequences, both good and bad.

The things that woke, or were reborn, were these: classical scholarship; the Greek ideal of the free individual and the versatile personality; intellectual curiosity; a sense of the values to be found in the joy of this life and the beauty of this world, unconditioned by any theological considerations; an approach to the problems of philosophy independent of theology.

The rebirth of classical scholarship, commonly called the "revival of learning," involved the rediscovery of the lost manuscripts of many forgotten classics of Latin and Greek literature, the study and publication of these works, the imitation of their style, the recovery and popularization of knowledge of the Greek language. Scholars at that time could become as much excited about anything Greek as scientists are today about jet propulsion or atomic fission. Men of fashion who were not scholars felt the contagion of that enthusiasm. Browning's bishop, in "The Bishop Orders His Tomb at Saint Praxed's Church," spoke to the condition of his worldly nephews when he promised that the saint would get them "brown Greek manuscripts" as well as beautiful mistresses. The popes became the greatest of all the collectors of classic manuscripts, and the Vatican Library—founded by Nicholas V, the first "Renaissance pope"—the greatest of all collections. Aldo Minutius, Venetian printer, employed Greek servants, made his household speak Greek, and announced his ambition to issue editions of all the known Greek classics and to make them "accurate, beautiful and cheap." (What better slogan could any publisher have?) Newly found pieces of Greek sculpture quickened the sense of bodily beauty and reinforced the other influences that were guiding artists toward its realistic representation. The reported finding of the perfectly preserved body of a beautiful Roman girl in a tomb on the Appian Way seemed a symbol of the resurrection of classic antiquity.

The ideal of the free individual, as portrayed in Graeco-Roman history and literature, was a stimulus to impulses that had long been in abeyance. Here was the picture of a culture in which there was no regimentation of minds. The Greeks had had their conventional religious beliefs and practices, to be sure, but they had neither dogmas nor creeds. They had priests but no hierarchy, temples but no apparatus for compelling conformity to any cult. Membership in the mystery cults was voluntary and unrestrained. The Romans had insisted only on a ceremonial gesture of recognition toward the "genius of the emperor"; beyond that, one could believe and worship as one pleased. Men of the Renaissance who read the ancient classics found in them more than an antiquarian interest. They heard a call to a kind of freedom that they had not known. The ideal of versatility found its exemplars in the personnel of the classics. Plato had been the best writer as well as the best philosopher, and a political scientist and the designer of an ideal state besides. Aristotle was the universal man, his works an encyclopedia in everything but alphabetical arrangement. Cicero was lawyer, philosopher, statesman, orator, essayist. The originally whimsical statement of a character in a Latin comedy, "I am a man and nothing human is alien to me," was taken seriously as encouragement to a multiplicity of interests and activities. This became one aspect of Renaissance culture. Consider Alberti—architect, painter, athlete, author of a Latin comedy good enough to be mistaken for a lost work of Plautus; or Michelangelo—sculptor, painter, poet; or Leonardo da Vinci—painter, sculptor, musician, military engineer, inventor. Others less notable achieved excellence in many fields, and no doubt many more cherished the ideal but lacked the requisite talent.

Intellectual curiosity is probably one of the essential conditions of versatility. Add to it a sense of freedom from outer or inner compulsion to conformity with established institutions and ideas, and the result is a critical attitude toward whatever may be proposed for one's acceptance. Presuppositions are examined. Authorities are scrutinized. Time-honored assumptions are questioned. The scientific spirit is in the making, though its processes may still be crude and its immediate results erroneous. Nothing is more characteristic of the Renaissance than this attitude of free inquiry. It can be very dangerous to existing institutions. To say that it is the spirit of individualism challenging authority and custom is only another way of describing the same attitude. The Renaissance man felt himself to be first of all a free individual. Later, the very classicism that had spurred him to demand freedom became a new norm to check the exercise of it, but it had not yet come to that and when it did it was only in limited fields of culture, such as an artificial and pedantic Ciceronianism in literary style.

It would be an insult to the medieval spirit to say that it put a low valuation upon man. On the contrary, it constantly held that man has infinite value, but this was man as a child of God and the church and therefore as a candidate for everlasting life. Because that value was so great, no earthly joy or beauty could be allowed to interfere with it—as they usually did if indulged to any degree, for "the flesh warreth against the spirit and the spirit against the flesh." The Middle Ages did not originate that thought, but they gave it heavy emphasis. Undoubtedly the medieval man had many innocent joys with the sanction of the church, and others not so innocent which could be enjoyed with a bad conscience but without too much risk because the church provided the means of expunging the guilt of indulging in them. The Renaissance spirit, by contrast, revived a sense of the value of the natural man and the life that now is. Men imbued with that spirit lost interest, more than they lost belief, in what the church was saying about future bliss and the conditions of attaining it. "One world at a time" might have been their motto, and this present world absorbed their attention. Their mood was "secular" in the sense that their concern was with the present saeculum (age), because it provided resources of joy and beauty that were rewarding in themselves. It was natural that the arts should flourish in such an atmosphere if this appreciation of the value of beauty were accompanied, as it was, by an outburst of creative energy.

For those who applied the new-found freedom in an intellectual approach to fundamental problems rather than to the visual arts, the result was a development of philosophy independent of theology. Medieval philosophers had been primarily theologians. For them, philosophy had been the handmaiden of theology, the "queen of the sciences." Renaissance philosophers were primarily *philosophers*. Their impulse was to hew to the philosophical line and let the theological chips fall where they might. Plato became the chief stimulus to Renaissance philosophy, especially after Ficino's translation of his work into Latin. Neoplatonism had an allure for those whose temper was at once speculative and mystical, such as Pico della Mirandola. When a synthesis of philosophy with Christian doctrine was attempted it was not by the Thomist method of setting limits to reason and letting revelation take it from there, but, rather, on the assumption that whatever in Christian doctrine did not parallel the findings of philosophy did not greatly matter.

The Renaissance man, whether philosopher or not, assumed man's competence to learn the truth and to find the fulfillment of his deepest needs by his own unaided efforts. Experience proved that this blithe self-confidence needed some discipline, but meanwhile it released a flood of intellectual and artistic energy which found expression in creative activities in painting, sculpture, architecture, secular literature, scientific research, philosophical thought, and geographical discovery. The recovered classical heritage made specific contributions in the fields to which it was relevant, but its general effect in all of them was to promote the sense of freedom to use new methods and reach new conclusions.

RENAISSANCE ART AND LITERATURE

Neoclassic Renaissance architecture supplanted the Gothic, which had never been at its best in Italy. If not better, the new was at least different. It drew its inspiration from Roman rather than Greek buildings. Its heavy rounded arches, its massive pillars, decorative pilasters, elaborated architraves, and swelling domes lent themselves to the construction of buildings expressing worldly splendor and human power. The church was the best client for the architects and builders of such structures. Brunelleschi's dome at Florence signaled the opening of an era. The Vatican, first occupied by the popes as their regular residence after the return from Avignon (1377), was rebuilt almost from the ground (beginning in 1447) as a Renaissance palace. The new St. Peter's, begun soon after and under construction for nearly a century, attained the maximum in sheer magnificence. Both carried out the determination of the first pope after the Great Schism to surround himself with such pomp and splendor at Rome that there could never again be any thought of moving the habitat of the Holy See or setting up a rival to its occupant. They are still the largest palace and the largest church in the world. Palaces also arose for the newly powerful and the newly rich. Italian nobles had palaces in the cities rather than castles on hilltops as in Germany or rural châteaux as in France.

Painting and sculpture, hitherto symbolic rather than representational and entirely religious in subject matter, became realistic and partly secular. The artists used models. All of them used their eyes. Some of them even studied anatomy. Pictures, even if intended for altarpieces, glorified physical beauty rather than the ascetic life. The saints became athletes, recognizable as saints by their "attributes" (gridiron, arrows, lion, etc.), not by their emaciation. The Christs were now healthy and sometimes heroic human beings, and the Marys were beautiful young Italian mothers. Thus the church took into its bosom the influences against which it had warred in its teaching and, by "visual education" through the media of the pictures above its altars, the sculpture in its aisles, and the very architecture of the edifices that housed its ceremonies, inculcated the humanistic doctrine that its dogmas denied. Adam and Eve and Susanna and the elders became favorite subjects because they gave opportunity for studies of the nude while still conforming to a popular preference for religious themes. Classic lore and mythology furnished an abundance of subject matter for pictures ordered by private patrons. There was also much portraiture, as always in a time when there is much recently acquired wealth. Private patrons often gave pictures to churches, generally of a "saint with donor," and there were civic commissions in sculpture as well as in architecture. In many an Italian city-state the prince who only yesterday had been a rough soldier of fortune felt the need of enhancing his prestige and proving the respectability if not the legitimacy of his status by becoming a patron of art. It was a good time for artists. Their main motivation was aesthetic or economic or both. This was true even of those who, like Michelangelo and Raphael, were truly devout and served the church for a mere pittance of pay.

As to literature, the most conspicuous fact is the appearance of a host of secular writers and lay readers. Medieval authors, with very few exceptions, had been priests or monks and their themes had been religious. Reading had been drastically limited no less by the prevalent illiteracy of laymen than by the shortage of manuscript books. Latin was the only literary language until late in the Middle Ages. Few laymen and not all priests could read it. The vernaculars, which were developing into the modern languages, were little used for written communication. Dante felt it necessary to defend himself for writing the *Divina Commedia* in Italian instead of Latin. Boccaccio more than any other was the creator of Italian prose style. With the Renaissance came the popularization of the vernacular for literary use, and this in spite of the new enthusiasm for the classical languages in intellectual circles. After the invention of printing there was a vastly larger audience of readers and a greater number of lay authors producing poetry and prose on every conceivable secular theme. Any history of Italian literature will furnish details to document these general statements. Literary humanism began with Petrarch. He and Boccaccio lived in the century before the main period of the Renaissance, but they both manifested its spirit. Members of the clergy, and even of the papal secretariat, contributed to the vernacular as well as to the Latin literature of the Renaissance, including some of its most secular examples. Under his own name, Aeneas Sylvius Piccolomini, Pope Pius II gained in early life a wide reputation as a poet and as the author of some very gamey literature, somewhat to his later embarrassment. In summary it may be said that Renaissance literature reflected the entire range of human interests in a secular and humanistic spirit, often using the patterns and imagery of pagan classical antiquity even when dealing with Christian themes.

What was the effect of all this on the church and religion? Absolutely none upon the church's basic structure and its system of doctrine. General public opinion had never been a decisive factor in determining these. They were now too firmly fixed in the minds of the ruling hierarchy and too strongly fortified by long usage and the conviction of their divine authority to be subject to change with the changing temper of the time. The influence of the Renaissance was indeed to play a part in a great revolt against this system in the sixteenth century. We shall come to that in the next chapter. One reason for the revolt was that the system itself resisted change from within. The Council of Trent, which was held just after the end of the period that is called the Renaissance (insofar as it was a period), further solidified the doctrinal and structural system of the Roman church precisely as it had been before the Renaissance. In these respects the church was impervious to change.

The church underwent great changes, however, in its externals and in the character of its leadership. Its worship and ceremonials took on an unprecedented degree of splendor. The Vatican became as luxurious as any court in Europe, and by far the most magnificent. The popes and cardinals and many of the other higher clergy from the middle of the fifteenth century to the middle of the sixteenth were worldly and sophisticated men. The bishop who "orders his tomb in St. Praxed's" is no caricature. Some of these men were splendid examples of Renaissance culture. Such were

Pope Leo X and Cardinal Bembo. This is not to impugn the sincerity of their belief in the doctrines of the church, but other interests determined their personalities and their behavior. Not since the tenth century had any pope laid himself open to such moral censure as did Alexander VI (1492-1503), the scandals of whose personal life and the malfeasance of whose administration made the name of Borgia a hiss and a byword to later generations. His case was too bad to be typical, but it fully exhibited the possibilities of moral deterioration when complete worldliness and freedom from restraint coincide with almost unlimited facilities for indulgence. On the credit side it must be recognized that many of the Renaissance popes were intelligent patrons of art, literature, and scholarship.

For the cultured laity, as well as for the clergy both high and low, the actual standards and the most cherished values of life tended to become those of Graeco-Roman paganism. As some of these standards and values were better and some were worse, the practical results were various and contradictory. For fine spirits, preoccupation with the temporal scene and the acceptance of unaccustomed liberty for the individual did not exclude a sense of spiritual realities and a moral order. We find, for example, Vittorino da Feltre the teacher, Michelangelo the artist, Castiglione the courtier. For base spirits, the "discovery of the world and of man" meant release for indulgence in lavish luxury, ruthless power, worldly pride, indecency, and the sins of the flesh. So we find Ludovico Sforza, the usurper of Milan; Aretino, the foul-mouthed and blackmailing "scourge of princes"; Filelfo, the racketeer of humanism; and Roderigo Borgia, the ecclesiastic willing to disgrace the church in order to win place and power for his illegitimate children. To put it mildly and generally, the relaxation of restraint upon thought was paralleled by a degree of laxity in behavior. There were probably as many sins, and of as many kinds, before as during the Renaissance, but more people now committed them openly, nonchalantly, and with no pretense of penitence.

As a partial corrective of excessive individualism amounting to lawlessness in conduct, there arose the ideal of the cultivated "gentleman." This found expression in many books which may be classed as books of etiquette though they were more than that.

The most famous, though not necessarily the first, of these was *The Courtier* by Baldassare Castiglione, a guide to the behavior, accomplishments, and moral principles that should be expected of a gentleman moving in polite society.

The fundamental characteristics of the Renaissance were a predominant interest in the values to be found in this present world, a sense of the individual's right and power to seek these values for himself, and a critical attitude toward any institutions or authorities that stood in his way. There was a consequent loss of interest in religion as represented by a church that was dogmatic and authoritarian on principle, and that was itself deeply penetrated in its personnel and administration by the secularity of the Renaissance, but that still resisted its demand for intellectual liberty. There was no general revolt against the church in Italy, because at that time it imposed no effective barrier to freedom of thought outside of the area of its dogmas, and few laymen were enough interested in these even to deny them. There was less real heresy in Italy during the Renaissance than in the thirteenth century. Few men were antireligious or antiecclesiastical, but many were nonreligious and regarded the church as an important part of the total sociopolitical structure but as entitled to no special reverence.

The church presently swept away its corruptions by a drastic house cleaning, known as the Catholic Reformation (see Chapter XX), and at the same time consolidated and reinforced its position on its historic ground. If immorality and worldliness are bad and if religious and intellectual liberty are good, then it can be said that the Roman church swept out both the good and the evil of the Renaissance. Those who think that the spirit of independence from hierarchical authority, the untrammeled search for truth, and a rational approach to the fundamental problems are themselves evil will necessarily consider the Renaissance as a disastrous period in the history of religion and culture. Those who regard these things as good will think that the movement is properly named—a Rebirth. In any case, the fruitful development and application of these attitudes came later and elsewhere. It may be that the consequences of the Renaissance were more important in the nineteenth and twentieth centuries than in the sixteenth.

XIX

The Protestant Reformation

When Martin Luther, Augustinian monk and professor of theology at the new University of Wittenberg in Saxony, posted his historic Ninety-five Theses (topics for academic disputation) on the door of the castle church the evening of October 31, 1517, he had no suspicion that he was precipitating a revolution that would divide Christendom. The act was like the dislodging of a stone that starts an avalanche. Posting the theses was pulling the trigger of a loaded gun. It was the occasion, not the cause, of the Protestant Reformation.

The Reformation began near the end of the period of the Renaissance and was to some extent a product of the forces that collectively bear that name. Not all the Renaissance characteristics were adopted, and other ingredients had to be added to make the mixture as explosive as it quickly became. The reformers rejected the pagan abuses of Renaissance classicism and the moral laxity that grew out of exclusive preoccupation with the beauties, joys, and values of this present world, but they followed the lead of the Renaissance men in claiming their right as individuals to form their own judgment as to the meaning of life, the values to be sought, and the ways of attaining them. If the ancient classics were to be taken as the guide of life, they chose as the object of their attention that ancient classic known as the Bible. If the "revival of learning" was to make ancient standards the norm for modern men, they would take the Scriptures as the authoritative classics of the faith and, relying on them as containing a standard more certainly valid than any of later origin, would restore the essentials of primitive and therefore perfect Christianity.

Italian humanists, with their critical attitude toward contemporary institutions, had satirized ecclesiastics and flouted the authority of the church even while remaining within its membership and sometimes in its pay. Consider Lorenzo Valla's devastating critique of the "Donation of Constantine" and his no less damning judgment upon the misgovernment of the "patrimony" which, as he proved, Constantine did not donate; Petrarch's almost libelous descriptions of the papal court at Avignon, his home town; Boccaccio's hilarious and bawdy mockery of licentious monks and clergy; Guicciardini's caustic comments on Vatican politics and morals; Michelangelo's sonnet on the apostasy of Rome, where "the blood of Christ is sold so much the quart"; Pomponazzi's general challenge of Christian doctrines and his specific denial of immortality. The freedom of criticism that these men and multitudes of others claimed, and could not be prevented from exercising, was now claimed and exercised by those who, not satisfied with criticizing abuses, felt compelled to undertake a reformation of the church in doctrine and practice. Every revolution from the beginning of time has been the defiance of constituted authorities by individuals, either separately or in association. The Renaissance had applied this method in the intellectual and cultural life. The reformers applied it in religion. As is usual in successful revolutions, the reformers checked the individualism of their movement and set up other authorities when they had gained freedom from the old ones; but the liberty that had been their initial assumption, and without which they could never have made a start, remained a potent though long latent factor in the institutions that developed.

The Renaissance also furnished the reformers with the apparatus and methodology of classical scholarship for use in the fulfillment of their purpose. Luther and Melanchthon knew their Greek and, what was rarer, their Hebrew. Zwingli and Calvin were linguistic humanists before they were religious reformers. The English reformers were practically all university men well trained in the new learning. Even the generally despised Anabaptists had their competent scholars who could match their knowledge of the classical languages against all comers.

MARTIN LUTHER

The impulse that started Luther on the path that led to the Reformation was an intense anxiety about the salvation of his own soul. It was not from the Renaissance but from the teaching of the Catholic Church that he derived a sense of the terrible nature of sin and its eternal consequences. While still a monk he was brought to the verge of despair by the consciousness of his own sinful state. It may be said parenthetically that it is not the people who commit the most sins but those who have the tenderest consciences who are most vividly conscious of sin. Luther's problem, then, was how to get his sins absolved. Study of the epistles of Paul and the writings of Augustine led him to doubt that this could be done by confession and priestly absolution and that salvation could be purchased by good works, penance, and appropriation of the merits of the sacraments and the saints. He became convinced that salvation was the free and unmerited gift of God conditioned only on man's appropriation of it by faith in Christ as Saviour through his atoning death. Such faith, he said, led to that inner transformation which St. Paul had called "newness of life" and to assurance of salvation. Man had direct access to God without the need of any intermediary—sacrament, priest, or saint. Virtuous living and the performance of religious duties were not the price by which man could purchase salvation, but were the natural result of the inner change that God wrought in the heart through faith.

Luther had got thus far in solving his own religious problem and discovering what he considered the true way of attaining forgiveness of sins and acceptance by God without the meritorious "works" prescribed by the church, when peddlers of indulgences put on an especially intensive campaign in Germany. This was what touched off his revolt against the whole system of which they were a part.

Pope Leo X needed money to carry on the building of St. Peter's at Rome, designed to be—as it became and still is—the costliest, largest, and most magnificent church in the world. Prince Albrecht, who had recently bribed his way to election as archbishop of Mainz, needed a papal dispensation to enable him to hold this post because he already had two other bishoprics and was under canonical age, and he also needed money both to repay to the great Fugger banking house what he had borrowed to finance his election and to pay the pope for the dispensation and for the pallium as archbishop. Between them they made a contract by which Albrecht was to be general commissioner for the sale of indulgences in Germany and the proceeds were to be equally divided between the pope and the prince. A secret clause in the contract had provided for Albrecht's getting his share, but the fact soon came to public knowledge. The whole sales campaign was handled very badly and not in conformity with sound Catholic doctrine. The theory of indulgences was that the purchaser must evince true penitence and that the cash payment was made in lieu of some other form of penance. There had been abuses of the system before, but none so notorious as when the Dominican Tetzel set forth as chief agent in what was a purely financial enterprise. The principal appeal was to buy release from purgatory for deceased relatives and friends—thus obviously eliminating the requirement of penitence from the transaction. Many good Catholics were indignant at this scandalous campaign, some on religious and some on other grounds. Conscientious priests found it demoralizing to their people, some of whom were led to believe that they could even buy forgiveness in advance for the sins they intended to commit. There were Dominicans who protested that it was giving their order a bad name. Merchants complained that their wares went unsold because the customers spent too much money for indulgences. Princes did not take it kindly that money was flowing out of their states into Albrecht's pocket. All these "nontheological factors" converged to create a wave of popular protest in northern Germany and there were rumblings of discontent elsewhere.

Luther's Ninety-five Theses, though technically only an announcement of propositions for discussion, were really an attack upon the theory as well as the practice and abuses of the sale of indulgences and the presuppositions behind it. Indulgences, when properly used and not exploited by ecclesiastical racketeers like Tetzel, were an integral part of the church's disciplinary system, which included confession, absolution, penance, the "bank of merits" accumulated by the saints, purgatory, and masses for the souls of the departed. To attack them was to deny the authority of the church that issued them. By implication it was to bring into question everything else that the church had authorized in both doctrine and discipline. Whatever the intention, the theses were an inflammatory manifesto. A German version of the Latin original went through Saxony and the adjacent German states like a prairie fire. Its religious appeal was reinforced by political, economic, and moral considerations, and the popular response was great and spontaneous. Pope Leo X had at first been inclined to consider the whole thing a mere tempest in a beer pot, stirred up by the temporary exuberance of a "drunken German monk." He was soon convinced that the matter was more serious, and in 1518 he summoned Luther to Rome. Luther evaded the summons by gaining strong political support for the claim that he ought to be examined or tried in Germany if anywhere. Consultations between Luther and representatives of Rome got nowhere. The reforming party had quickly come to the conviction that the church needed not only a correction of administrative abuses—it got that a little later from within—but a thorough reformation of its doctrine and structure.

In 1520 the pope issued against Luther the bull *Exsurge Domine*, denouncing forty-one errors in his writings, the "pestiferous virus" of which he could no longer tolerate, and threatening, rather than actually pronouncing, excommunication. Luther burned the bull when it finally reached him. In that year also he wrote and published three brief treatises, in two of which he violently attacked practically every doctrine and practice that now distinguishes Roman Catholicism from what can be regarded as the common ground of Protestants. This is where he really crossed his Rubicon and reached the point of no return.

The next year Luther was summoned before a Diet of the empire, at Worms, by the young Emperor Charles V, a grandson of Spain's Ferdinand and Isabella. He went to Worms under the emperor's safe-conduct and the protection of Elector Frederick of Saxony; replied to the charge of departing from Catholic orthodoxy by saying he would recant if, and only if, he could be proved wrong by the authority of Scripture; summed up his defense by the famous dictum "Here I stand, I can do no other, God help me, amen"; and got away alive.

How did it come about that a man already excommunicated, and now flinging such defiance into the faces of an emperor and a papal legate, could escape the flames that had consumed so many lesser heretics? It was not the emperor's safe-conduct that saved him. John Huss had carried with him to the Council of Constance a similar guarantee from the Emperor Sigismund, but he was burned nonetheless. The explanation is to be found in the political changes, and to some extent in the religious changes, of the intervening century. The German states had gained more independence; the German princes were more nearly sovereign in their territories; their allegiance to the emperor, never more than a vague respect for the high dignity of his office, did not include any obligation to support his policies. The feudal empire was dissolving into nations. Spain itself, of which Charles had been king before he became emperor, was a nation outside of the empire. This circumstance further weakened his authority over the states that were the empire's constituent parts. Furthermore, Luther's program of reform had already won a significant following among the common people, the scholars, the knights, and the princes of some of the German states. Most important of all, Luther had the backing of his own prince, the Elector Frederick of Saxony.

Luther's situation at the Diet of Worms was dangerous but not desperate. Apprehensive that assassination might accomplish what formal condemnation could not, his friends kidnaped him as he started on his return journey to Wittenberg and hid him in Wartburg Castle for eight months. While there he translated the New Testament from Greek into German. This was not the first German version, but it was the first to gain wide circulation. This, with the later addition of the Old Testament, became one of the cornerstones of the Reformation and also the most important monument of modern German prose.

The political factor was of crucial importance in the Protestant Reformation. Church and state had been working together ever since the days of Constantine and Theodosius for the defense and support of what was deemed the true religion. In Saxony now, and soon in other German states, the civil powers came to the aid of what, under Luther's tutelage, they had come to consider the true religion. So rapid was its spread that, when another imperial diet was held at Speyer five years after the one at Worms, it was agreed that Lutheran states might remain Lutheran and Catholic states Catholic and each should be tolerant toward followers of the other faith. This was going pretty far in legalizing the new movement. Three years later another diet at Speyer modified this arrangement to the advantage of the Catholic side by destroying this legal equilibrium. The new plan was that Catholics should be tolerated everywhere but that followers of the reform need not be tolerated in Catholic states. Several princes and cities that had adopted the reform protested ineffectually against the inequity of this program and thereby earned the name of "Protestants," which was later extended to cover the whole reform movement.

We need not trace the tensions and conflicts of the next few years. Luther always insisted that he was not at war with the church and had never left it, but, on the contrary, that he was trying to save it from a hierarchy that had usurped control of it and to cleanse it of the corruptions of doctrine and practice that had crept into it. He and his colleagues were reluctant to give up hope of a reconciliation with Rome, but any such hope was so obviously foredoomed to disappointment one wonders that it could ever have been entertained for a moment. Its fulfillment would have meant the abdication of the pope and the radical revision of what had become established doctrines and practices of the

Catholic Church. Meanwhile, the parties were solidifying in Germany, and always along political lines. States whose rulers were Lutheran became Lutheran states; those whose rulers were Catholic remained Catholic. This principle was clearly stated in the Peace of Augsburg (1555), which fixed the rule *Cuius regio eius religio* (He who rules the territory determines its religion). This is a basic doctrine in the state-church system. Its presupposition was that all the citizens of any state must profess the same religion. The same principle was reaffirmed nearly a century later in the Peace of Westphalia (1648), which ended the Thirty Years' War.

Luther himself, the undisputed leader of the German Reformation, was a compound of strangely contrasting qualities. His physical and mental vigor were such that he evidently seemed to many observers to be a bigger man than he actually was. An eyewitness of his debate with Eck at Leipsic in 1519 described him as "of middle height, emaciated from care and study so that you can almost count his bones through his skin," but immediately adds that "he is in the vigor of manhood." One can see that, whether in his youthful emaciation or in his middle-aged corpulence, he exhibited a high degree of both somatic and cerebral energy. In his prime he seemed bursting with animal spirits and intellectual dynamic. His sermons and tracts seemed to erupt from him in a torrent. His clarion voice could summon to spiritual battle in tones that echo across the years as one reads his greatest writings. At home with his wife and family—for he dramatized his repudiation of clerical celibacy by taking a wife—sitting at his table drinking "good Wittenberg beer" while he regaled his countless guests with the "Table Talk" that still makes good reading, playing his flute in the orchestra he formed with his children, or like a good pastor visiting the sick and poor, he was a Luther of infinite fascination. But there was also the Luther who could fly into a towering rage, who could vilify his opponents with abusive language dredged from the gutter, and who could call upon the princes to crush with the utmost ferocity the social uprising of what he called "the murderous and thieving rabble of peasants," who had been driven by starvation to disorderly and desperate measures. There was the Luther of deep inner devotion spending hours in prayer before dawn, the author of the battle hymn of the Reformation, *Ein feste Burg ist unser Gott,* the scholarly and voluminous Biblical commentator, and the dogmatist who would not take the hand of a fellow reformer because they differed as to the mode of Christ's presence in the bread and wine of Holy Communion.

The Protestant Reformation was not one movement that later divided. It was at least four movements which never united. Luther was the leader of the first, John Calvin of the second. The third was the English Reformation. These three gave rise to state churches all of which perpetuated as long as they could the medieval design of permitting no rival or dissenting church to exist within their respective areas of jurisdiction. The fourth, with roots reaching farther back, gave rise to those Protestant communions which on principle stressed voluntary membership, religious liberty, and separation between church and state.

JOHN CALVIN

John Calvin was as different from Luther in personality as one man can well be from another. He was a wispy intellectual with a rigidly logical mind, with a Frenchman's clarity of thought and expression, and with the legalistic bent which training as a lawyer had given him. He belonged to the generation after Luther. Reformation ideas had filtered into France while he was a student at Paris, and they appealed to him. Forced to flee from France, he stopped overnight at Geneva and stayed there the rest of his life. The city had recently gained freedom from its overlord and driven out the bishop who had been on the losing side of this little revolution. The city was ripe for reorganization, and Calvin reorganized it as a theocratic community with such insistent oversight of the morals of its citizens that at one time, before he was well set, the more worldly element drove him into banishment. After three years they were glad enough to call him back from Strasbourg, where he had been carrying on a similar but less strenuous program. He never held public office but, since the members of the church and the voting citizens were identical bodies, and since the advice of the council of ministers to the civil authorities was considered mandatory, John Calvin, as chief minister, was virtually the ruler of Geneva until his death.

Calvin's great contributions were the systematization of Protestant theology and the development of a presbyterial form of church government. His formulation of the Reformed doctrine began with his *Institutes of the Christian Religion,* written in its first form when he was only twenty-six years old and addressed to the king of France. Its primary purpose was to convince the king that the Protestant faith was not heretical and that its adherents should not be persecuted. In subsequent editions the original six chapters were elaborated into eighty-one and it became and has remained the greatest of all Protestant theological treatises. The central thesis of this system of theology, the Augustinian doctrine of the absolute sovereignty of God, was developed with remorseless logic to the conclusion that before the beginning of time God had determined the precise number and chosen the particular individuals who were to be saved and had either consigned the rest of the human race to everlasting damnation (the "double decree") or at least permitted them to drop into hell by the weight of the guilt of their "original sin" inherited from Adam. This is the famous doctrine of election and predestination in its absolute form. Presbyterian and Reformed churches today, still cherishing Calvinism as their spiritual heritage, have found ways of interpreting it in less rigorous terms and of stressing the sovereignty of God without such ruthless damnation of "non-elect infants" dying in infancy. Whether or not Calvin's doctrine of irresistible predestination is logically consistent with human freedom and responsibility, the historical fact is that nowhere has the demand for freedom been stronger or the sense of moral responsibility more rugged than among the spiritual heirs of Calvin.

Out of the Geneva church came also a form of church organization and government which, by the place it gave to elders ("presbyters") elected by the congregation, not only recognized the laity as the source of ecclesiastical authority, but also set a pattern for a republican form of representative government.

The figure of Calvin in history remains as cool, remote, desiccated, and repellent of familiarity as was the living man when, accosted by an enthusiastic refugee as "Brother Calvin," he answered frostily that the proper form of address to him was "Monsieur." Calvin's Geneva was, nevertheless, hospitable to refugees, and there were plenty of them as Protestants fled to escape their persecutors in many parts of western Europe. For this reason Geneva became a school of theology. Returning refugees carried the *Institutes* with them in their baggage and in their heads when they returned to their former homes. Calvinism became the doctrine and Presbyterianism the polity of Protestantism west of the Rhine, and in no small degree east of it. In England and in colonial America it became Puritanism.

It was consistent with Calvin's idea of the "holy state" that the heretical Servetus should be brought to trial, condemned, and burned (1553) when he trespassed on the soil of Geneva. This bold Spaniard was a scientist ahead of his time and a free-lance theologian of rationalistic temper. He had already been condemned by the Inquisition in Spain but had escaped from its prison. While a fugitive, he had engaged in acrimonious correspondence with Calvin and had been warned to stay away from Geneva, but he came. Calvin did not actively instigate his trial and condemnation, but he approved and consented. His associate, Theodore Beza, published an extended defense of the action but the event shocked the larger Protestant community. It was never repeated, though of course that was not the end of either Protestant or Catholic persecution. Sébastien Castellio wrote a reply to Beza which, though Castellio himself was regarded as a heretic, had far-reaching influence in turning Protestants away from the use of inquisitorial methods in the defense of their faith. Years later, Genevan Calvinists erected an "expiatory monument" on the site of the burning, not to signify approval of Servetus's views but as a testimony to their disapproval of violence as an instrument for the defense of orthodoxy.

There were other liberal thinkers, somewhat akin to Servetus and Castellio, who were on the side of religious reformation but did not come within any of the three groups of orthodox and "respectable" reformers. Faustus Socinus—or, in its original Italian form, Fausto Sozzini—was one of these. Unlike the leaders of the three great groups of reformers (Lutheran, Calvinistic, and Anglican), Socinus did not regard Nicene trinitarianism and the supplementary decisions of the so-called Ecumenical Councils as theological bedrock beneath which reforming thinkers could not drill. His views were by no means identical with those of fourth-century Arius, which the Council of Nicaea had rejected, but the similarity was such that the two terms, Arianism and Socinianism, have ever since been linked as designating denial of the "deity of Jesus" and of the "identity of substance" between the Father and the Son. Socinus became the progenitor of modern Unitarianism. Other influences, especially in English thought in the seventeenth and eighteenth centuries, were more directly responsible for the development of this phase of Christian "liberalism." Socinus was never in any sense its "authority," but he was its best known fore-runner. Dissatisfaction with traditional trinitarianism ran as a current of thought beside—or at times inconspicuously beneath—the main stream of Protestant orthodoxy. It found an ally in deism and an intellectual resource in the philosophy of the Enlighten-ment. It gave its own coloration to a large segment of English Presbyterianism in the eighteenth century, and came conspicuously to the surface in the revolt against New England Calvinism and the establishment of Unitarianism as a distinct denomination early in the nineteenth century. Though this denomination has remained small in numbers, it has included many American intellectuals, and the influence of its type of thought has been out of proportion to its statistics.

THE REFORMATION IN ENGLAND

The Reformation in England was less revolutionary, less radical, and more complicated than the movements led by Luther and Calvin. The insular position of England encouraged her nationalistic spirit and her resentment toward any interference from the continent. Patriotic Englishmen, the laymen more than the clergy, had a sense of the distinctive character of the church *in* England for centuries before separation from Rome made it the Church *of* England. Henry VIII had personal and dynastic reasons for desiring the annulment of his marriage with Catherine of Aragon so that he might marry another. The pope had political reasons for refusing to annul it, since Catherine was the aunt of Emperor Charles V, whose friendship and help he desperately needed. The only kind of "reformation" (if one can call it that) that interested Henry was the transfer of the supreme ecclesiastical authority for England from Rome to England. When that was accomplished by act of Parliament, there was an independent Church of England.

But the matter was not so simple as this might suggest. Other reformatory influences had been at work. There was the "evangelical underground" of Wyclif's successors, the Lollards. There was the new learning of the Renaissance, flourishing at both Oxford and Cambridge and partly devoted to the study of the New Testament in Greek. There was William Tyndale translating the New Testament from Greek into English. There was a strong infiltration of Lutheran ideas—so strong, indeed, that Henry himself felt called upon to write a book against them, for which the pope gave him the title "Defender of the Faith." Before the end of Henry's reign—which was the year after Luther's death—leading clergy and laity in England were embarked on a vigorous reformation of doctrine and cultus, though Henry had done little to help it except to repudiate the authority of the pope and confiscate the property of the monasteries. It advanced still farther under the boy king Edward VI, who succeeded Henry. The five-year reign of Mary Tudor, daughter of the divorced Catherine, brought a violent restoration of Roman Catholicism, with the burning of something like three-hundred prominent Protestants. Many fled to Geneva, whence they presently returned more Protestant than ever and with a pronounced coloration of Calvinism. Thereafter there were two main parties—those who wanted a conservative reform maintaining bishops in continuity with their long line of predecessors and a liturgical service according to the Book of Common Prayer, and those (the Puritans) who would do away with both and Presbyterianize the Church of England. The Elizabethan Settlement, which was itself a middle way between Roman Catholicism and Puritanism, established episcopacy. Even then the matter was not finally determined, for the Puritans were a continuing and increasing factor until their very success during the fifteen-year interregnum between the execution of Charles I and the return of Charles II became their undoing.

During that stormy hundred years between the Elizabethan Settlement and the restoration of the Stuarts, it was a settled certainty that the Church of England was going to be Protestant, but one could never be sure whether it would turn out to be Episcopal or Puritan. One of the strongest infusions of thoroughgoing Puritanism in its Presbyterian form flowed southward over the border from Scotland. There John Knox—a blazing reformer who, after escape from the Catholic Scotland of his youth, a term in the French galleys, and a short period in England, had drunk deep of the Calvinistic waters of Geneva—had carried through a strictly Presbyterian reformation of the Church of Scotland. He had forced the abdication of the beautiful but willful Mary Queen of Scots and driven her to seek asylum (and another throne) in England. Elizabeth could scarcely thank him for that, for Mary had many Catholic friends who pressed her adverse claim to Protestant Elizabeth's crown. To Knox as much as to anyone is due the Puritan tradition of defiance of the secular powers when these set themselves against what Puritans deemed their religious and civil rights. English dissenters and American colonists of later times learned much from Knox.

When James VI of Scotland, Mary Stuart's son, became James I of England, it was the hope of English Puritans that he would revise the Elizabethan Settlement and Presbyterianize the Church of England. He did nothing of the kind. On the contrary, the terms of the settlement were more strictly enforced. It was not, however, until his son Charles I came to the throne that the lot of the Puritans became insufferable. Two contrasting results followed: the great Puritan migration to New England in the 1630's, and the alliance of English Puritanism with the parliamentary party that grew up in opposition to the royal autocracy which the bishops were supporting. Parliament and Puritans triumphed together. Charles and Archbishop Laud went to the block. It was in this period that the Westminster Assembly, summoned by

Parliament and thus ostensibly representing the Church of England, drafted the Westminster Confession, which is to this day the standard of Presbyterian orthodoxy.

Not all Puritans were Presbyterians. Of almost equal historical importance, though less in numbers, were the Independents, progenitors of modern Congregationalism. Countless minor groups complicated the situation. Some of them, such as the Levelers, were such sturdy fighters for individual liberty and democratic rights that they seemed to their own time revolutionaries, and to ours, prophets. John Milton, hard to classify ecclesiastically, was one of these left-wing Puritans. It fell to the lot of Oliver Cromwell to rule the realm as Lord Protector, suppress revolt, end a civil war, and hold in leash the conflicting forces that could not be harmonized. The task was impossible for anyone but him. When death loosened the grip of his strong and often ruthless hand, the Commonwealth was doomed and England was glad to restore its monarchy. Charles II came back from France.

The Elizabethan Settlement was restored along with the Stuarts with the addition of even stronger measures against Puritanism in all its forms. All dissent from episcopacy was outlawed. Almost to the end of the seventeenth century England remained as firmly committed as Rome had ever been to the principle that only one form of religion could be permitted to exist and that it was the business of the state to apply what pressure might be necessary to prevent any other from existing. But England was never very good at practicing a consistent and continuous policy of religious persecution. A good many nonconformists were imprisoned but there were no burnings or hangings under the restored Stuarts.

The end of England's long regime of religious intolerance seemed to come almost as a by-product of the "bloodless revolution" of 1689—just a hundred years before France's bloody one—when the autocratic rule of the Stuarts was followed by the liberal reign of William and Mary. The fact that Mary was the daughter of James II provided the "legitimacy," and the statesmanship of her Dutch husband furnished the liberalism. The Toleration Act in the first year of their reign suspended the penal laws against nonconformists and introduced the modern era of religious tolerance.

Episcopacy remained firmly established as the structure of the Church of England, but dissenting bodies of Presbyterians, Independents, and Baptists could exist and function with security, though still with some social disadvantages and some restrictions on civil rights. Just four years earlier (1685) Louis XIV, moving in the opposite direction, had outlawed Protestantism in France by revoking the Edict of Nantes, by which Henry IV had given legal status and a limited measure of religious liberty to Protestants. In the preceding years Louis had done his best to exterminate them. He explained the revocation of the edict by saying that protection of Protestants in France had become unnecessary because they no longer existed! This may be one reason why Roman Catholics in England, though still not persecuted, got no restoration of full civil rights from the Toleration Act.

What was earlier referred to as the "fourth movement" that contributed to the totality of the Protestant Reformation included the Socinians, who have already been mentioned, but it began with the Anabaptists. Even before Luther had sounded his note, there were some little groups of earnest souls who had become convinced that the church should consist only of those who voluntarily joined it by making their personal commitment to Christ, that the Church should have no connection whatever with the civil power or the state, and that the Roman Catholic Church with its hierarchical dignitaries, worldly power, sacramental system, and elaborate rituals had fatally departed from the primitive pattern. There are no reliable historical data upon which to base a judgment as to how many of these radically dissenting groups there had been, how early they arose, how continuous had been their testimony, or how complete had been their acceptance of the points that have just been enumerated. They were, at best, a religious underground in the times when nonconformity with the existing order was punishable by death, and they were humble people whose thoughts and actions would not have been conspicuous enough to attract much attention even if considerations of safety had not made it wise to remain as inconspicuous as possible. Some Baptists of today believe that there had been an unbroken succession of such from Apostolic days, but the evidence is too fragmentary to convince any except those who consider it important that it should be so.

Certainly the three basic beliefs mentioned above do not seem terribly shocking to Protestants of today, especially American Protestants, but they were violently revolutionary in the fifteenth and sixteenth centuries. Catholics, of course, regarded all three as nothing short of religious anarchy. The first two gave offense alike to Lutherans, Calvinists, and Anglicans, all of whom held that the church is an institution into which the infant children of believers should be inducted at the earliest possible moment, and that it was right and proper for the state to lend its support to the "true" religion and to suppress all others. Zwingli approved the judicial drowning of the Anabaptists when they appeared in Zurich. Luther sanctioned the death penalty decreed against them by that same Diet of Speyer (1529) at which the resistance of his followers to what they deemed unfair treatment won them the name of "Protestants." Melanchthon instigated the execution of some Anabaptists at Jena in 1536. They were long regarded as an embarrassment to all the respectable reformers, as left-wing extremists are likely to be in any liberal or reforming movement.

This intolerance was bad enough, but not quite as reprehensible as it may seem. Although the Anabaptists included in their number some men of sober character and sound scholarship, and although they embodied an idea that was destined to be of decisive importance in the development of Protestantism, democracy, and civil rights, they had a lunatic fringe which attracted more attention than their basic ideas, and it was a very broad fringe. First, they became entangled with the Peasants' Revolt, which appeared to involve them in a campaign of terrorism against landlords. The connection was incidental rather than fundamental. Many Anabaptists were peasants, and the lot of the peasants was so bleak that their violent measures to obtain redress of grievances are understandable now, though then they seemed subversive of the whole social order. Further, many of the Anabaptists became obsessed with chiliastic ideas—the end of the world was just around the corner, the Second Coming of Christ was at hand, they were the prophets of the New Age, they would soon be sitting on thrones of glory while the rest of the world would be groveling at their feet. John of Leyden and his colleagues undertook to set up an apocalyptic kingdom at Münster. Though this was actually only a minor episode precipitated by a crazed enthusiast, the scandalous proceedings gave the Anabaptists such a bad press that, under that name, they virtually faded out of the picture.

The real ideas back of their movement did not fade out. A former priest, Menno Simons, salvaged the movement and gave his name to the continuing representatives of its basic principles—the Mennonites. What was more important in the long run, there was an element among the English Puritans that adopted the Anabaptist principle of separation of church and state. These Separatists are conspicuously represented by the members of the Scrooby congregation, who, after a stay in the Netherlands, migrated to New England and became the Pilgrim Fathers. Hence arose Congregationalism, combining the ideas of independence from the state (an idea that was in abeyance in colonial New England) and the autonomy of each local congregation. Some of the Separatist Puritans adopted also the first item of the Anabaptist doctrine, individual responsibility for the Christian decision, and, therefore, "believers' baptism." They became the Baptists.

It would be an exaggeration—indeed, a perversion of history— to say that the free church idea and the American pattern of separation of church and state were derived chiefly from the Anabaptists, but it is only doing them belated justice to say that they were the first in modern times to assert these ideas, and that they exercised an influence at a crucial point in the development of Protestantism.

XX

Catholic Reformation and Expansion

The Catholic Church needed a reformation in the sixteenth century—no doubt about that. An able French Catholic historian who has written an excellent book on this subject* states this fact very positively and adds: "There was no need, however, of reformation such as the Protestants understood it." That is a question about which, of course, opinions differ. Since we have considered the Protestant movement toward reforms in the doctrines and structure of the church, let us now look from the Catholic point of view at the reformation in the life and work of the church which was carried through by leaders who held that no change in its doctrines or structure was either necessary or possible because they were already infallibly right. This latter movement is sometimes called the Counter Reformation. But that is not a fair name for it because it seems to imply that it was only a reaction against Protestantism, and this is not true, though certainly one of its motives and objectives was to check the Protestant advance and win back some lost ground. More fundamentally it was an inner awakening, a self-cleansing, and a revitalizing of the Catholic

* Pierre Janelle, *The Catholic Reformation*, Bruce Publishing Co., 1944.

211

Church—a Catholic revival in contrast with the Protestant Reformation and the Renaissance, stimulated by both but not a mere reaction to either. Its proper name is the "Catholic Reformation."

Conditions within the church in the fifteenth century had become very bad. The low morals of the higher clergy were an open scandal. Many of the Renaissance popes were wicked and all of them were worldly. Simony, nepotism, luxury, and sins of sex were rife. Of course there were faithful bishops and pious abbots —probably more than the other kind—but the proportion of the other kind was outrageously high. Good moral character was not among the required qualifications for ecclesiastical advancement. The lower clergy were for the most part ignorant and untrained. The modern high standards of education for the priesthood had not been thought of. It would be mere guesswork to say anything of the average level of priestly morality. General belief in the importance of the sacraments together with the theory that the efficacy of the sacraments was independent of the moral character of the ministrant—a sound and sensible doctrine under any conditions—made it possible for the laity to employ the services of priests for whom they had no respect as persons. This was a dangerous and demoralizing detachment of religion from life. The monastic orders, also, were in a sad state of deterioration. The Cluniac and Cistercian reforms were in the distant past. The monasteries had become too rich for their own good, had admitted too many candidates with no pretension to any authentic "calling" to the religious life, and could find nothing useful for them to do. The one who traditionally finds work for idle hands to do did not neglect this shining opportunity. Here we are not left to rumor or conjecture, for the reports of official "visitations" to the monasteries paint a dark picture of their demoralization, revealing at the same time that many of the visitors had the conscience to discern, even if they had not the power to correct, the evils that they found.

Ecclesiastical order and discipline were in a sad state of confusion. At the very time when Martin V and his successors were rescuing the papacy from schism and from conciliar supremacy, the administrative authority of the popes was being whittled away by secular patronage in appointments to benefices, by the independence of monasteries from episcopal oversight, and by the growing spirit of nationalism which challenged some papal prerogatives. All this cut into the income of popes, bishops, and parish priests. The pinch had been felt by the papacy in Avignon days, but the emergency had been met then by inventing new sources of revenue and a more effective system of collection. But as luxury and lavish expenditure increased it became necessary to put a tighter squeeze on laymen by exacting higher fees for every form of service. The abuses in connection with the sale of indulgences were part of this process. Every thoughtful Catholic knew that a reformation was needed.

The Catholic Reformation was promoted chiefly by three agencies: the papacy itself and the papal court; the Council of Trent; and the religious orders. The first and third of these were fields for reform as well as centers of reforming activity.

The papal court was shocked and sobered by the sack of Rome in 1527 by the army of Charles V, but the new era at the Vatican began a little later with the election of Paul III as pope in 1534. He and his successors, with varying degrees of earnestness and energy, took up the work of removing the flagrant abuses that were closest to them. The Renaissance frivolities and worse were swept away. There were no more boy cardinals, no more infant or adolescent "nephews" holding rich benefices. There was a revived sense of the dignity and responsibility of high office in the church. It was no longer possible for any pope to say, or even to think, as Leo X is reported to have said, "God has given us the papacy, therefore let us enjoy it." Discipline was tightened and administration made more efficient. The deeply devotional life of Catholic Christianity —always continuing though it had been eclipsed by luxury and worldliness in high places—came again to its proper prominence. With the quickening of religious zeal came also an access of energy for the suppression of heresy. There had been stirrings of liberal religious thought in Italy. The ideas of Luther and Calvin had crossed the Alps and found some acceptance in literary circles, though none among the common people, so far as the record shows. The Protestant impulse, if it can be called that, was confined to literary cliques and coteries. It never reached the grass roots as it did in the north. Moreover, it had no political protection, as it had in the states that became Lutheran or Calvinist. The Inquisition was re-established, and Renaissance freedom of thought was swept out along with Renaissance secularity and paganism.

Paul III (1534-49) was not at heart a reformer. He would have preferred to be a Renaissance prince. He was a member of the noble Roman family of the Farnese, and he had gained his first preferment in the church through the relations of his sister Giulia with Alexander VI, in grateful remembrance of which her semi-nude figure in marble adorns the base of the tomb of Paul III in St. Peter's. He showed little personal interest in the reform of abuses, but the movement of the times was in that direction. He was more concerned with the development of agencies for fighting the tendencies toward free religious thought. It was he who gave official recognition to the Jesuit order (1540), established the Inquisition in Italy (1543), and at last, after much pressure from the emperor, called the Council of Trent (1545) but insisted that it should give its first attention to the reaffirmation of Catholic doctrine and postpone the reform of abuses until the doctrinal formulations had been completed. He was pressured into the appointment of a commission to report on the abuses and possible methods of curing them. Almost in spite of himself, Paul III initiated the Catholic Reformation.

Paul IV (1555-59) was a reformer in heart as well as act. This noble Neapolitan, Giovanni-Pietro Caraffa, was a person of mystical temper but powerful initiative. He ran away from home at fourteen to join the Dominican order, but did not. Presently he became an official of the papal curia. At Rome, says an eminent Catholic scholar, "he lived chastely and purely throughout the scandalous pontificate of Alexander VI." He became a bishop, then a member of the pious society of the Oratorians. As pope he gave the papal court the house cleaning that was long overdue. His unbending hostility to all "heretics" led him to denounce the Peace of Augsburg (1555), which gave Protestants a legal right to exist in German states with Protestant princes, but he was a man of deeply devout spirit and pure life.

THE COUNCIL OF TRENT

The Council of Trent met intermittently for eighteen years (1545-63). At one time Luther had clamored for a general council before which he could argue his case. There were some Catholics, including Emperor Charles V, who still hoped that the Protestants could be won back and the church reunited if some concessions were made. Paul III was reluctant to call a council, doubtless being realistic enough to know that the Protestants would not be satisfied with a mere reform of abuses or with any concessions that a council could offer. Charles V wanted to have the Protestants represented at the council and to take up first the reform of the abuses, which he still thought were the chief ground of their separation. Paul III excluded them by the terms of the call and won his point that the matter of abuses should be postponed until the council had reaffirmed the Catholic doctrines, which—as he knew and the emperor did not—were the real ground of the Protestant separation from Rome.

The first thing that the Council of Trent did, therefore, was to restate the Catholic doctrines in a more uncompromising form than ever and thus to shut, lock, and double-bolt the door against any possible return of the Protestants unless they came in complete surrender—which, of course, there was not the slightest chance of their doing. It required years of intermittent sessions to produce the full set of doctrinal canons. Though the council was constituted in 1545, it was not until October, 1551, that the decree concerning the sacrament of the Eucharist was adopted, and the ones covering purgatory, the veneration of saints and their relics, and use of images and the validity of indulgences were adopted on the last two days of the council, December 3 and 4, 1563.

After the first few years, and when the possibility of doctrinal compromise had been completely foreclosed, and when the council had bestowed copious anathemas upon any who did not accept its doctrinal pronouncements, attention was directed to the reform of abuses and the improvement of administration. The achievements here were very substantial. Control over dioceses was restored to the bishops, absenteeism of priests from their parishes and the holding of a plurality of benefices were forbidden, seminaries were established for the education of priests (a step of incalculable importance), simony and nepotism were condemned, the granting of benefices to boys (except those studying for the priesthood) was checked, and many abuses were corrected in connection with the sale of indulgences, the worship of images, and high-pressure methods of collecting fees and alms. In warning against abuses, the council took occasion to reaffirm the validity of all the religious practices that the Protestants rejected. Thus in both ways—in restating with emphasis and elaboration the traditional doctrinal and hierarchical system, and in purifying but defending the whole program of religious practice—the Council of Trent built higher and stronger walls around the position of the Roman Catholic Church. By recognizing the equality of "tradition" (that is, the teaching of the church) with Scripture as a source and guarantee of truth, the council prepared the way for later dogmatic declarations, especially those defining the infallibility of the pope and the Immaculate Conception and bodily Assumption of the Virgin Mary.

LOYOLA AND THE JESUITS

While providing for its defenses, Catholicism was also preparing for attack. The most effective instruments of its aggressive action were the religious orders—the old ones, improved and invigorated, and the new ones that were being formed. The glory of the Catholic Reformation, as seen from the Catholic point of view, was the organization, growth, and achievements of the Society of Jesus. This order, commonly called the Jesuits, stopped Protestantism in its tracks in Hungary, almost annihilated it in Poland, won back to the papal allegiance much of Germany, blocked the reform movement in France, and virtually wiped out its beginnings in Italy except for the continuing Waldensians, who survived by hiding in Alpine fastnesses. At the same time, it scattered over Europe its excellent schools, which specialized in enrolling the children of titled and wealthy families, gave the

Catholic community an organized system of moral teaching, which standardized the working of the confessional, and spearheaded the thrust of Catholic missions into India, Japan, China, and the New World.

Ignatius Loyola, the founder of the Society of Jesus, is as fascinating a figure as any that his age of picturesque personalities produced. A Spanish grandee whose military career had been ended by battle wounds, he had a revolutionizing religious experience during his months of recovery and resolved to become a soldier of Christ. With patience and industry he made good his lack of early education. Later, as a student at the University of Paris, he gathered half a dozen devoted companions, one of whom was Francis Xavier, afterward to become the great missionary saint to India and the Far East. One day in August, 1534, in the church of St. Mary on Montmartre in Paris, this little group, fired by Loyola's contagious enthusiasm, formed an oath-bound band which became the Society of Jesus. Pope Paul III gave this company formal recognition and authorization as a religious order in 1540. As a former soldier who had dedicated his armor to the Virgin, the founder created a military company with discipline as strict and demand for obedience as unquestioning as in any army. Ignatius Loyola was its "general" until his death. By that time his order had grown into a great company in which every recruit was sworn in only after long mental and spiritual preparation. The *Spiritual Exercises* of Ignatius Loyola are the world's most famous manual, not only for the devotional life, but for the discipline of the individual will to absolute obedience. Once trained and enrolled, the Jesuit was ready to go anywhere on earth instantly on command and undertake any task to which he might be ordered.

Some other new religious orders must be passed over with brief mention, though they deserve more. The Capuchins were a derivative from the Observants, who had seceded from the Conventuals, the strictest division of the Franciscans. They practiced rigorous asceticism, and many of them became effective preachers. Their churches were plain and bare. Some of them even yet are notable for the amazing display of skeletons in their crypts. The Theatines, taking their name from the original see of their most eminent member, Giovanni-Pietro Caraffa (Paul IV), were a development from the Oratorians. They specialized in the intensive training of exceptionally able young men, so that their houses became, as Caraffa's biographer says, "seminaries for bishops," not for mere priests. Naturally they remained a small order. The Barnabites, on the contrary, were expansive and missionary. The Oratory grew out of the work of St. Philip Neri, about whom gathered a group of young men who formed a confraternity for spiritual exercises. It became an association of secular priests and clerics who practiced devotion with cheerfulness and, avoiding worldliness, made a point of avoiding also any appearance of supersanctimoniousness. These are but samples of the many movements that embodied a genuine determination to cultivate the spiritual life. Some of them began, in a small way, a little before the period that we have designated as that of the Catholic Reformation.

CATHOLIC MISSIONS

The times were ripe for missionary expansion, for the known world was expanding. Dreams that seemed as imaginative as today's "space travel" were being realized when Portuguese ships crept around the tip of Africa into the Indian Ocean, Columbus and Vespucci found the shores of new continents, and Magellan's ship sailed around the world. The Far East was indeed known to exist. Marco Polo had brought incredible (but true) reports about it, and other traders had come back with travelers' tales, but all this was as misty and mysterious as the legendary Prester John. America was something absolutely new. So little did even the most advanced geographers suspect that there was room for a continent between Europe and Asia that when they found it, not knowing what they had found, they called its inhabitants "Indians."

Catholic Christianity expanded in both directions, east and west, to fill what seemed to be a religious vacuum. The eastward drive, a Jesuit enterprise, was the most spectacular; the westward, in which Dominicans and Franciscans also played an important part, was the most fruitful and permanent. From the beginning, it was Jesuit policy to exercise influence on and through the ruling classes of society. Remember that Luther, too, had addressed the first of his three Reformation treatises to "the Christian Nobles of the German Nation," since, though all laymen were true priests in his view, the nobles were the laymen who could help most in doing what needed to be done. Similarly, the Christian conquest of barbarian Europe had been accomplished chiefly by first winning the tribal or national leaders, whose subjects then accepted the new religion of their chiefs as a matter of course. The same method was applied in the mission to the Far East, with the addition that, since these lands had ancient cultures of their own, with scholars and priests, the approach was now to the intellectual and religious leaders as well as to the rulers and nobles. The results were highly encouraging. When the reports of what was being done got back to Europe, many thought that the missionaries had permitted their message to be corrupted by adapting it too cleverly to the ideologies and vocabularies of the Indian and Chinese religions. The controversy grew heated and there were warnings from Rome. This was only one among several things that brought criticism upon the Society of Jesus from other Catholics and especially from other orders that may have been jealous of their conspicuous efficiency and growing influence. After flourishing for a time, the Jesuit missions in the Far East were wiped out by a wave of anti-Christian and antiforeign reaction which added to the roll of the church's martyrs and saints.

The expansion of Christianity into the Western Hemisphere had begun before any of those changes that together constituted the Catholic Reformation, but the missionary effort in America derived fresh impulse from them. When Columbus sailed from Palos it was only a matter of months since Ferdinand and Isabella had completed the task of driving the Moors out of Spain by the conquest of Granada. The Jews, also, had been driven out. The Spanish Inquisition was working at top heat—and that quite literally—to make Spain, now politically united, a solidly Christian and soundly Catholic nation. The operation had something of the character of a crusade. The discovery and military occupation of new lands with pagan populations opened a vast new field for the extension of this process. The method was necessarily different from that which had been employed either in the Far East, where the missionaries were entirely without military backing and had to make their way by persuasion with the leaders of highly advanced civilizations, or in Spain, where the problem had been to intimidate or eliminate a non-Christian minority. In the Caribbean, in Mexico, and in South America, the Spaniards were a minute minority which quickly gained complete domination. The gathering of gold and the creation of a Spanish empire may seem to have been the principal motives both of the crown and of the conquistadors and explorers, but it was unthinkable that there should be a Spanish empire that was not Christian. Even the gold-hungry conquerors knew that, and with them went monks and friars who had no other interest than the salvation of souls and the extension of the church's domain. No help was asked from the political or religious leaders of the conquered peoples. Neither Montezuma in Mexico nor the Incas in Peru were expected to lead their subjects to the acceptance of Christianity. They were simply killed, the indigenous social and political organizations were destroyed, and the ceremonials and apparatus of the pagan religions were wiped out as quickly and completely as possible. Crosses were erected, Masses were said, and the monks and friars set about the work of converting the people and teaching them the rudiments of Christianity. As compared with later Protestant missionary efforts among the American aborigines, Catholicism had the advantage of presenting symbols and ceremonies that made a strong appeal to the eye and the ear. The result in the long run was that Latin America became Catholic. Until the nineteenth century all other forms of religion were prohibited by law. There were relatively few martyrdoms, because the Spanish power was so overwhelmingly dominant that resistance seemed impossible. An exception was the Pueblo revolt in New Mexico (1680), which cost the lives of many priests and drove all Spaniards out of that area. Diego de Vargas effected the reconquest twelve years later.

There were some great characters among the missionary priests. Bartolommeo de las Casas, a Dominican, began in the Caribbean, where he became the first champion of Indian rights. When he saw that the enslaved Caribs were being killed off by the excessive labor demanded of them and that his protests were of no avail, he made the unfortunate suggestion that African natives might be imported as slaves. Later he was in Guatemala. His bust may still be seen topping a fountain in the old capital, Guatemala Antigua, once the seat of government for all Central America. Again he protested against the harsh treatment of the Indians, and was told that there was no other way to handle them. When he offered to prove the efficacy of kindness under even the hardest conditions, they sent him to what is now the state of Chiapas in Mexico, then a far frontier where the natives had the worst possible reputation for stubborn hostility. He went, and saw, and conquered—by his own mild methods.

Alvar Nuñez Cabeza de Vaca, not a priest but one of the rare Spanish lay humanitarians of his time, was wrecked on the coast of Florida; made an almost impossible journey along the Gulf Coast to Mexico, taking with him a company of Indians who had held him in friendly custody for several years somewhere near Corpus Christi; successfully resisted efforts of the Spaniards to set his Indian friends to work as slaves in the silver mines of Zacatecas, and sent them home with gifts. Then he went back to Spain to beg the crown to protect the Indians of Mexico from those who were exploiting them. After that he went to Paraguay to start another campaign for Indian welfare. The Jesuits, also, set up a humane though thoroughly paternalistic regime in Paraguay, without military protection, and conducted it successfully for many years.

Father Kino, a Jesuit, was the missionary pioneer in what is now Arizona. His monument is the beautiful mission of St. Xavier near Tucson. New Mexico was first explored by Pedro de Alvarado in 1540-42, but the first permanent settlement, Santa Fe, was not made until about 1605. Its full name, translated, is "The Royal City of the Holy Faith of Saint Francis of Assisi," for the Franciscans founded the missions and converted the Pueblo Indians. Almost by chance it was the Franciscans who became the missionaries in California. The Jesuits were ready to start, late in the eighteenth century, when the pope dissolved their order. The

Franciscans, led by Fra Junípero Serra, took up the task and established the line of missions (including Los Angeles) from San Diego to San Francisco.

No amount of legitimate criticism of the manners and morals of the Spanish conquerors, or of some of the techniques of evangelization that were employed, should be allowed to cast a cloud upon the heroic devotion of the many friars and priests, some known but many more unknown to fame, who endured the labors and dangers of those years. They gained the result that they and the soldiers and administrators all sought. They did make Latin America Catholic.

There can be only passing mention here of the French exploration and occupation of Canada. On its religious side this, too, was, of course, Catholic. The Society of Jesus furnished the forces for the conversion of Canada. There the problem was in every way different from that which the Spaniards faced in the south. The native population was sparse and primitive. There were no such mature and literate cultures as those of the Aztecs, Mayas, and Incas and no such substantial pagan religious institutions. The economic interest of the French was in furs. They wanted the Indians to bring in beaver skins to trade for tin whistles and glass beads, and then go back to the forest to trap more beavers and bring in more skins. That meant that they must be treated kindly. There could be no slaughtering of them for their gold and emeralds as in Peru or enslaving them to work in the mines or cultivate the encomiendas as in Mexico. Since the profits were less immediate and spectacular, the influx of fortune seekers and the military forces of occupation were less. The Jesuit missionaries, fired with zeal and with the enthusiasm of their order's youth, forgot considerations of safety and carried their message of salvation into the depths of the forests. Many of them met martyrdom. The many-volumed *Jesuit Relations* tells in detail the story of their exploits.

The expansion of Catholic Christianity into Asia and America could scarcely have occurred without the prior features of the Catholic Reformation, but it also contributed to that Reformation by bringing to the church a widened outlook, a fresh sense of mission, enlarged resources, and a heightened morale.

XXI

Protestantism Reaches America

The transplanting of Protestant Christianity to American soil was a feature of the English colonization movement from its very beginning. Without exaggerating the importance of the religious motive to the exclusion of all others, as some of the pious writers of American history were formerly inclined to do, one must not go to the other extreme and write it off as something secondary and incidental. It is probably true that a majority of the colonists who came to America in the seventeenth century came primarily to improve their economic situation. The expectation of finding sudden wealth along the Atlantic Coast, as the Spaniards had found it in Mexico and Peru, may have inflamed the minds of early investors in the Virginia Company and some of the first colonists who came to Jamestown, but this hope soon faded. More substantial and significant was the prospect of getting land. The feudal system had been operative so long in continental Europe and in England that for the ordinary citizen there was no possibility of becoming a landholder. The middle and lower classes were land-hungry. The promise of a "freehold" in a new continent, sometimes described as virtually a duplicate of the Garden of

223

Eden, was a potent lure. Even in the most religious of the early English colonies, there were many whose motivation was chiefly economic. It was wholly so for the Dutch and Swedish colonists.

Nevertheless, the religious motive was a powerful factor in American colonization as a whole. In some colonies it furnished the initial impulse and the controlling force. To understand the nature and the varieties of this appeal, one must look at the European background as well as the American situation.

As to America, the parts of it that had been explored and settled before 1600 were solidly Roman Catholic. England and the other Protestant powers were a century late in starting. Pope Alexander VI had assumed the right to divide the whole of America between Spain and Portugal. His Line of Demarcation did not stand, but between them the two countries had taken everything south of the Rio Grande and a good deal north of it, and Florida as well. The French had begun to occupy Canada. (Santa Fe, Quebec, and Jamestown were all founded within a period of three years.) The "colonization sermons" preached in England late in Elizabeth's reign on behalf of the Virginia Company stressed the necessity of erecting a "Protestant rampart" against a threatened closing of the gap between the Catholic colonies to the north and south. It may be doubted whether this was ever the decisive argument with any prospective colonist in the absence of more personal considerations. Such personal religious reasons for migration were not far to seek.

At the beginning of the seventeenth century, every country in Europe had its established church and put forth every possible effort to suppress dissent or to prevent the open profession and practice of any other form of faith. The theory was that religious homogeneity was essential to the stability of the social order and the strength of the state. This heritage from the Middle Ages had become common to Catholic and Protestant countries. The principle that "he who rules the territory determines its religion" had been explicitly avowed in the Peace of Augsburg (1555) and was to be reiterated and confirmed in the Peace of Westphalia (1648). Obviously there is no place for religious toleration in such a system. Yet within the preceding century Protestant movements had sprung up in Catholic countries, various types of Protestants had come into existence with representatives in Protestant countries, where they constituted illegal minorities, and there were remainders of Catholic populations in countries that became Protestant. For all these people who were at outs with the intolerant religious establishments in their native countries there was one road of escape—to America.

It was not that these seekers of religious liberty necessarily believed in religious liberty for everybody. The Puritans who came to Massachusetts Bay certainly did not if they were good Calvinists, for Calvin did not believe in it. The Catholics who came to Maryland certainly did not if they were good Catholics, because religious liberty for all is contrary to basic Roman Catholic principles and is acceptable only as a compromise when the proscription of non-Catholics is impracticable. With no convictions as to the fundamental human right to religious liberty, these oppressed ones could come in the hope of finding a new field in which they could establish a regime in which *they* could worship God in the way they deemed right. This actually was the guiding motive of the founders of those colonies in which religion was a primary consideration.

In England the Elizabethan Settlement had fixed on a somewhat ritualistic episcopacy as defining the character of the Church of England, but even then there was a large Puritan element in the church. In the reign of James I and the early years of Charles I that element became stronger and the measures for its elimination became more violent. The Virginia Company, which founded Jamestown, was formed while it was still possible for Episcopal Anglicans and Puritans to co-operate; both elements were represented in the directorate of the company. The motivation of its investors and colonists was chiefly economic and patriotic; it was religious only in the general sense of building a "Protestant rampart" and in the announced purpose, never very seriously pursued, of converting the natives. They were not specially concerned about religious liberty. There, as in most of the other colonies, the European state-church system was transferred to America so far as the conditions of colonial life permitted. Anglican Episcopacy was established in Virginia, but popular interest in religion was mild. A "gentlemanly conformity" with the form of worship "authorized by the laws of England" was expected, but even this could scarcely be enforced on the residents of plantations scattered all along the rivers of eastern Virginia and the Tidewater country. In the earliest days there were fines—seldom collected— for failure to attend church twice on Sunday. After the tightening up of intolerance in England with the Act of Uniformity (1661) there were penalties for failure to have an infant child baptized by a "lawful minister," and for a time heavy fines were imposed on Quakers and any who might harbor them. In general, Virginia and the other southern colonies represented efforts to import the European system of compulsory uniformity and do the best that could be done with it under the circumstances.

NEW ENGLAND SETTLEMENTS

Radically different was the Plymouth colony. The little congregation at Scrooby, in Nottinghamshire, was regarded even by its fellow Puritans as a left-wing group. Rejecting the state-church idea, they affirmed the autonomy of the local church and, instead of trying to capture Parliament and make the Church of England Puritan by law, as the Presbyterians did, affirmed the policy of "reformation without tarrying for any." They escaped the hostile climate of England by seeking asylum first in the Netherlands and then in lands that had been granted to the Virginia colony, but landed by mistake near Cape Cod. Their little settlement at Plymouth became an exemplification of the Congregational order. Even after it merged with the larger Massachusetts Bay colony, it maintained a more tolerant attitude than was common among early Puritan communities.

The more rigorous enforcement of English laws against the Puritans by the autocratic Charles I, aided and abetted by Archbishop Laud, brought about the great Puritan migration that led to the founding of Salem, Boston, and the Commonwealth of Massachusetts. Most of these Puritans were not "separatists"— that is to say, they had not wanted to withdraw from the Church of England; they wanted to capture it, if possible. A few years later in England they did just that and controlled it under Cromwell and the Commonwealth. But no such good fortune as that could be foreseen when Charles and Laud were giving the screw another turn every day. These Puritans came to America with the intention of creating a "holy state," a society in which it would be safe to be a Puritan and unsafe to be conspicuously anything else. Nothing was farther from their thought than the establishment of liberty for all communions. They brought with them what we are persistently calling "the European system" because it had been the universal pattern of church-state relationship for a thousand years and still persists to a great extent in the European churches. The wonder is not that the Puritans were intolerant of forms of religion not authorized by the state and its one church. The wonder is that they so soon relaxed the compulsions of that system and began to develop the "American system" of free and legally equal churches and of complete religious liberty. Even in the period of their stiffest intolerance, the Puritans did not try to force everyone into their church. In fact, they made it rather difficult to get into it. The worst they did was to require church attendance, to prevent the establishment of any other church, to limit the exercise of full civil rights to church members, to exile a few of their own vociferous heretics, and to bar some wandering Baptist and Quaker preachers. Even these measures did not outlast the first generation. The sturdy partisans of the old order were all immigrants who had brought it with them. For example, John Cotton, stoutest of all the New England defenders of the practice of religious persecution, was almost fifty years old and had been minister of a Puritan church at old Boston in Lincolnshire for twenty years before he ever set foot in the new Boston.

The earliest and most conspicuous rejections of the theory of compulsory conformity were in Rhode Island, Maryland, and Pennsylvania. These colonies were, respectively, Baptist, Roman Catholic, and Quaker in their initial impulse.

Rhode Island owed its founding as a "shelter for persons distressed in conscience" to one of those perennial "seekers" whose consciences cannot endure any restraint upon their search for truth or their utterance of it when found. Roger Williams, a graduate of Cambridge University and an ordained Anglican clergyman, had some training in law under the celebrated Sir Edward Coke and imbibed some Puritan ideas before coming to Boston in 1631. Among his subversive ideas were these: that church membership should be voluntary; that the state had no right to compel church attendance or Sabbath observance or to restrict the freedom of thought and utterance about religion; that, since the land in the New World belonged to the Indians, the king of England had no power to grant a charter for the possession of it. The colony gave him more latitude than might have been expected, but finally banished him. He fled to the shores of Narragansett Bay and there put his principles into practice by buying land from the Indians and founding the settlement of Providence on the basis of complete tolerance and equal civil rights for all regardless of their religion or lack of it. Together with other rebels against the theocratic rule in Massachusetts, he formed the first Baptist church in America. It is doubtful whether he ever actually joined this church; if he did, he withdrew after a few months to pursue his independent way. While on a visit to England, where he became a friend of Milton (five years his junior) and won the esteem of Cromwell, he came upon a pamphlet by John Cotton, the "unmitred pope of Boston," denouncing the dangerous idea of granting religious liberty. Williams replied with *The Bloudy Tenent of Persecution for the Cause of Conscience* (1644). Cotton replied to Williams, and Williams replied to Cotton, but the gist of the argument was in his first pamphlet. It was that the true principles of Christianity and the peace and security of the civil order alike demand that the minds and consciences of all men—whether Christian, Jew, or Turk—be left free from compulsion, and that all these can live together in a "firm and lasting peace" in a state or kingdom that will grant such liberty. Let error be fought against with no other sword than the Sword of the Spirit, "which alone, in soul matters, is able to conquer." Roger Williams and the Baptists were the pioneers and prophets of religious liberty. They sounded their note and set up their standard at a time when

Lutherans, Roman Catholics, Episcopal Anglicans, and all Puritans except a few radical individuals and groups stood stoutly for compulsory uniformity of religion.

MARYLAND AND PENNSYLVANIA

Maryland, the second tolerant colony, was under a Catholic proprietor. Actually, its proprietor, Lord George Calvert, was a gentleman of mild and tolerant temper, but his tolerance was never put to the test. He held his grant from a Protestant king and there was no possibility of getting religious liberty for Catholics in his colony except by granting liberty to all. It is rather surprising that Charles I let him go so far. Moreover, Calvert needed Protestant colonists, and he could not get them if his colony were rigidly Catholic. A majority of the colonists from the start were Protestants. Later, about the time when Louis XIV was cracking down on the Protestants in France, Maryland became a royal colony with established Episcopacy, and Catholics were the victims of Protestant intolerance. Because of the peculiar circumstances of its founding—a colony with a Catholic proprietor under a Protestant king—it does not illustrate any real progress toward what was to be the American system of religious liberty.

Pennsylvania made a real contribution in that direction. It was a Quaker colony. The Quakers were the followers of George Fox, who was one of the great religious geniuses of all time. His basic idea was that religion is a matter of the individual's direct relation with God. Consequently the highest authority is the voice of God as each man hears it, not the decision of any ecclesiastical authority or even the word of such a useful book as the Bible. Fox won many followers in England and on the European continent. One of them was William Penn, the son of a British admiral to whom the crown was indebted to the amount of a good many thousand pounds. That debt was discharged, without any strain on the treasury, by giving the son a huge grant of land in America that had cost the crown nothing. Since it was believed to be a wooded area, Penn proposed to call it "Sylvania," but without his connivance this was enlarged by the addition of his name, so it became "Pennsylvania." Penn and George Fox visited continental Europe, especially the Netherlands and northern Germany, seeking converts and colonists. The fortunes of the colony need not be traced further than to say that, with such principles of religious individualism as those of Fox and Penn, it is obvious that the colony could have nothing like an established church and that there could never be any question of making any citizen's civil rights dependent upon his conformity to some authorized standard of doctrine or worship. Pennsylvania never had an established church. More persons "distressed in conscience" came to Pennsylvania than to Rhode Island —chiefly because there was more room for them. In the seventeenth and eighteenth centuries there were successive waves of immigration of persecuted minorities from central Europe. Some were Mennonites (Anabaptists), a group from which President Eisenhower is a direct descendant. Some were Lutherans who fled from persecution in Catholic German states, such as those who escaped from the principality ruled by the Archbishop of Salzburg. These and others became the "Pennsylvania Dutch" (really German), whose very presence was a testimony to that colony's hospitality to Europe's persecuted religious minorities and whose industry and stalwart character added to both the economic and the moral resources of their new home.

French Protestants (Huguenots) furnished another valuable element, though more of them came to other colonies than to Pennsylvania. Louis XIV had first persecuted them to the point of extinction (as he supposed), then took away all their legal rights by revoking the Edict of Nantes (1685), then forbade their emigration from France. Consistency was never Louis' strong point. Though forbidden to emigrate, they came to America in thousands. The restrictions placed on Catholics, and especially on priests, in many of the colonies were rather directly related to the fact that everybody in America knew what Catholic France was doing at that very time to its Protestant population. Many had learned about it at first hand from Huguenot neighbors.

More than any other of the incipient American commonwealths, colonial Pennsylvania had such a diversity of religions that the establishment of any one of them as the state church would have been impossible even if it had not been contrary to the principles of a majority of its citizens.

SEPARATION OF CHURCH AND STATE

What was true of Pennsylvania was true of the colonies as a whole when the time came to organize a national government after the Revolution. Nine of the thirteen colonies still had established churches, but when the colonies are viewed as a group, no communion had a majority of all the church members and all the church members together were only a minority of the total population. Further, it is almost certainly true that not one of the nine established churches commanded the allegiance of a majority of the people in the colony that gave it legal sanction and support. The establishment of an American state church for the new nation would have been a political impossibility. Moreover, the very idea of legal compulsions and restraints in the field of religion had become an odious anachronism in the minds of the people generally. The concept of civil and political liberty, which was also an import from England, had so far developed in the American climate that the separation of church and state was inevitable and imminent.

Virginia led the way. Its Declaration of Rights—adopted two weeks before the signing of the Declaration of Independence—asserted that "all men are equally entitled to the free exercise of religion according to the dictates of conscience." Ten years later —and just a year before the writing of the Federal Constitution— the Virginia Act for Establishing Religious Freedom, drafted by Jefferson, declared that the state has no right to tax a citizen for the support of any religion, even his own, and that civil rights and eligibility to public office "have no dependence on religious opinions." This meant absolute disestablishment. The act was all the more emphatic because before enacting it the Virginia lawmakers had defeated a compromise proposal to set up a sort of establishment of Christianity in general and levy church taxes that would be prorated among all the churches. The widely publicized debate on this latter proposition should dispose of the argument—sometimes heard in our own times—that the framers and supporters of the First Amendment could not have thought of prohibiting tax support for the churches if only it were fairly distributed among them.

The Articles of Confederation (1777), which created "The United States of America," had declared that the thirteen states enter into a firm league "for their common defense . . . against all force offered to, or attacks made upon them, or any of them, on account of religion, sovereignty, trade, or any other pretence whatever." The inclusion of religion, and at the head of the list of the possible grounds of attacks that are to be resisted, is not without significance. In view of the religious diversity of the Americans and the steps already taken and about to be taken to guarantee complete religious liberty, it is obvious that what they were banding together to defend was not some one preferred church but the vital principle of freedom in religion.

Next came the Ordinance of 1787, in which Congress, still under the Articles of Confederation, decreed religious liberty throughout all the territory held by the United States outside of the several states—the old Northwest Territory. Then came the Constitution, which, by its silence on the subject, implied the absence of any establishment of religion by the new nation. This was followed by the First Amendment, which absolutely forbade it. Most of the colonial establishments of churches were abolished either shortly before or soon after the colonies became states. In two or three there were vested interests and contractual obligations of such a nature that the abolition took a little longer. The "standing order" in Connecticut lasted until 1818. Massachusetts, following tardily in 1834, disestablished the last state church on United States soil.

For the first time in history a people entered upon its career as a nation composed of religious minorities all free and legally equal, none (except the disappearing vestiges of establishments just mentioned) enjoying any special favor from the state governments or from the Federal government, and with no citizen's civil rights limited or conditioned by his religious faith or his lack of it. It was a revolutionary event in both political and religious history. It was possible only because of the preceding immigration of so many left-wing Protestants who had been not members but victims of the European state churches, and because of the growth of concepts of civil liberty (of which religious liberty is simply a special case) in England as well as in America. Thus was born the "denominational system," which still prevails. The freedom that it implies is fundamental to the American ideal, but it did not solve the whole problem or guarantee the success of the Christian enterprise in the new nation.

XXII

Religion on the American Frontier

The United States was practically all frontier at the beginning of the nineteenth century. This might have been denied by the proud residents of Boston, with its 24,000 inhabitants, or of Philadelphia, with 28,000, the country's capital during the decade ending in 1800, or of New York, with 60,000. Let us grant to these and some other towns along the Atlantic Coast with an honorable colonial history whatever of culture and urbanization they may claim. Even so, their nearness to the frontier was the most important fact about them. Their earlier outlook had been to the east, while they barely glanced over their shoulders to notice occasionally the wilderness behind them. Now they were facing westward with growing awareness of the vast open spaces and unknown resources that lay in that direction. Ninety per cent of the country's 5,300,000 population (by the 1800 census) was east of the Alleghenies, and more than half of the other ten per cent was in Kentucky and Tennessee. The whole Northwest Territory—which was later to become the states of Ohio, Indiana, Illinois, Michigan, and Wisconsin—had only 51,000 inhabitants. The

234

Mississippi River was the country's western boundary, but three years later the scope, the mystery, and the lure of the great open spaces were to be increased by Jefferson's reckless purchase of the vast Louisiana Territory, the exact limits of which no man knew.

All this created a unique set of problems, as well as of opportunities, for the nation and also for the churches. It was a situation without known precedent for a young nation, the offspring and heir of a mature culture and strong enough to have won its independence from the parent country, to find itself in possession of a vast and habitable hinterland into which it might expand beyond the limits of imagination. Young America had more lebensraum than it knew what to do with, and more than any other nation, young or old, had ever had before. The space into which the United States was about to expand was a vacuum—except for the Indians. That seemed a negligible exception, or at most a minor and temporary obstacle. It must be admitted that the Indian matter was handled badly, and at times ruthlessly, yet the main course of events was inevitable. In a clash between a hunting economy and an agricultural economy the outcome is never doubtful. The Indian population was sparse and impermanently settled, as always in a hunting economy. The invading settlers wanted nothing from the aborigines except their land. As always in such a conflict of cultures, the more intensive users of the soil prevailed and the permanent drove out the nomadic. It might have been done more kindly and more honestly, but it had to be done. The population of the states on the Atlantic seaboard was pressing forward to occupy and cultivate the western lands. For some years the growth of the eastern states was checked because the number of those who migrated to the west was greater than the natural increase plus the number of immigrants from Europe.

The situation in America posed a unique problem for the churches, too. In the first place, since there remained only a few vestiges of the European system of church support by taxation and by accumulated endowments, support by voluntary offerings was the only possibility. Even good Christians who have been accustomed to regarding their church as either independently wealthy or a financial ward of the state do not find it easy to dig into their own pockets to finance its work, and that is just what the Americans had to learn to do. In the second place, and even more important, the church members were a surprisingly small part of the population. Estimates range from five to ten per cent. The Great Awakening in the middle of the eighteenth century—an evangelistic movement in which the great names were those of Jonathan Edwards and George Whitefield—had seemed to set the colonies on fire with religious zeal, but the fires had died down. It was not merely that there was widespread indifference to religion. The rationalistic mood induced by the philosophy of the Enlightenment found popular expression in a wave of skepticism. French thought of the Revolutionary period made a powerful impact. Though the effort to found a deistic church in New York never got far, deism had many followers. While out-and-out infidelity and atheism never became formidable, there were thousands to whom "natural religion" seemed sufficient and by whom Christianity and its institutions were regarded as superfluous. Against these obstacles as well as the hardships of the frontier, the divided church had to make its way as best it could.

Under these conditions, and since religion was now entirely a voluntary matter under the new American regime, the church had either to evangelize or die. Since the people were moving by thousands into the western lands where there were no churches, the church also had to go west. Here was a new kind of missionary expansion—not, as in Christianity's first three centuries, the infiltration of an old established pagan culture by preaching and persuasion; not, as in the conversion of northern Europe and the lands that were to become Latin America, by the use of political pressure or military conquest in addition to moral suasion to Christianize the existing population of an area in which the church was a newcomer; but a migration in which the migrants themselves were the object of the evangelizing effort and the church was one of the institutions that traveled with them into the unknown and shared with them the pioneering venture. The church, though often in a rudimentary form, became part of the basic social structure of almost every new settlement and village.

THE FRONTIER CHURCHES

Methodists, Presbyterians, and Baptists plunged into the wilderness with almost reckless zeal. These became the great "popular churches" in the early stage of occupying the frontier and pushing it ever westward. Their preachers went wherever pioneering settlers went. Self-supporting churches with full-time ministers were still far in the future in the new country, but various devices met the needs of the transition period.

It is notable, but natural, that the formation of national organizations by several denominations so nearly coincided with the beginning of the nation. The Methodists, who had been only the left wing of the Evangelical Revival in the Church of England until the American Revolution cut them loose, organized themselves as a church in 1784 (see Chapter XXIII). They at once adopted a system of centralized control which seemed strangely out of keeping with young America's passion for individual liberty but worked marvelously well. Francis Asbury was the principal architect of this system. He may have been an autocratic master, but he was such a prodigious worker and was so indefatigable in the toilsome tasks and perilous travels of a peripatetic frontier ministry that his example counted for even more than his commands. Methodist bishops, presiding elders, circuit riders, and class leaders formed a network which expanded to keep pace with the advancing edge of settlement and provided nurture and control for the infant communities as they moved toward maturity.

The Presbyterians, who had formed presbyteries and synods in colonial days, organized their general assembly in 1787. They had a vigorous evangelistic tradition, partly a heritage from the Great Awakening, which sometimes strained the tethers of the church's courts and creeds but more often utilized its organization to give stability and maintain standards of culture. While the churches were still weak, ministers often divided their time between two or three within easy reach. In any case, the Presbyterian minister was expected to be a gentleman of sound education and some theological training, and it was the business of the presbytery to see that he met its criteria before locating him with one or more churches.

The Baptists, who had been the pioneers in the demand for absolute religious liberty for individuals as against the government and independence for the local congregation as against control by any higher ecclesiastical authority, carried on their expansion with little system but with great zeal. A despised minority during most of the colonial period, they had outdistanced the Episcopalians in numbers and almost overtaken the Congregationalists and Presbyterians by the opening of the new century and were about to pass these. Their division into "General Baptists" and "Particular Baptists" need not detain us—as, indeed, it did not greatly detain them in their numerical and geographical advance. Though they had no courts or synods, they had "associations" of churches, on about the scale of the Presbyterian "presbyteries"; and though they prided themselves on having no creed, they had a highly Calvinistic "Philadelphia Confession," allegiance to which was required for membership in most associations. The Baptist device for coping with the sparsity of population and the smallness of the frontier churches was the "farmer-preacher." While the Methodists had circuit riders who were full-time preachers giving part-time service to each of several communities, the Baptists had part-time preachers living where they served and supporting themselves largely by farming.

Out of the evangelistic activities of these three denominations grew that characteristic early American institution the camp meeting. It really began among the Presbyterians, and was a feature of that surge of emotional religion known as the Western Revival which flourished especially in Tennessee and Kentucky about 1800-1803, but the Methodists soon took it over, reduced it to a standardized pattern, and gave it as much sobriety as it ever had. It did exhibit some traits of primitive religion, and in the backwoods it developed abuses which have invited satirical comment, but for a time it served a religious purpose while also alleviating the isolation of the frontier and furnishing a temporary change of scene for people who had never heard of taking a vacation trip purely for recreation.

A native American movement with Presbyterian and Baptist backgrounds was that of the Disciples of Christ. Beginning with a revulsion against the division of Christians into sects and against the creeds which they considered the grounds for these divisions, they preached "Christian unity," but, by formulating a specific basis of union which they considered scriptural but others did not, they became a separate denomination in spite of themselves. They developed a type of rational evangelism which had a strong appeal for many who were unmoved by the emotional methods of the time. During and after the 1830's they took a place of increasing prominence among the "popular churches" on the advancing and maturing American frontier.

The Congregationalists, who still had nearly all their constituency in New England, did their migrating chiefly along isothermal lines. Their first home missionary work was done in co-operation with the Presbyterians, with whom they formed a Plan of Union for that purpose which lasted during the first third of the nineteenth century. They did not profit much denominationally from this, but it was a great help to the Presbyterians. Then, moving slowly but building solidly and founding colleges as well as churches, they penetrated Ohio, Indiana, Illinois, and Iowa.

The Episcopalians, recovering rather quickly from the unfortunate position in which the toryism of most of their clergy had involved them, formed a national organization in 1785 and got their first American bishops the next year. They were in no hurry about westward expansion. A generation had gone by before their pathbreaker, Philander Chase, acting on his own initiative and at his own risk, took to the winding trail which led him to establish a church in New Orleans, do missionary work in Michigan, become a bishop in Ohio, and found two colleges in Ohio and Illinois, for both of which he successfully solicited funds in England. After that it was easier for the church to appoint its first official missionary bishop, Jackson Kemper, whose diocese included a considerable part of the upper Mississippi Valley and had no western boundary.

The reader of American history must give due weight to the

fact and the influence of the frontier, but he must not so linger upon it as to forget how rapidly the conditions were changing behind the rapidly advancing line of continuous settlement. The churches did indeed "follow the frontier," but they also grew up with the country, and they were among the chief agencies in the transformation.

One of the ways in which they effected its transformation was by the establishment of colleges. Harvard, Yale, Princeton, and the other early colleges on the East Coast had been founded by the churches. This was in line with a long tradition, for the medieval universities, with one or two exceptions, had been religious foundations. As new communities sprang up west of the Alleghenies, the churches planted new colleges among them. Soon the prairies were dotted with colleges. Meagerly equipped at first and inadequately staffed by ill-paid faculties, many of them rendered invaluable service before they died of starvation, but many survived to become strong centers of sound learning. They bore the chief burden of giving the churches an educated ministry and an educated laity, insofar as these objectives could be attained, and of lifting the cultural level of the heart of America. Half or more of the country's colleges today owe their existence to the churches.

AMERICAN CATHOLICISM

Roman Catholics were less than one per cent of the country's population at the end of the Revolutionary War. Their number is estimated at 18,000. Most of them were English, with a sprinkling of French who had filtered down from Canada by way of Detroit and along the Mississippi and the Wabash. The Irish had not yet come. (The Irish who gave such valiant support to the Revolution were all Presbyterians from Ulster.) Most of the religious intolerance in the colonies in the eighteenth century had been directed against Catholics—regrettably, but understandably, because Protestants were still being persecuted in every Catholic country in Europe. Yet during the Revolution the bitterness faded out, and after it the new nation began business on the principle of

equal civil rights for Catholics, Protestants, and unbelievers alike
—a program then unparalleled elsewhere. The first Catholic bishop
in the United States, John Carroll (1790), was a gentleman and
scholar of the finest type. The church got off to a good start. Its
growth was not rapid until the great potato famine in Ireland
brought a flood of Catholic Irish pouring into the country in the
early 1840's. What had previously been a fairly steady but never
great flow of immigration became a torrent, and all of one kind.

After the Irish came the Germans; later the Italians, the Poles,
and multitudes from other countries of eastern Europe. With
increasing numbers and with constant reminder by Catholic
authorities that education is the function of the church, began the
establishment of the system of parochial schools and the continuing campaign to secure public money for the support of these
schools. Concordats between the Vatican and many European
states had secured either virtual control of public education by the
Catholic Church or at least the inclusion of Catholic religious
teaching in tax-supported institutions. Neither of these arrange-
ments was possible in the United States, a country predominantly
Protestant in its beginnings and with the unique principle of
separation of church and state and complete religious liberty for
all.

Most of the early Catholic immigrants remained in eastern cities,
where their competition in the labor market was the more resented
because there were as yet no effective labor organizations. The
resultant "nativist" movements, which were primarily antialien,
automatically became anti-Catholic because all the aliens in question were Catholics. This shift of emphasis was the easier because
for a time most of the priests were also recent arrivals, since there
had been no time to train American priests and few bishops to
ordain them, because it was commonly believed that the be-
wildered new Catholic citizens took orders from their priests
(who got theirs from Rome) in regard to their political activities,
and because the papacy was then in its most reactionary mood.
For one brief period there was a Catholic party, organized by
Archbishop John Joseph Hughes, which had its own slate of
candidates in a New York State election. The nativist organizations

always had a tinge of fanaticism about them. They were a fever which burned itself out, partly because political power was shifting toward the trans-Allegheny West, which was not confronted by the real or supposed perils that were their reason for existence. The last of the series was the Know-Nothing Party, which flashed into prominence because it seemed to offer a way of side-stepping the slavery question, and disappeared as suddenly when that became the inescapable issue.

SOCIAL RESPONSIBILITY AND SLAVERY

Up to this time the churches had had little to say about any social question. The early documents are full of records of church trials in which members were disciplined or expelled for such sins as drunkenness, gambling, profanity, adultery, fighting, and various breaches of the peace. There was a large segment in which the "works of the devil" were succinctly defined as, chiefly if not exclusively, "dancing, card-playing and theater-going." Political skulduggery and offenses against social justice had not drawn the attention of the churches. Neither did slavery until it loomed large as a social, economic, and political problem. Then slavery became the first great social issue upon which the churches developed a conscience. In fact, they developed two contrasting consciences. In the North, slavery was seen as a sin; in the South, as a divinely established institution opposition to which was sheer infidelity. Julia Ward Howe voiced the sentiment of the northern churches when she wrote:

> In the beauty of the lilies Christ was born across the sea . . .
> As he died to make men holy, let us die to make men free.

The Alabama Methodist conference declared in January, 1861: "African slavery is a wise, humane and righteous institution approved by God." Bishop Elliott, Episcopalian, in a sermon at Savannah, Georgia in 1862, described opposition to slavery as "presumptuous interference with the will and ways of God." The general assembly of the southern Presbyterian Church voted in 1864: "We hesitate not to affirm that it is the peculiar mission of the southern church to conserve the institution of slavery and to make it a blessing to both master and slave."

Slavery and secession became the occasion for division in the national bodies of the Methodists, Baptists, and Presbyterians. Only the Methodists, who were the first to divide, have healed their Civil War schism, after almost a century. Among the Episcopalians, committed by tradition to the theory that units of government are units of church organization, the southerners calmly organized a Protestant Episcopal Church in the Confederate States of America in 1861, and as calmly disbanded it and returned to the fold in 1865 when the fortunes of war had proved that the Confederate States of America did not exist as a separate nation. Since the northerners did not admit that the secession had ever been a political reality, they had not recognized the withdrawal of the southern dioceses, so the reunion was automatic and immediate. The Disciples of Christ did not divide because their organization was so loose that there was virtually nothing to divide. During the war years their southern members and ministers could not attend the annual conventions, then always held in Cincinnati; after the war they did; and that was all there was to it. The Congregationalists did not divide because they had no churches in the south. The Roman Catholic Church had taken no position on slavery either before or during the war. "By their silence," says Peter Guilday, "our prelates divorced this burning political question from Church affairs." Immediately after the war the Second Plenary Council of Baltimore said: "We could have wished that a more gradual system of emancipation could have been adopted." But since it had expressed no sentiments about emancipation by any system until it was an accomplished fact, naturally it did not divide on this issue.

THE WESTWARD MOVEMENT

The end of the Civil War left the South disorganized and depleted, and during the next decade the unwise policies of reconstruction imposed upon it made bad conditions worse. The North was not only flushed with victory but buoyant with energy and hope. It was for the most part energy for the pursuit of wealth and hope of getting it. Again the West beckoned. The westward movement of population beyond the Mississippi and the Rockies and the expansion of the churches to keep up with the advancing frontier were a continuation of the great trek that had its impetus in the discovery of gold in California in 1848. The panic of 1857 had destroyed for many in the East every reason for staying where they were, and new discoveries of gold and silver in Nevada, Colorado, and Idaho had alerted them to the call of the West. Meanwhile, the railroads were building. The last link in the transcontinental line was closed in 1869. These circumstances destroyed the earlier pattern of migration, which could be represented—with some oversimplification, to be sure—as the steady westward movement of the outposts of settlement forming an irregular but continuous north-and-south line across the country. The Santa Fe Trail, the Oregon Trail, the Mormon Trail with its continuation, the rise of settlements on the Pacific Coast, and the growth of mining camps wherever precious metals were found had already greatly disturbed that pattern. The railroads destroyed it. Homesteaders and town builders could now overleap empty spaces and establish nuclei of settlement at any accessible spot that seemed to possess natural advantages. As the Union Pacific, building westward, and the Central Pacific, building eastward, had met at Promontory Point to form a continuous railroad from the Mississippi to the Pacific, so the frontiers of settlement moved in both directions to close the gap between them until by 1890 it had come about that the frontier, in the old sense, no longer existed—though it must be admitted that there were still some "great open spaces" and that it was a very loose and uneven network of settlements that covered the great plains and the mountains.

The churches accepted the challenge of the new needs and opportunities and created new agencies to promote their work of expansion. New home missionary societies and church extension boards were formed. The strategy of the Christian campaign to evangelize the West and plant churches in the new towns along the railroads became more systematic and had more adequate financial backing from the East. Individual missionaries penetrated to remote spots, and devoted laymen often started churches wherever they happened to be, but the national organizations determined the main lines of development. When Robert G. Ingersoll, the most militant infidel of his time, declared that the church was dying out, Chaplain C. C. McCabe, assistant secretary of the Methodist Church Extension Society, gave a reply that became a slogan: "We're building two a day." That was, in fact, an understatement, for before 1890 that society had aided in building 9,000 churches.

Some great personalities emerged in this campaign for the Christian conquest of the West. Some of them also performed notable services of other kinds. Going back to the early days, there was Peter Cartwright (Methodist), a rough-and-ready frontier evangelist who became such a "character" that before his death in 1872 he was made the subject of two articles in the French magazine *Revue de Deux Mondes*. Marcus Whitman (Congregationalist), apostle to the Northwest, played a part in bringing the importance of the Oregon country to the attention of the government in Washington and preventing our claim to it from going by default. Pious legend may have exaggerated the importance of his contribution in this matter, but it was substantial even if not crucial. His heroic ride from Oregon to the nation's capital was a supermarathon, executed not to bring tidings of a victory but to give warning against a threatened diplomatic defeat. When he was murdered by the Indians in 1847, the case for doing something about Oregon got an emotional stimulus that helped to stir Washington to decisive action the next year. William Taylor, a Tennessee backwoods Methodist preacher, went to San Francisco in 1848, was a street preacher there for several years, and then evangelized widely in all directions, but his later labors on five continents were so remarkable that he rates a larger entry in connection with the story of foreign missions. Starr King (Unitarian) went from Boston to San Francisco in 1860, became the most popular preacher in the city, and was so influential in keeping California in the Union that he is commemorated by a bronze statue in Golden Gate Park. Sheldon Jackson (Presbyterian), a graduate of Union College and Princeton Theological Seminary, superintendent of Presbyterian missions in the Rocky Mountain area, ranged from Montana to New Mexico and founded many churches. In 1884 he went to Alaska, where the next year he became superintendent of public instruction and organized a public-school system. He held this office until his death twenty-five years later. Meanwhile, he had helped to lay out mail routes (since he knew the country better than anyone else), had assisted in organizing the territorial government, and had introduced the domestic reindeer, which became an important element in the economy of the Alaskan natives. But he always remained at heart a missionary.

Revivalism continued to be a favorite American method for the promotion of religion even after the camp meeting passed away. It had begun earlier. The Great Awakening before the middle of the eighteenth century, in which George Whitefield and Jonathan Edwards were the outstanding figures, echoed through the colonies for many years. The Great Western Revival of 1800-03, in which the camp meeting was born, initiated a series of waves of revivalism in which some of the notable names are Charles G. Finney, Dwight Moody and Ira Sankey, Sam Jones, Billy Sunday and Billy Graham. In most of these "campaigns" many churches and many denominations co-operated. There was also continuing revivalism on a smaller and more local scale. Several denominations regarded it as part of the normal calendar of every congregation to have a revival, or "protracted meeting," every year, with preaching every night for two or three weeks. The pastor might do the preaching, but the preferred practice was to engage the services of a traveling evangelist. There were hundreds who made this work their profession. This procedure was at its height in the latter part of the nineteenth century and the early years of the twentieth.

Not all the growth of the churches came by evangelization and natural increase. As immigration increased the population of the country, so also it increased the number of church members. The percentage of church members among the immigrants was larger than in the country as a whole. The reason for this was that most of the immigrants came from European countries having state churches of which a vast majority of the people were at least nominal members. The churches that gained most in this way during the years of heaviest immigration in the nineteenth century were the Roman Catholic and the Lutheran. Ireland, Italy, southern Germany, and Poland have furnished the largest Catholic immigration. Northern Germany and the Scandinavian countries sent throngs of Lutherans. The immigrants from Ireland before the Revolution were almost all Presbyterians from Ulster. The German immigrants in colonial days had come chiefly under the spur of religious persecution in their old homes. They included Mennonites and other dissenters from established Lutheranism (these became the "Pennsylvania Dutch") and Lutherans who had been driven out or escaped from German states under Roman Catholic rule. It is to be remembered that Germany was then not yet one country, but many autonomous principalities, and that it was still an accepted principle, confirmed by the Peace of Westphalia, which ended the Thirty Years' War in 1648, that "he who governs the territory determines its religion." The later and greater German immigration in the nineteenth century had an economic and political, rather than a religious, motivation.

The Lutheran immigrants from whatever source tended to retain the language of the country of their origin, at least for religious purposes, and to retain their church organizations on the same lines. For this reason, American Lutheranism has continued to have a strongly foreign coloration. Its growth has been chiefly by natural increase reinforced by successive waves of immigration. Its many divisions are largely based on linguistic differences or on issues having their origin in Europe, such as acceptance or rejection of the union of Lutheran and Reformed churches in Prussia and Hesse under governmental pressure in and shortly after 1817. All the Lutheran groups have remained stoutly conservative theologically, though with enough variation to impede the process of unification which has been making headway among them. The most rigidly conservative, the least co-operative, and one of the strongest is the Missouri Synod, organized in 1847.

The Roman Catholic Church, though profiting by immigration even more than the Lutherans, has not been equally limited by this fact. It is true that many congregations, institutions, and schools continue to use the language of their constituents' country of origin. This fact and the tremendous development of the separate system of Catholic schools and colleges, the conditions imposed upon the intermarriage of Catholics with non-Catholics, and the fundamental allegiance of priests and people to an overseas ecclesiastical authority have tended toward the establishment of a cultural pluralism and to the imposition of limits upon communication between Catholics and other Americans. Nevertheless, Roman Catholicism, with no change whatever in doctrine or discipline, has in many respects been Americanized to a remarkable degree. This is a broad generalization to which many exceptions could be cited—and, from the Catholic point of view, justified. It is not based on the record of such universally honored characters in the 1880's and '90's as Cardinal Gibbons and Archbishops Ireland, Keane, and Kain, for the liberal and co-operative practices of these men were checked by instructions from Rome and they have no contemporary parallels. It is, rather, that, by and large, Catholics in America are not generally regarded by non-Catholics as primarily persons of foreign origin.

In recent years immigration has brought from the Near East enough members of Eastern Orthodox churches to give the twenty-one churches of this order as listed in the 1957 *Yearbook of the Churches* a claimed membership of more than two million.

Two other religious movements of magnitude and importance have originated on American soil. The Mormons (Church of Jesus Christ of Latter-day Saints) began with the alleged discovery of *The Book of Mormon* by Joseph Smith near Palmyra, N. Y., in 1827. The book was a record, amounting to several hundred pages, inscribed on golden plates in characters of "Reformed Egyptian," which were translated through a pair of miraculous spectacles that automatically turned them into English with a strong flavor of the King James Version of the Bible. Organized into a church in Ohio, the Mormons became a compact and exclusive group—not merely a church but also a social and economic unit and, so far as possible, a governmental unit. They migrated first to Missouri, then to a site on the Mississippi River in northern Illinois, where they founded the town of Nauvoo, which, under the autocratic leadership of their prophet, became the largest town in Illinois, the center of a strong community with its own standing army, and a political power in the state. The murder of Joseph Smith and the armed hostility of the surrounding population indicated the impossibility of carrying out their ambitious plans in that location. Brigham Young led them across the plains and mountains to Utah and the site of what was to become Salt Lake City. When the first settlers arrived (July, 1847) this area was a part of Mexico, but so remote from its seats of government that there could be a lively hope of soon breaking away and forming an independent state, as Texas had recently done. Six months later the treaty ending the Mexican War brought it within the boundaries of the United States. Missionaries sent to Europe won many converts, especially in England and Sweden. Migration to Utah, the new Promised Land, was part of the gospel they preached. Polygamy—until it was outlawed by the church in 1890 —increased the population but intensified the antipathy of non-Mormons. Industry and good management made the entire Utah enterprise as successful a colonization project as history records. Religious zeal, the careful indoctrination of the young, and continued missionary efforts have brought the Mormon Church to a membership of more than a million and a quarter, with a concentration in Utah and the mountain states but with congregations throughout the country. The radio concerts of the superb Tabernacle Choir and the "spoken word" of Richard Evans, over a period of thirty years, have won the admiration of all who hear them.

Christian Science is a system of religious teaching and drugless healing discovered and organized by Mary Baker Eddy in successive steps about 1866. Its Textbook, *Science and Health,* was published in 1875. Keeping a closely knit central control in Boston, and using none of the traditional evangelistic techniques of propaganda and expansion, it has gained a body of adherents which, though no statistics are given out, must be of the order of a million. One of the agencies by which it has gained the respect even of those who reject its philosophy and regard its opposition to medical research and practice a menace to public health is the highly intelligent and widely circulated daily *Christian Science Monitor*, which contains a minimum of distinctively Christian Science material.

An important feature of contemporary American Christianity is the large number of independent and energetic religious groups about which scarcely any descriptive statement can be made that will apply to all except that they stand apart from the older historic denominations and from one another. They enter into no conferences, are members of no councils of churches, co-operate with nobody, but promote their own programs with great zeal and devotion. All are basically Fundamentalist in their theology, but with many variations in detail. There can be only bare mention of a few: Seventh-day Adventists, Jehovah's Witnesses, Amy Semple McPherson's Four-Square Gospel, the Churches of God (fourteen listed organizations), Nazarenes, the various Pentecostal Holiness bodies, and the Churches of Christ. No similarity in doctrine, worship, or methods of promotion, except as indicated above, is implied by listing these together in a single sentence. In general these movements are not in the slightest degree affected by anything that could be called modern scholarship, and the more successful of them are growing more rapidly than either the old-line Protestant denominations or the Roman Catholic Church.

So by natural diffusion, by the work of missionaries who were half explorers, by the systematic efforts of national church boards and societies, by planting churches and colleges which both shared in and promoted the growing culture of what had only lately been frontier settlements, and by education, evangelism, revivalism, and the proliferation of new and unconventional movements, religion had more than kept pace with the development of the country. If mere statistics mean anything, it may be noted that between the beginning and the end of the nineteenth century, while the population of the United States had increased from 5,300,000 to 75,900,000, the percentage of church members in the total population had increased from less than ten to thirty-six per cent.

XXIII

Christianity in Europe

While Christianity was making a place for itself in the New World, it was in danger of losing that which it had held in the Old. It had already lost in England, and was about to lose in most countries of continental Europe, the status of an institution to which the state compelled conformity. The question was whether it could hold the allegiance of the minds of men who were asserting their freedom in all other fields. Empirical science, foreshadowed by Aristotle, had entered its modern phase with Galileo and Bacon. The way to find truth was to study observed facts. John Locke had declared that "sensation and reflection" were man's only means of gaining knowledge. Almost simultaneously with the release of Locke's principal work, Sir Isaac Newton published (1687) his *Principia* (*The Mathematical Principles of Natural Philosophy*). These marked the dawn of what was hailed as the Age of Enlightenment. Bacon and Locke told how all true knowledge must be obtained, and Newton explained everything! As Alexander Pope, the poetical spokesman for the Enlightenment, hymned it:

Nature and Nature's laws lay hid in night;
God said, Let Newton be, and all was light.

For the men of the Enlightenment there remained problems but no more mysteries. The belief spread that man could be lifted to perfection by using his own mental powers in accordance with scientific method, that such religious teachings as could not be certified by observation or reason were to be rejected, and that if God had created the world and its inhabitants—before Hume it did seem that the law of causation required the assumption of a First Cause—he had left the world to run according to natural law and man to work out his own salvation with the aid of an inquisitive mind to whose achievements no limits could be set. The consequence, in Newton's nation, was a cool Deism which, rejecting the supernatural and worshiping natural law, produced a somnolent church with neither the power nor the will to exercise moral leadership or to minister to the spiritual needs of men. On the Continent, and especially in France, which was then the center of European culture, it led to the polished skepticism that, in Voltaire's phrase, made God a character to whom he bowed but with whom he was not on speaking terms.

The 1700's in Europe have been called "the glittering century." The term does the period some injustice by implying that its brilliance was wholly superficial. The truth is that there was much solid intellectual substance beneath its brilliant surface. One cannot speak lightly of the century of Leibnitz and Hume, of Addison, Swift, and Gibbon, of Rousseau, Goethe, and Schiller, of Handel, Bach, and Mozart, and of the opening of the British Museum and the first edition of the Encyclopaedia Britannica. It was in a sense a revival of the spirit of the Renaissance, with its intellectual liberty tending toward a self-sufficient rationalism, its appreciation of beauty and joy (for those in fortunate circumstances), and its declining interest in either faith or morality. The state of organized religion and of personal morals was low in every country of Europe. To speak only of England, which concerns us most nearly, the church paid by loss of moral authority and spiritual leadership for its long preoccupation with the externals and temporalities. Alike among the common people and in high society, the general level of morality had perhaps never been lower.* In Germany the state-dominated church had consciously adopted the policy of noninterference with anything outside of the narrow circle of its own doctrines and sacraments. Its theologians were either bogged down in a stultifying Protestant scholasticism or frustrated by accommodation to the prevailing rationalism of the time. Roman Catholicism in such Catholic countries as France, Spain, and Italy had suffered a decline from the high level of the Catholic Reformation to a painful position from which it was later to be rescued by the conservative reaction to the French Revolution and Napoleon.

JOHN WESLEY

In Protestant Germany, Christianity's recovery from formalism and sloth was largely due to the rise of Pietism—an emphasis upon the individual's direct communion with God, the validity of religious experience, and the necessity of not only nurturing the devotional life by prayer but also giving it expression in deeds of mercy and benevolence. In England, the saving event was the breaking out of that Evangelical Revival with which the name of John Wesley is forever linked. These two reinvigorating movements met at the point where Wesley, the high church Anglican, in his early gropings found himself in Moravian company, first on a ship in distress during an Atlantic storm and later in the quiet of a Pietistic meeting in Aldersgate Street, London, from which he emerged with his "heart strangely warmed."

In many ways John Wesley is reminiscent of Ignatius Loyola. He was as completely a child of his age and culture, eighteenth-century England, as was Loyola of sixteenth-century Spain. Like the founder of the Jesuit order, he cared less for theology than for religious results. When, after his preaching had begun to win converts by the thousands, he was reminded of the doctrine of predestination with its teaching that most of mankind has been

* For details and documentation, see J. W. Bready, *England Before and After Wesley*, Harper, 1938. For more scandalous particulars, L. C. Jones, *The Clubs of the Georgian Rakes*, Columbia University Press, 1942.

elected by God's decree to eternal damnation, Wesley swept Calvin aside and gave slight heed to his own church's somewhat milder assertion of the limitation of God's mercy to the elect (Art. XVII of the Thirty-nine Articles), and cried: "What will you prove by Scripture? That God is worse than the Devil? It cannot be. Whatever that Scripture proves, it never can prove this; whatever its true meaning may be, this cannot be its true meaning. . . . No Scripture can mean that God is not love."

In every sense of the word, Wesley was a general. (Geneticists might find interest in the fact that his distant cousin, whose name was Arthur Wesley until the spelling was changed to Wellesley, was to become the Duke of Wellington, the victor at Waterloo.) He demanded absolute obedience from his lay preachers and laid down rules for the conduct of the members of his societies so detailed that the name "Methodists," first flung in derision at Wesley and his companions at Oxford, became fastened on the entire Wesleyan movement. He was not as "moving" a preacher as others in the Evangelical Revival, such as George Whitefield, but he saw to it that his converts were organized into disciplined companies which would become something permanent. To this day Methodist churches and clergy are governed by a *Book of Discipline*.

Wesley drove himself incredibly—an average of 4,500 miles every year on horseback over what then passed for roads; at least 45,000 sermons preached in his lifetime, the first each day at five o'clock or earlier; 450 books either written or edited; and a volume of correspondence conducted that would weary a modern tycoon equipped with dictograph and a bevy of secretaries. Then, at the end of each day, there had to be the entry in that *Journal* which historians acclaim as the best picture we have of the England of the first three Georges. In fifty years Wesley with his followers broke up the cold formalism of English church life, made Christianity a transforming power for hundreds of thousands of miners, artisans, farm laborers, and small tradesmen, and set in motion philanthropic and reform impulses that led to John Howard's crusade against prison horrors, William Wilberforce's against slavery, and Robert Raikes's Sunday schools, originally intended to lighten the mean and stunted lives of children in the slums.

Wesley was no separatist. He was an ordained clergyman of the Church of England and wanted to work within that church. Even to the end of his life he was never quite willing to admit that he had left it. When his adherents became numerous they were organized not into local churches but into "societies." But the actual functioning of these societies, the conferences of Wesley's preachers, and the total disregard of the Anglican authorities made it more and more difficult to maintain the fiction that Methodism was only a movement for the revival of religion in the Church of England. Affairs were in this tentative state when the first Methodist lay preacher came to America in 1760. Twenty years later, when there were more than a hundred preachers and almost 10,000 Methodists, they still regarded themselves as extrazealous and free-wheeling members of the Church of England under the special direction of John Wesley. The winning of American independence (to which Wesley had been opposed) made it impossible for American Methodism not to assert its independence. This was done, with Wesley's approval, at the famous Christmas Eve conference, 1784, at Baltimore. Then and there was born the Methodist Episcopal Church, which became a potent factor in evangelizing America.

THE EVANGELICAL REVIVAL

The Evangelical Revival of the eighteenth century did more than produce German Pietism, which remained within the bosom of Lutheranism, and the Methodist Church, which ultimately separated from its parent, the Church of England. It became a permeating influence in all the churches. Its warm devotional life, its deep concern for the salvation of souls, and its active interest in the betterment of living conditions for the common people—all these worked for good at a crucial time. The mystical and humanitarian qualities of the Evangelical Revival furnished no answer to the Enlightenment's empirical philosophy or its rationalistic arguments against revealed religion, but they were a steadying and sustaining influence for thousands, ultimately for millions, of the common people, who, knowing little about the intellectual issues involved, were in danger of being swept along by the popular current of unbelief, which was the Enlightenment's most immediate but least admirable consequence.

It is no mere coincidence that the beginnings of the great modern missionary expansion of Christianity came just as the Evangelical Revival was reaching its crest. German Pietists and Moravians had sent some missionaries to Greenland, Labrador, and the Danish West Indies early in the eighteenth century. The Church of England's Society for the Propagation of the Gospel in Foreign Parts, organized in 1701, had worked in the British West Indies as well as in the American colonies. It was toward the end of the century, and under the influence of the Evangelical Revival, that the missionary impulse began to reach out beyond the limits of colonial possessions. When William Carey, an English Baptist minister, joined with others in forming a Baptist missionary society in 1792 and soon thereafter went to India, it was the beginning of a new era of Christian expansion. We shall sketch the development of this wider expansion in a later chapter, at present only noting that it was largely the result of that revival of evangelical zeal which—strangely, it may seem—paralleled the Age of Enlightenment.

England's "bloodless revolution" of 1689 had put that country a century ahead of the European Continent in civil and religious liberty and in democratic government. In France until late in the eighteenth century royal absolutism prevailed, Protestantism was legally nonexistent—but only driven underground, not exterminated, by the dragonnades and the revocation of the Edict of Nantes—and the higher Catholic clergy were solidly on the side of the privileged class, to which they belonged, though the parish priests were generally on the side of the oppressed, among whom *they* belonged. The French Revolution was antiroyalist and anticlerical, but not antireligious except in one brief period of madness. When the Revolution was over, and when Napoleon had risen and fallen, the badly frightened powers of Europe joined in a Conservative Alliance to restore the old order of things and to defend all "legitimate" monarchs against the threatening rise of liberal sentiments.

CATHOLICISM IN EUROPE

Catholicism profited greatly by this reaction. Napoleon had carried off the pope to Fontainebleau and compelled him to sign away his sovereignty over the Papal State. When Napoleon fell, the pope naturally returned to Rome and to the exercise of his temporal sovereignty. This gave general satisfaction, for even those who did not love the pope hated Napoleon and were glad to see his redrawing of the political map of Europe erased as completely as possible. But with the pope back in the Vatican, acknowledged as the absolute monarch of a state covering a considerable part of central Italy, and acting in close alliance with the reactionary governments of Europe, new troubles arose. The French Revolution, in spite of some appalling excesses, and Napoleon, in spite of his imperialistic ambitions, had left a residue of advanced political thought—a stronger demand for the recognition of basic human rights, and the concept of a secular society in which all men would enjoy freedom of religion and no ecclesiastical authorities should dominate the civil government. Italy was seething with this new spirit. It was the achievement of the Vatican in the nineteenth century that it fought off these revolutionary forces until the progressive political unification of Italy ended its temporal sovereignty in 1870, and that simultaneously it was reviving its inner strength, decreeing new dogmas, reasserting its absolute refusal to compromise with the liberal spirit of the times, and putting the capstone on its pyramid of power by the decree of papal infallibility.

The church was fortunate in having successively two strong popes with unprecedentedly long pontificates: Pius IX (1846-78) and Leo XIII (1878-1903). The decree of the Immaculate Conception of the Virgin Mary (1854), the first promulgation of a dogma on the authority of the pope alone, foreshadowed the *non ex consensu ecclesiae* ("not from the consent of the church") which was

included, sixteen years later, in the definition of the pope's infallibility in matters of doctrine and morals. The Syllabus of Errors
(1864) served notice that the Vatican adhered in principle to the
medieval position that governments should co-operate with the
"one true Church" and should protect their citizens from the
poisonous teachings of any other. One of the "errors" denounced
in this document is the claim "that the church ought to be separated from the state and the state from the church." Leo, more
diplomatic in his approach to the problems of the modern world,
showed himself a no less stalwart defender of the same position
in his great encyclical *Immortale Dei* (On the Christian Constitution of States, 1885), in which he deplored the "lamentable rage
for innovation" that has led to the false modern theory "that everyone is to be free to follow whatever religion he prefers, or none at
all if he disapproves of all," and that has brought it about in
states embracing such principles that "the Catholic religion is
allowed a standing in civil society equal only to societies alien from
it"—that is, other churches. While thus condemning the American
principle of religious liberty as strongly as his predecessors had
done, Leo recognized that it was not always practicable for the
church to insist upon its unique prerogatives and that, where it
does not have the power to enforce what it considers its rights,
it may temporarily concede the legal, if not the theological, right
of other "churches" to exist. In more modern mood, Leo XIII
championed the cause of labor and was among the first religious
leaders—perhaps the very first—to demand social and economic
justice for the common man.

When the popes lost their temporal sovereignty in 1870, by the
withdrawal of the French troops from Rome to meet the demands
of the Franco-Prussian War, they became, in their own view,
"prisoners in the Vatican," and so remained until by the treaty and
concordat with Mussolini in 1929 the independent state of Vatican
City was established, with an area of 108.7 acres.

XXIV

Christianity and Modern Thought

What is commonly called "modern thought" is, to a great extent, a delayed result of the Renaissance. Then men began to break away from established authority, question what had hitherto been accepted without questioning, and seek for truth by reliance on their own powers of observation and reasoning. Modern science and modern philosophy were both born of that revolt against authority. The Renaissance, checked in Italy, the land of its origin, burst forth with fresh vigor in England and then in France. There its chief manifestations were not in painting and sculpture, but in science and philosophy. The resulting prevalence of empiricism and rationalism did indeed create a peril for the Christian faith. Faith had built upon some unquestioned and unquestionable presuppositions. For Protestants, the chief of these were revelation and the Bible as its infallible channel. But science and philosophy felt free to question everything, including these. In reality they rather ignored than investigated them.

We have already spoken of the intellectual movement that is called the Enlightenment in England, the *Eclaircissement* in France and the *Aufklärung* in Germany, the threat that its skeptical temper offered to Christian faith, and the defense against this threat by Pietism and the Evangelical Revival. In secular thought the Romantic movement furnished a somewhat similar escape. These movements all stressed emotion more than reason and tried to find a cognitive value in "feeling." They were evasions rather than solutions of the issues presented by the Enlightenment. There was nothing discreditable about this, for few philosophical battles are fought out on the ground on which they originate. But it was not long until some Christian thinkers began to reflect that there were in these new and apparently dangerous movements some elements that might be a positive resource for the Christian faith. Perhaps one might get a truer knowledge of what God has done and said by studying the evidence by the same methods that the critics of Christianity were using.

The Enlightenment contained an element that was not crude rationalism or materialistic empiricism. This was a common-sense demand that beliefs should be examined, and if necessary revised, in the light of the known or knowable facts. Modern science was born out of this respect for evidence as the necessary ground of any conclusions that can be held with assurance. What did this mean for religion? Some, enchanted by the new methods of science, would now believe nothing that could not be proved as Newton's law of gravitation was proved. Religion became for them a mass of superstitions to be put away along with the other playthings belonging to the infancy of the human race. On the other hand, there were those pious ones who thought it little less than sacrilege to subject to the test of evidence any of the cherished beliefs they had received on authority. But there were some also who felt that, though the basic truths of Christianity might be neither provable nor disprovable by scientific methods, there was a great body of Christian lore and tradition that stood in need of just such a clearing up as the principles of the Enlightenment might furnish. Here was the beginning of what may be called evangelical liberalism.

The Enlightenment, from the English Hume to the French Encyclopedists, had carried itself entirely outside the orbit of Christian thought. The early years of the nineteenth century saw a new series of intellectual events which had more significance for Christian thought because they were not anti-Christian.

These new ideas and discoveries were scientific rather than philosophical. All of them involved, directly or indirectly, questions as to the nature of the Bible: What kind of book is it? What is the nature and extent of its inspiration? What is the scope and what are the limits of its authority? These questions were especially important for Protestants because, when they had rejected the authority of the church as constituted in the Middle Ages, they had reaffirmed with emphasis the authority of the Bible. William Chillingworth's phrase "The Bible and the Bible alone is the religion of Protestants," originally intended only as a denial of the co-ordinate authority of ecclesiastical tradition, had come to be an assertion that the Bible was the very bedrock of all truth. The Reformers and their followers for the next two or three centuries had not realized that the theory of Biblical infallibility was itself an item in that Catholic "tradition" which they thought they were rejecting completely.

The first issue had to do with the age of the earth. Archbishop James Ussher (Anglican, Dublin) had arranged a chronology, drawn from the data given in the Old Testament, which acquired such prestige that it was printed in all standard editions of the King James version until recent years. By this chronology the earth was created in the year 4004 B.C. In any case, since Genesis says the world was created in six days and the line of the patriarchs begins on the sixth day, it could not have been much earlier than that. Yet the new science of geology was saying that certain fossils were millions of years older, and that the strata of sedimentary rock indicated a vast age for the earth. Which was right—Genesis or geology? It became a hotly debated issue. Books were written on both sides. Clerical reputations were made and lost. The belated thought that the "days" of Genesis might mean geological epochs furnished a rather narrow avenue of escape. It had never occurred to any exegete until geology gave its testimony to the earth's antiquity, but it served the purpose for those who could not bring themselves to deny facts as hard as rocks but who felt it necessary that Scripture should be infallible on every subject it mentions.

The real issue, of course, was not the age of the earth but the nature of the Bible. This preliminary skirmish suggested to many that perhaps it was not intended to serve as an infallible guide in science. But strict orthodoxy long maintained that the Bible would be "untrustworthy" in religion if it contained any statement in the area of science or history that is not absolutely correct.*

EVOLUTION AND THE BIBLE

The fight over evolution was longer and more serious. The idea of organic evolution had been stated by many earlier scientists, but Darwin's great book *The Origin of Species* (1859) presented massive evidence in support of the hypothesis. In this and in *The Descent of Man* (1871) was a theory of the origin of the human race and of man's relationship with the rest of the animal world which was radically different from the account given in Genesis. No ingenuity of exegesis could make it appear that the author of Genesis really meant what Darwin said. Furthermore, the idea of evolution quickly began to be applied in fields other than biology—in the study of the development of social institutions, of law, of language, of religion itself. In the first forty years few religious leaders dared face the implications of the scientific doctrine and the philosophy that grew out of it. One who did was Henry Drummond, natural scientist of Edinburgh University and for a time the associate of Dwight L. Moody, the evangelist. Drummond wrote *The Natural Law in the Spiritual World* and *The Ascent of Man*. He was the first conspicuous "Christian evolutionist." Another was Henry Ward Beecher, who, being then the most popular preacher in America, contributed a proevolution article to the *North American Review* in 1880. From this, most pious Americans probably reached the conclusion not that evolu-

---

* My own boyhood Bible, the flyleaf of which testifies that it was given to me by my father on Christmas Day, 1890, not only carries the Ussher chronology at the head of every page of the historical books—including the date of creation as September 1, 4004 B.C.—but also asserts, in the "Helps" at the back of the book, that the religious "ideas" in the Bible cannot be believed unless all its statements of "facts" are accepted as true. —W.E.G.

tion was compatible with Christianity but that Beecher, though an incomparable preacher, was just a loose-thinking liberal. Beecher's more scholarly successor, Lyman Abbott, lectured widely on "The Evolution of Christianity" and wrote a book entitled *The Theology of an Evolutionist* (1897).

The idea of evolution as "God's way of working" gradually won acceptance by most Christian scholars, but so heavy was the conservative drag that most ministers cautiously refrained from saying a good word for evolution and left their flocks to assume that it must be contrary to their religion since they never heard it defended except by "infidels." The continuing conflict was dramatized by the Scopes case in 1925 when William Jennings Bryan and Clarence Darrow faced each other in the trial of a high-school science teacher for violation of a Tennessee law forbidding teaching in any tax-supported school "the theory that denies the divine creation of man as taught in the Bible." Immediately thereafter antievolution laws were enacted in Mississippi, Arkansas, and Texas. The crux of the question was still whether or not denial of the inerrancy of the Bible is an attack on Christianity.

BIBLICAL CRITICISM

A few had approached the question of the nature of the Bible on a broader front and in a scientific spirit long before Darwin and evolution took the spotlight. Even in the eighteenth century there were Christian scholars who, as they read the Bible, saw that it did not exhibit a constant level of divine inspiration, that its writers seemed to express diverse and not always harmonious views, and that some of the books appeared to be of composite origin and to have been written later than the dates traditionally assigned to them. By the early years of the nineteenth century, methods of more rigorous historical research and literary analysis had been developed in Germany, and it was inevitable that these should be applied to the Bible. To scholars on whom the spirit of the Enlightenment had made its impress it seemed reasonable and necessary that the most intelligent processes of historical and literary analysis should be applied for the better understanding of the world's most important body of literature. The result was what came to be called "higher criticism."

"Lower criticism" was the study and comparison of manuscripts to determine the most accurate text of the Biblical books. No one objected to that, but to the more conservative minds it seemed presumptuous to continue the research by examining these texts as other pieces of ancient literature are examined with a view to discovering their authorship, dates, structure, and relation to the periods that produced them. Some of the results of such study were radically at variance with traditional views. Among them were the "documentary theory" of the Pentateuch, the division of Isaiah into at least two parts separated by about one hundred and fifty years, and the late date of Daniel. These and other discoveries involved a thorough revision of earlier ideas about the course of Hebrew history and the development of Hebrew thought. What was even more important, this "new view of the Bible" made it impossible to prefix "The Bible says" to a verse taken at random from any part of it on the assumption that this settled the matter. The application of the same principles to the New Testament was even more disturbing to many.

There was lively and continuing controversy on these themes, in England as early as the 1860's, in the United States beginning almost a generation later. It was long before this new method of Biblical study and its results reached any considerable numbers of the laity (if they have even yet), but the denominational leaders, the seminary professors, and most of the clergy knew enough about them to take sides. In many circles one's attitude toward "higher criticism" became the touchstone of orthodoxy. The conservatives were quite right in saying that much more than a question of literary history was involved. If this new view prevailed, the Bible could no longer be used as an "arsenal of proof-texts." If it were agreed that the Biblical writers viewed truth from the standpoint of their own time and place, then moderns might feel themselves free to see it from the point of view of the best culture of their own day, including its scientific and philosophical insights. It was quite certain that there would be revisions of some of the doctrines that had been formulated in the fourth century and in the sixteenth. And so, indeed, there were. It is rather surprising that there were only a few heresy trials. By the end of the nineteenth century, a strain of "evangelical liberalism" ran through the leading Protestant denominations. The root of it was a demand for freedom of thought on the basis of unrestricted scholarship, not only in interpreting the words of the Bible (that had been an original principle of Protestantism), but also in determining what kind of book the Bible is.

A similar tendency in the Roman Catholic Church was promptly checked. Its first manifestation was the rise of liberal political and social movements in Catholic European countries. Leo XII had already denounced the democratic movement and the principles of religious liberty before Pius IX in his Syllabus of Errors (1864) made clear the church's continued claim to absolute control over the intellectual life of mankind. His promulgation of the dogma of papal infallibility (1870) made clear the locus of the church's authority. Leo XIII's encyclical *Aeterni Patris* (1879) established the thirteenth-century system of St. Thomas Aquinas as the permanent standard of Catholic philosophy, and his *Providentissimus Deus* (1893) was directed against critical methods of Biblical study. This was followed by a decree prohibiting doubt as to the textual authenticity of the "three heavenly witnesses" passage in I John 5:8 (1897). Under Pius X, the first pope to be canonized in almost two and a half centuries, the condemnation of independent scholarship came to a climax with a decree of the Mosaic authorship of the Pentateuch (1906) and two encyclicals (1906, 1907) completely crushing "Modernism," which included Biblical criticism and much more. This was followed by the requirement that a special "anti-Modernist oath" shall be taken by all teachers in Catholic seminaries and colleges by which they bind themselves to agreement with "all the condemnations, declarations and proscriptions" in regard to Biblical interpretation that have been put forth by the church's constituted authorities. To bring the record down to date, in 1950 the question of the transfer of the Virgin Mary's body from earth to heaven was taken out of the hands of the theologians and historians by Pope Pius

XII when he promulgated the dogma of the Assumption; and in the same year the encyclical *Humani Generis*, while speaking appreciatively of the work of Christian scholars, reminded them that they must stay within the boundaries prescribed by the Vatican and that, for example, they must regard the early chapters of Genesis as neither myth nor legend but as literal and accurate history.

Paralleling the line of "liberal" development which derived its impulse and method largely from science, and which aimed to apply scientific methods to the study of the data of religion while remaining within the boundaries of evangelical Christianity, there were other streams of thought which were less concerned about maintaining their evangelical status and diverged from the orthodox current. The rise of the Unitarian movement has been mentioned in an earlier chapter. It gained new vigor on American soil as a revolt against New England Calvinism, but it was a revolt against much more than that. It was a rejection of the concept of a "redemption religion" in which the cross and the atonement were central features, a general repudiation of the miraculous, a strong ethical emphasis, and a declaration that the untrammeled quest of truth and "salvation by character" were the highest objectives of the religious man. Many of the oldest churches in Boston and its neighborhood became Unitarian, and Harvard came under Unitarian control. William Ellery Channing (1780-1842), the saintly, eloquent humanitarian and tolerant apostle of Unitarianism, took the lead in forming the American Unitarian Association (1825). Emerson and his associates in the Transcendentalist movement represented a different phase of liberalism, but found Unitarianism congenial to their mood and consistent with their doctrine. Universalism, which had had a long history of the reaction of individual thinkers against the doctrine of eternal torture for sinners, became an organized religious body at about the same time.

The failure of the Unitarians and Universalists to gain any large number of adherents—for neither group has ever had more than 100,000 members in the United States—was doubtless due in large part to the wide spread of the liberal movement of which they were the most extreme exponents. With the slackening of insistence upon a strict interpretation of the traditional creeds, it became easily possible for ministers and laymen to maintain their connection with their "orthodox" churches while questioning the authority of the Nicene *homoousion* terminology, rethinking the meaning of Christ's "Sonship," emphasizing the ethical teaching of Jesus more than his redemptive function, and letting the blood atonement and eternal punishment drop out of their thought.

THE SOCIAL GOSPEL

Protestants both enjoyed the benefits and paid the penalties of liberty when they confronted the issues posed by the "new view of the Bible" and other phases of contemporary thought. Since they recognized no ruling power which, itself immune to the impact of modern thought, could impose its restrictions upon them by arbitrary authority, they were free to accept or reject these newer views as individual judgment might direct, subject only to such restraints as general opinion in the several denominations might impose. Few denominations cared to bring the matter to a sharp issue in their highest judiciaries. Those of higher educational standards and closer contacts with the currents of modern thought were deeply permeated with the more liberal views. Even in such soundly "evangelical" bodies as the Congregationalists, Presbyterians, Methodists, and Northern Baptists, there came to be a great host of ministers and laymen who, without becoming avowed partisans of either higher criticism or the evolutionary philosophy, found themselves thinking more about the natural goodness of human nature and how it could be developed by the influence of "the teachings of Jesus" than about original sin, the election of a favored few to be saved by the power of a "substitutionary atonement," and the sharp distinction between the "saved" and the "lost." Hell was seldom mentioned in the "better pulpits." Dean Shailer Mathews said that the reason the Universalists did not grow more rapidly was that now they "would first have to prove that there is a hell before proving that nobody goes to it." These negative aspects do not fairly represent the moral and spiritual vigor of evangelical liberalism. It had these qualities. It stirred the Christian conscience in regard to economic questions, the rights of labor (before the unions had grown strong enough to take care of themselves), the problems of the slums, and the issues of social justice. It is notable that interest in these practical and present-day applications of Christian principles to the betterment of the social order found its most active expression at what seemed to be the church's opposite poles—on the one hand, evangelical liberalism; on the other, American Anglo-Catholicism and Roman Catholicism. The "social gospel" became the word to conjure with in liberal Protestant circles. From the standpoint of the older Protestant orthodoxy, the "social gospel" seemed to be an evasion and the liberal theology a complete surrender of the essentials of the faith.

FUNDAMENTALISM VERSUS LIBERALISM

The organized opposition to "modernism" in all its forms came from the Fundamentalist movement. This arose, late in the nineteenth century, in various "Bible conferences" and "prophetic conferences." These were undenominational. All of them stressed the inerrancy of Scripture, blood atonement, and the predictive element in prophecy, certain passages of which when literally interpreted could be made to indicate the imminent end of the world. Out of these conferences issued the "five points" of Fundamentalism. These were: the plenary inspiration and inerrancy of Scripture, the deity and virgin birth of Jesus, the substitutionary blood atonement, the bodily resurrection, and the premillennial second coming of Christ. *Jesus Is Coming* was the title of a book which had a subsidized circulation of millions of copies both in America and abroad in many translations. A popular slogan was "Millions now living will never die." This emphasis on the Second Coming as something now to be expected at any time gradually lost its centrality though it was not abandoned. The stress was upon the infallible truth and divine authority of every word of Scripture and upon the classic doctrines of atonement, redemption, and salvation. "Bible institutes" were established, and some of them very substantially financed, to prepare preachers of this conservative

gospel, now that the theological seminaries of the principal denominations were deemed to have been fatally infected with the
heresies of Biblical criticism and modern thought. The institutes
continued to function usefully, especially in training religious
workers who lacked the college education required by the theological seminaries as prerequisite to admission.

Long before the middle of the twentieth century these also
had lost their fighting temper, though not their basic convictions,
and had reverted to the type of conservative doctrine that was
practically identical with that of seventeenth-century Protestantism but with less emphasis on the specific tenets of Calvinism and
with more evangelistic drive. Popular evangelism—the case of
Billy Graham is the most conspicuous example—has rested on this
theological foundation. The results of a century of Biblical study,
now accepted by the vast majority of accredited scholars in this
field, are neither denied nor discussed but are blandly ignored,
and "the Bible says" is assumed to be bedrock authority. The term
"Fundamentalism," however, as carrying with it the connotations
derived from its earlier use, has become an anachronism except in
very limited circles.

LIBERALISM, NEO-ORTHODOXY, AND ECUMENICITY

At the same time, partial eclipse has overtaken the "liberalism"
of the late nineteenth and early twentieth century. The tragic
events connected with two world wars, and between the two and
after the second, seemed to render implausible its optimistic view
of man and its hope of a progressive realization of the kingdom of
God on earth through a growing application of "the teaching of
Jesus" and the social gospel. Leading theologians found the liberal
estimate of man's inherent goodness and the accompanying philosophy of history shallow and unrealistic. The fact of *sin*—a term
that had become almost taboo to the thoroughgoing liberals—was
brought back and restored to its earlier prominence, with fresh
and profoundly thoughtful interpretations of Christianity as a
"redemption religion." In this movement the initiative was taken
by Germans, who had seen their world collapsing around them

and to whom the "naïve optimism" of the earlier liberalism, especially as it had found expression in prosperous America, seemed particularly odious. There was more to it, however, than an equally naïve pessimism derived from generalization on their own misfortunes. There were authentic insights into the human situation. The suggestion was quickly taken up by British and American thinkers. "Neo-orthodoxy" and "neo-Reformation theology" are terms that have become familiar, but neither is acceptable to those who take this position. It is certainly neo-something, for its leaders have frankly accepted the results of critical study of the Bible while still finding in the Bible, as well as in the study of man and history, the basis for their conviction that even the good are fatally sinful, that the church as well as the world "stands under the judgment of God," and that the grace of God is their only hope. Karl Barth and Emil Brunner are eminent among those who have contributed to the formulation of a new and thoroughly evangelical Biblical theology which yet accepts the findings of modern Biblical scholarship.

The rediscovery of Kierkegaard after almost a century of oblivion has added new depth—some would say new confusion—to theological thought. While the great Dane launched his most direct attacks against the Hegelian philosophy and the lethargy of a church that had come to comfortable terms with the world, the acid of his criticism bit deeply into the complacency both of optimistic liberals and of tradition-bound conservatives. He found in man's condition and in the divine imperatives paradoxes that defy smooth rationalization. From Kierkegaard came Existentialism in all its manifold varieties from the atheist Sartre to the Roman Catholic Gabriel Marcel—not a system of thought but, rather, a mood of "concern" for the total human situation, or "anguish" for one's own, together with the conviction that Life and Truth are such that no rational conceptual system is possible. Such sensitive awareness of the irreducible complexities and contradictions of the "existential" situation skirts the edges of a new and fashionable type of anti-intellectual obscurantism. Strong minds do not fall into that pit, and weak ones can do no more than use the novel terminology as conversational catchwords.

Among the strong who have been stimulated but not dominated by this influence are such thinkers as Reinhold Niebuhr and Paul Tillich.

Modern Biblical scholarship has produced not only a "new view of the Bible" but new translations which are widely accepted and used even by those who do not accept the "new view." The Revised Version of 1882-86 never went far toward replacing the King James Version of 1611, and the American Revised Version of 1902 had even less popular appeal in spite of scholarly approval. Among many private translations the most notable were the Moffatt Bible (1822-26) and the Smith-Goodspeed "American Translation" (1927-31). More recent is the Revised Standard Version (1946-52), which certainly carries as much "authority" as the so-called "Authorized Version" of 1611 ever had, since it was made by a widely representative company of scholars under the auspices of the International Council of Religious Education, an organization embracing about fifty denominations and now constituting the educational division of the National Council of the Churches of Christ in America.

Since the beginning of the modern Protestant ecumenical movement, which may be dated from 1910, there has been an almost continuous series of theological conferences involving representatives of a great number of religious bodies in all parts of the world. The coloration of these conferences has been basically that of the older confessional theologies of the participating groups, but greatly affected by the movement of which we have just been speaking. The visible influence of the older liberalism has been slight, probably because of the preponderant representation of continental churches into which it never penetrated, but it cannot be assumed that it has become a negligible factor in Christian thought. A striking result of these ecumenical conferences and of the present free circulation of theological literature across sectarian lines and of the training of thousands of ministers in undenominational seminaries (such as Yale, Union, and Chicago) is the blurring of the theological lines between the denominations. There is now no telling what a minister's theology may be from the fact that he is a Methodist, a Presbyterian, an Episcopalian, a

Baptist, or a Congregationalist. For some denominations the lines are still fairly clear, but it is a matter of some significance that the planes of cleavage in Christian thought now so seldom coincide with the historic issues upon which Protestantism became divided, and that this is even truer of the laity than of the clergy.

Every European observer comments—unfavorably, as a rule— on the multiplicity of sects in the United States. The *Yearbook of American Churches for 1958* gives the number as 268. It is in many ways a distressing phenomenon, yet the explanation is not wholly discreditable. Because there has been religious liberty, there has been freedom to divide and for separatists to form new organizations. The weakened hold of traditional authorities and the independence in thought and action characteristic of a new country have given rise to a great variety of religious views. Immigration from every country in Europe has brought representatives of every form of religion that existed in the countries of origin. The one traditional idea generally retained was that every pattern of religious thought and practice should have a separate "church" to maintain and propagate it. The result could not fail to be a multiplication of sects. But with all the divisions and subdivisions, the situation is not so bad as may at first glance appear. Of those 268 sects, 213 have less than 100,000 members; 120 have less than 10,000 each. About eighty per cent of all who are counted as church members are in one of six groups: Baptist, Lutheran, Methodist, Presbyterian, Episcopalian, Roman Catholic.

The process of denominational fission seems to have stopped and the reverse tendency has set in. It began early in the nineteenth century with the co-operation of Christians across denominational lines in such practical matters as temperance and antislavery societies, the Y.M.C.A. and Y.W.C.A. Then in Bible societies, and in such voluntary associations as the Evangelical Alliance. Denominations co-operated in the Sunday School Association, and in the Young People's Society of Christian Endeavor. The modern developments in religious education could furnish material for a chapter. The Sunday school began as an undenominational enterprise, but that phase soon passed. The apostle of co-operation for the improvement of the Sunday schools—and Heaven knows they needed it—was Methodist Bishop John H. Vincent, the founder of Chautauqua. (And why not a chapter on that, too, "the most American thing in America"?) The Sunday School Association's "uniform lessons" furnished a beneficent revolution in a curriculum that had usually begun with the first chapter of Genesis and usually petered out by the time it got to Moses. Later, the Religious Education Association, fathered by President William R. Harper, enlisted the interest of educational experts in making Christian education really educational. The International Council of Religious Education inherited the task and the resources of both and had the co-operation of about fifty denominations in the United States and Canada. This was the solidest piece of co-operative religious work that had been undertaken in the entire history of Protestantism, and it was carried forward with great efficiency.

The rising tide of interest in foreign missions overflowed sectarian dykes in the Student Volunteer Movement, which had far-reaching effects in creating bonds of unity among Christian youth. Denominational missionary societies gave expression to their common interests by forming the Home Missions Council and the Foreign Missions Conference of North America. From these it was but a step to the World Missionary Conferences at New York (1900) and Edinburgh (1910). Issuing directly from the last of these were the Faith and Order and the Life and Work organizations, which merged in 1948 to form the World Council of Churches.

Meanwhile, the discovery of Christian duties in the field of social betterment and the appeal of what was called, not too aptly, the "social gospel" gave rise to the Federal Council of Churches (1908), the first full-scale co-operative organization of leading American denominations as such. By the union of this with the International Council of Religious Education and other interdenominational agencies, the National Council of Churches was formed (1950). Beginning with the opening years of the twentieth century—and even earlier in a few cases—city, county, and state councils of churches were being formed until, by mid-century, there were literally hundreds of them. All these were co-operative agencies rather than unions. But in the past half-century there have been fifteen denominational mergers in the United States, besides such more comprehensive unions as the United Church of Canada, the United Church of South India, and united churches on a national scale in other countries in which Protestant Christianity is a minority religion.

The tide of division has definitely turned; the flow is now in the direction of unity. The goal may be far distant, but the direction is sure.

XXV

The Field Is the World

At the beginning of the nineteenth century, Christianity scarcely existed outside of Europe and America. Asia was untouched by it, except for a fringe of the Moslem Near East, a slight residue from very early evangelization (perhaps by St. Thomas) in south India, and the still smaller trace in the East Indies where the Dutch had taken over from the Portuguese. Africa was a completely "dark continent" from the Christian standpoint except for the Copts in Egypt and Ethiopia and the negligible results in South Africa deriving from the Dutch occupation and from the English who succeeded them in 1795. White settlement in Australia did not begin until the last years of the eighteenth century, and the first effort to give the gospel to the natives was some time after that. On the map, Christianity was far from being a world religion. It was not even seriously trying to be that. But a new era was at hand—an era of earnest effort to win converts to Christianity among the adherents of the ancient and highly developed religions of Asia and also among the nature-worshiping and magic-mongering primitive peoples of Africa and the islands of the sea. This tremendous surge of missionary action was a characteristic of the nineteenth century continuing into the twentieth. It was not altogether unrelated to the expansion of the political power and economic interests of the great Christian nations.

In this new aggressive expansion of Christianity into non-Christian lands, the new thing was not the mere fact of expansion. What was new was the methods employed, which were radically unlike those by which Europe and Latin America had been Christianized. This new wave of expansion advanced wholly by persuasion and by the conversion of individuals. There were no mass conversions of entire populations by military or political pressure or by police methods. The result was that Christianity became a minority religion in almost every "pagan" land but none of these lands (with a few very small exceptions) became a Christian country. To get the full meaning of this contrast, let us look again at the whole sweep of Christianity's advance through the centuries and across the map.

Christianity had been from the start an expanding religion, conceiving of itself as having a mission for all mankind. The Gospel of Matthew had quoted Jesus as saying, "Go ye into all the world and preach the gospel to every creature." Even in its earliest days, when some thought of Christianity as a kind of reformed and improved Judaism, the question was not whether Gentiles should be admitted but whether they had to become Jewish proselytes in order to qualify. This limitation did not last long. The expansion of Christianity in the Graeco-Roman world during the first three centuries remains one of the marvels of history. The records of the details of that growth are sadly incomplete, but we do know that no sort of social or political compulsion played any part in it. There are reasons to believe that even before Christianity had escaped the perils of persecution it had won something like five per cent of the population of the Roman Empire. Then came a tremendous acceleration of its growth, first by imperial favor, then by the compulsion of imperial laws. As the barbarian tribes came on the scene, they, also, were the object of mass conversion in which the preaching of the missionaries was always backed by pressures of an entirely secular sort. So it was with the conversion of the parts of Europe more remote from the older centers of influence. It was not until after the year 1000 that it could be said that all the tribes and nations of Europe—including Russia, the Balkan and Baltic lands, and Scandinavia—were Christian territory. In every case the conversion had been a mass operation.

The discovery of America opened a new continent for evangelization as well as for conquest and colonization. These processes went on together. In Mexico and in Central and South America, where there were large native populations with cultures and religions far above the primitive level, the old cults were swept away by the conquest, except insofar as some features could be assimilated. Devoted priests and friars taught the new converts how to practice the religion of their conquerors, but the acceptance of it was not optional. So these vast areas were added to the territory that could be called Christian. In the parts of America that were occupied by the English and the French—the parts that were to become the United States and Canada—the native population was sparse, nomadic, and relatively primitive. The colonization of these regions by Europeans soon reduced the natives to a small per cent of the total population. For a long time they were so far beyond the reach of the invading whites that compulsory conversion would have been impossible even if it had been attempted—as it was not. The expansion of Christianity in this part of America was achieved by the influx of Europeans who brought Christianity with them and whose descendants became the people of these lands. Whether or not the United States can be called a "Christian country" depends on the definition of terms. The point to note in this connection is that here Christianity did not expand by winning a previously pagan population, as it had done in all previous expansions, but by moving into a vacuum.

The new feature of the expansion of Christianity in the nineteenth century was that it was a concerted and organized attempt to convert individuals in non-Christian countries, and to do this without employing any apparatus of compulsion. To be sure, nothing is ever absolutely new. There had been earlier missionary efforts which approximated this character. Such was the Nestorian effort in central Asia in the sixth century and after, and the Jesuit missions in China and Japan in the sixteenth, and the work of some heroic Jesuits, Dominicans, and Franciscans who pioneered in early America far beyond the reach of any military protection. In spite of their ultimate failure, these deserve honorable mention. But even so, there was a new quality in the nineteenth-century missionary enterprise which did not aim first to gain the favor of the political and religious leaders and through them gain status in the country, but went directly to the common people with a presentation of the Christian message.

Actually this nineteenth-century movement began late in the eighteenth. The Evangelical Revival in England furnished the impulse, as German Pietism had done a little earlier on a smaller scale. The London Missionary Society (interdenominational), the Church Missionary Society (Anglican), the Baptist Missionary Society, the Wesleyan Missionary Society, and the British and Foreign Bible Society all got their start at this time. Much earlier there had been the Society for the Propagation of the Gospel in Foreign Parts (Anglican), but this had been concerned chiefly with the religious welfare of British colonists and gave only marginal attention to such natives as might be within easy reach. The new missionary societies began with great zeal but with meager resources and with only vague ideas as to methods of procedure. It could not have seemed a very important event when young William Carey—who had been first a shoemaker and then a Baptist preacher—took ship from England to India under the auspices of the Baptist Missionary Society which he had helped to organize, nor did the significance of the event quickly become evident. He had been in India seven years before he won his first Indian convert to Christianity. The day was December 28, 1800.

William Carey discovered that the first problem of a missionary in the field was one of communication. India had many languages and dialects. Missionaries going out from England knew none of them, and there were no grammars or other textbooks from which to learn them. Fortunately, Carey had a gift for languages. He cultivated this gift so assiduously that in his thirty-four remaining years he became eminent as linguist and philologist. Besides writing much Christian literature in the Indian languages, he compiled dictionaries or grammars in at least six of them. If his own work was more linguistic than evangelistic, he furnished the language tools to the many missionaries who came after him.

Pioneer missionaries in all parts of the world have found themselves confronted with this same necessity to become pioneers also in the study of languages previously unknown in the Christian world. They have reduced to writing hundreds of dialects of preliterate tribes in the more primitive areas. The British and American Bible societies have played a great part in this. It was no exaggeration when a volume containing samples of Bible translation was called *The Book of a Thousand Tongues,** for the actual number was about eleven hundred. The first publication of any part of Scripture in a non-European language for evangelistic purposes was a Malay version of Matthew in 1629, and the first such complete Bible (and the first Bible printed in America) was John Eliot's Algonquin translation, 1663. Though this linguistic work began so early, its great development was in the nineteenth century.

The British East India Company, which had been the virtual ruler of India since 1763, was exercising its full power in Carey's time. It was not enthusiastic about missions. Its interest was in profits. Most of its representatives, living free and easy lives and enjoying to the full their sense of racial superiority, regarded the missionaries as meddlesome interlopers who sometimes even had the effrontery to defend the native peoples against exploitation and abuse by their white masters. After the Sepoy Mutiny of 1857 the British government took control, to the great advantage of Indians and missionaries alike. Missionaries, both Protestant and Catholic, European and American, came in greater numbers, and the infiltration of Christianity became more rapid through educational and medical as well as evangelistic activities.

During the years of British rule in India, Christianity derived some advantage from its association with Western power and prestige, though there was never any attempt to force it upon the Indian people. But for the same reason it labored under the dis-

* American Bible Society, 1938.

advantage of being regarded as a foreign religion. With the rising sense of Indian nationalism, and especially since the attainment of independence, the disadvantage was intensified.

These two themes run through the whole story of the modern missionary advance. On the one hand, Christianity and its spokesmen have been respected as representatives of nations more advanced in literacy, medical science, agriculture, industry, economic sufficiency, and general welfare. Schools, hospitals, and social services have, therefore, been acceptable offerings by the spokesmen for Christianity. The "missionary doctor," in particular, has become one of the most admirable types on the modern missionary scene. In most cases these humanitarian services have been all the more acceptable because they were offered in the spirit of pure Christian compassion for the needy and were not used as mere propaganda devices. But on the other hand, the "white superiority" idea bred a natural resentment among dusky peoples—sometimes with such ancient and mature cultures as the Indian and Chinese though with less literacy and industrial know-how than the great Christian nations—especially after contact with the more-or-less democratic West had quickened the desire for such national independence and such popular rights as they had really never known in the old days. The growth of this latter spirit has profoundly affected the character of Christian missions in the twentieth century. We shall come back to that.

A new field was opened, and one destined to absorb more missionary funds and energies than any other, when the London Missionary Society sent Robert Morrison to Canton in 1812. China was not then hospitable to Western culture. This first Protestant missionary in the Far East became a pioneer in almost every kind of missionary work: in linguistics, for he published a grammar and a monumental dictionary of the Chinese language and a translation of the Bible; in education, for he founded a school with the double purpose of teaching the classics of Chinese and European literature and training native evangelists; in medicine, for he established a dispensary and provided for the training of native attendants. Other missionaries followed, living dangerously and subject to the variable moods of local mandarins. In the Opium Wars of

1840 and 1858-60 the British got title to Hong Kong and trade concessions in several coastal cities and, incidentally, secured a guarantee of the right of missionaries to operate freely in any part of the country. It was an unfortunate combination of military power, commercial interests, and evangelization. The missionaries had no responsibility for these campaigns that blasted a way for them into the interior and at the same time made their task more difficult by embittering those whom they had come to convert. A flood of missionaries now poured into this most ancient empire. Practically every missionary society in the world sent its representatives. Schools and hospitals were established as well as churches. The appeal was chiefly to the lower classes, but many bright young men presently discovered the advantage of a Western education and many of them accepted the religion of their teachers.

Christian forces could not enter Japan until after the doors of that "hermit nation" had been opened by the treaty that Commodore Matthew Perry negotiated in 1854.

Robert Moffatt went to Africa in 1816 under the auspices of that same London Missionary Society that had sent Morrison to China four years earlier. Himself one of the great, Moffatt scarcely more than touched the fringe of the continent as compared with the stupendous labors of his son-in-law, David Livingstone, who explored it from ocean to ocean. After a few years of missionary work in a fairly limited district, though never long in one place, Livingstone became convinced that what was most needed was knowledge of the geography of Africa, the terrain, topography, and river systems of which were unknown to the civilized world. He took the assignment of opening the way for whatever Christianizing influences might follow. He did not bother too much about making converts, but he established friendly relations with many tribes, aroused world sentiment against the barbarity of the slave trade, traveled with incredible hardship through vast areas that no white man had ever seen, making careful scientific observations as he went, and opened the Dark Continent for those who would come after him. Many came, and there are now many thousands of both Protestant and Catholic Christians in central Africa.

Except for the Moslem nations, which then as now sternly repressed all efforts to proselyte the adherents of the Prophet to any other religion, the whole world seemed to lie open to those who would go to "preach the gospel to every creature." The Pacific islands, made known largely through the voyages of Captain James Cook late in the eighteenth century, had already become missionary fields. Among some jungle tribes the missionary's calling might still be full of hazard but, with the exceptions mentioned, the world was an open field. A favorite text for missionary sermons was Matthew 9:37: "The harvest truly is plenteous but the laborers are few."

Organized American foreign missions began when the American Board of Commissioners for Foreign Missions, an undenominational organization but chiefly supported by Congregationalists, sent Adoniram Judson and Luther Rice to Asia in 1812. Their conversion to Baptist views while on the voyage led to the formation of a Baptist missionary society to support them. They went to Burma, where Judson became the most memorable of missionary pioneers in southeast Asia. His colorful career included a period in prison in France after the English ship on which he was making his first voyage was captured by a French privateer, and two years of imprisonment in Burma during a period of hostilities between that country and the British East India Company. But these were only minor episodes in his forty years of missionary work. Like Carey, he became a linguist, and translated the Bible into Burmese and wrote a grammar and a dictionary of the language. A century after his death Judson's name is still one to conjure with in the promotion of missions.

Within a few years after these American beginnings, every important denomination in the United States had organized its foreign missionary society, and the conversion of the "heathen" became one of the major concerns of local congregations in every city and town in the country, stimulated by the continuous activity of local societies and women's organizations, "children's days for foreign missions," occasional visits from missionaries on furlough, periodical campaigns for offerings, and, more recently, the inclusion of support of foreign missions as a large item in regular church budgets. This has come to be one of the most characteristic features of American church life. It is not that America has any monopoly on foreign missions. On the contrary, every Christian country has been active in this kind of work, and many churches in non-Christian countries have become "sending" churches for still needier areas even while they themselves are on the receiving end. A glance through any recent edition of the *World Christian Handbook* (World Dominion Press, London) reveals a bewildering number and variety of organizations in many countries engaged in promoting and conducting foreign missions. But it may be doubted whether this cause has occupied as large a place in the thought and action of the laity and the local churches elsewhere as in the United States. While the American churches have done much for foreign missions, foreign missions have also done much for the American churches in widening their horizons and quickening their zeal.

Secular events necessarily have a profound effect on missionary work. For example, after the Spanish-American War the assumption of some national responsibilities for regions outside of the country's continental territory was accompanied by a fresh burst of energy for a corresponding expansion of Christianity. More recently, and more importantly, the passing of the colonial era and the world-wide rise of the spirit of independence and the demand for nationhood among previously dependent peoples have profoundly altered the missionary situation. Christianity no longer enjoys the prestige of being the religion of the master race or the superior people. The masters have lost their mastery, and their superiority has become a discredited assumption. The white man's religion now has to overcome, as best it can, the disadvantage of being the religion of those whose mastery is resented even where it has not yet been thrown off. Many native churches which were controlled and financed by missionary boards have become, or are on the way to becoming, "indigenous" churches. The term is inaccurate, but its meaning in this connection is clear. The Roman Catholic Church has taken the lead by appointing natives as bishops in every country sufficiently advanced to provide competent candidates. Protestant churches have adjusted to the demand for native leadership, and have generally welcomed it. The expansion of Christianity thus enters on a new phase, in which the spirit of colonialism and foreign control tends to disappear, and the enterprise becomes one of the strong helping the weak without that odious assumption of dominance and tutelage.

Perhaps the missionary must always be the zealous propagandist convinced that his religion is right and all others wrong, but direct evangelization has not always been his immediate aim. Because Christianity has in it a strong element of humanitarianism, the missionary has been concerned about the relief of physical suffering and the improvement of standards of living. This has led to medical work and the establishment of hospitals and orphanages, and in some cases to agricultural missions (like that of Sam Higginbotham in India) and other efforts to improve economic conditions. Because Christianity is also a system of ideas the appropriation of which requires a certain level of culture and is facilitated by literacy, the missionary has often become a teacher. So schools have been conducted in almost every mission field, and colleges in many of them. Frank Laubach is at heart a Christian missionary, but his amazingly successful world-wide literacy campaign has been carried on as a disinterested service to humanity without regard to any advantage that might accrue to the Christian cause.

The changed conditions in the modern world, together with the changing ideas in many minds as to the essentials of the Christian message and the apparent futility of expecting ever to convert the populations of such countries as China and India, since only about one per cent of them have been converted by a century and a half of missionary effort, suggested that the whole project needed a fresh study to see whether a different approach might not be indicated. The Laymen's Foreign Mission Inquiry, headed by Professor W. E. Hocking of Harvard, undertook such a study (1930-32). The result, published in the book entitled *Rethinking Missions*, proved to be too controversial to serve as a guide to action. Its critics felt that it was predicated on a too liberal view of Christianity. It was clear that the mission boards and the greater part of their supporting constituencies regarded direct evangelization as an indispensable feature, indeed the basic feature, of missionary work. Yet it was evident that the enterprise of foreign missions—which has always had more angles than most of its critics realize—had been feeling its way along new paths in the work of such men as C. F. Andrews, the intimate friend of Gandhi, in India; Albert Schweitzer, the many-sided Alsatian genius, in Africa; Kagawa, the Japanese saint plying back and forth between his country and ours to the enlightenment of both; and E. Stanley Jones, evangelizing alternately in India and America and at the same time promoting his own plan for the union of all the churches. Embodying the missionary spirit, though not specifically missionary in the traditional sense, is the work of the great Christian relief agencies—Church World Service, the American Friends Service Committee, the Unitarian Service Committee, the Lutheran Service Committee, the relief division of the World Council of Churches, and the various Catholic relief organizations.

Out of Christianity in non-Christian lands has come one of the most powerful influences in the making of the contemporary ecumenical movement. To native Christians in India or on the Congo, the historic grounds of separation that keep apart the denominations in Europe and America do not seem profoundly significant. United churches have come into existence under native leadership in several such countries, with the full approval of the missionaries. The important mission boards work in close cooperation. The International Missionary Council is their most comprehensive agency. The organizations that led to the formation of the World Council of Churches in 1948 were direct outgrowths of the World Missionary Conference at Edinburgh in 1910. What has been said of the reciprocal relations between the American churches and their missionary enterprises can be repeated in more general terms. If the Christian lands have done much for foreign missions, the missions have done no less for them. They have made it difficult for Christianity to be either sectarian or parochial.

XXVI

Christianity in the Modern World

What is the status, what are the problems, and what are the prospects of Christianity in our day?

Of the two and one half billion people in the world, one third are Christian, one third of the Christians are Protestant, and one third of the Protestants are in the United States. These statistics are very inexact. Some of the figures that enter into the total for Christianity are the total (or almost the total) populations of countries in which a certain church had been long dominant and is established by law. Some churches in the United States count all the members of their families as members of the church. Others count only communicants. The totals therefore are only rough approximations. They doubtless exaggerate the numerical strength of Christianity. Figures for the adherents of the other great religions are no more accurate, being entirely based on population statistics. However, these statistics are not without value. Some inferences that can be safely drawn from them are: that Christianity has more adherents than any other religion in the world; that in a world-wide view none of the great religions is making serious inroads on the constituency of any other; and that there is no statistical ground for an expectation that Christianity or any other religion will "take the world" within the predictable future.

More detailed reports for the United States, though open to the same doubt as to their accuracy, indicate on their face that the nearly ninety-five million counted as Christians constitute fifty-seven per cent of the population, that this percentage is steadily increasing, that a little less than two thirds of these are Protestant and a little more than one third Roman Catholic, and that the rate of growth of the larger churches is near enough the same to dispel any reasonable hope or fear that any one of these will capture the whole field. Even if all the statistics that have been cited are even more inaccurate than the authors think they are, it is obvious that institutional Christianity in the United States is a going concern. People go to church in great numbers—a larger proportion of them, it seems, than in any other country that is reputed to be Christian—and they give hundreds of millions of dollars a year to support the local operations of their churches and many millions more to finance their missionary, educational, and benevolent activities. The expenditure for new church buildings in the United States in 1957 came to not much less than one billion dollars, the largest amount on record. If it is true that "where a man's treasure is, there will his heart be," it cannot be said that the American people have lost interest in religion. Any intelligent student of society, whether sociologist or historian, ought to be able to see that organized religion is one of the major factors in American life.

In the British Isles it is no less true, though for somewhat different reasons, that Christianity is a conspicuous and significant element in the total scene. Institutionally and ceremonially it is even more conspicuous. As an American president takes the oath of office at his inauguration he kisses the Bible—whatever that may mean. But the coronation of a British sovereign is a high religious ceremony from first to last, with Westminster Abbey as its scene and the archbishop of Canterbury and other bishops in key roles. One cannot picture an England without its cathedrals and its hundreds of beautiful old parish churches. Though these are monuments of an age when religion was a more universal interest than it is now, the sight of them can scarcely fail to be a reminder even to those who seldom see the inside of them, and this means the great majority of the people in England. A survey in 1957 found that only fourteen per cent of the population went to church even occasionally. This is probably an underestimate, for the church membership is about eighteen per cent, of which the Church of England has a little more than one third and the rest is divided not very unequally between Protestant Nonconformists and Roman Catholics. Though data of every kind suggest that the secular attitude predominates, those who know the English people cannot avoid the conviction that there is a deep undercurrent of religion which continuously influences social action and comes to the surface in times of emergency. It is the judgment of many who are not prejudiced in favor of Christianity that the frankly socialist British Labor Party and the whole program of the British "welfare state" is a derivative not from Marxism but from the Christian socialism of the nineteenth century and the humanitarianism of British Nonconformity.

Scotland is much more obviously religious. And the tensions between Eire and Northern Ireland, based in a large degree on religious differences, testify that both still take their faith seriously.

Continental Europe presents a complex situation that cannot be briefly analyzed. Though established churches still exist everywhere, except in France, and their reported membership approximates the total populations in most of the countries, the number who "practice" the religions in whose ranks they are counted is conjectural. This is no less true in a Protestant country like Sweden than in Catholic countries like Italy and Spain or in countries where Eastern Orthodoxy is the official religion, as in Greece.

Any estimate of the continuing vitality and influence of Christianity must be based on other than statistical grounds, and such an estimate will probably depend largely on the point of view of the one who makes it. Such facts as the following must at least be taken into account. Governments find it politically expedient to continue the formal recognition of religion and the establishment of their traditional churches. The Communist power, which has done what it could to obliterate religion in Russia, finds it more advantageous to permit the churches to exist and to try to make them its allies in the iron-curtain countries than to suppress them. Czechoslovakian Protestants make a brave but not wholly successful effort to show the world that they are as free as ever while making the necessary adjustments to a Communist-dominated regime. The Vatican continues its policy of protecting its own status and maintaining what it considers the unique rights of the Catholic Church by making concordats with governments wherever possible, especially with a view to maintaining the freedom of its episcopate from secular control, protecting its property and the functions of the religious orders, and controlling public education wherever that can be done. In several countries there are specifically "Catholic" political parties, either with or without that word in their names. As of December, 1957, the Vatican had diplomatic relations with forty-eight national governments—more than ever before. There is a substantial body of opinion—and this not only in the churches—that the Christian ideology is the strongest antidote to the Communist poison that threatens to enter the West by infiltration when it cannot by force of arms. Add this to the admitted fact that it was only the churches that offered any organized opposition to the Nazi madness when Hitler was at the top of his power, and that it is only certain men with a Christian motivation—some Protestant, some Catholic—who can be remembered now as the heroes of the resistance movement in Germany. Add also the fact that Christian scholarship is vigorous in the higher intellectual circles and that there is a solid body of the faithful and the devout in the middle ranks of society. It would be misleading to paint too rosy a picture of Christianity in Europe, but it would be even more erroneous to depict it as in a state of collapse.

Though sociologists and historians usually give to religion far less attention than its actual prominence in the social scene deserves—chiefly because they do not know what they can say about it without offending some group by exalting another or giving still more offense by criticism—the influence of Christianity as a force in social progress has been immense. Every promoter of a "good" cause knows where he can find a ready-made constituency from which he can expect support. Christianity—at its

best—has been, from the beginning, on the side of social betterment, and its programs have been oriented toward the common welfare and social justice. Often it has fallen far short of the
ideal, but for long centuries it was virtually the only force operating in that direction. The European state churches in Protestant
countries have tended to limit their concern to doctrine, worship,
and sacraments. In England, however, the "nonconformist conscience" became a powerful influence in support of social reforms
of every kind.

American churches have often been accused of "activism" by
overseas critics because of their participation in movements for
social betterment even though these sometimes required political
action. Their reply is not to deny that they have been active but
to assert that it is an essential part of Christianity's business to
Christianize the social order. There is nothing essentially new
about this. The preceding chapters must have made it clear that
this purpose has run through the whole stream of Christian history,
however varied may have been the concepts of a Christian social
order and the methods employed for its realization. In America
both the concepts and the methods have been in large measure
determined by the prevalence of the democratic ideal, which has
itself found support in the Christian understanding of the nature
of man. When the founding fathers of this republic were laying
down the first principles of freedom, they gave to these principles
a religious sanction by declaring that all men were "*created* equal"
and that they were "endowed by their *Creator* with certain
unalienable rights." Citizens, including church members, claim
these rights as against any possible attempt by either state or
church to control their political actions, and most of the churches
have themselves practiced the democratic process. There has therefore been little temptation for the churches to lay down the law
to the government in regard to such social reforms as can be
effected only by legislation. They cannot even control the votes
of their own members and they repudiate any desire to do so.
Church conferences and councils often make pronouncements on
social questions that are also matters of public policy. These,
together with the general body of opinion in a denomination and

exhortations from its pulpits, may produce a certain concentration of sentiment which is registered at the polls. But this is far short of being bloc voting by churches, and farther still from any sort of undemocratic determination of public policy by ecclesiastical authority.

It is a reasonable conclusion that no church or combination of churches will impose its will upon society in our time. American Protestant churches, at least, are ill adapted to act as pressure groups even if they had the desire to do so. Yet the churches in the aggregate do exercise an influence on public opinion, and thus on the determination of public policy in matters that involve moral issues and human values. They do this because there is, in general, a higher degree of humanitarianism in the churches than outside of them. Christians do not automatically have any gift of superior political or economic wisdom that would enable them to select the most effective programs for promoting the general welfare, but their religion is a force that moves them in that direction. History supports the generalization that those who love their God with all their heart, soul, and mind have a more than average inclination to love their neighbors as themselves. At least from the time of the great social encyclical of Pope Leo XIII, *Rerum Novarum*, and the Social Creed of the Churches—to go no farther back—the churches have taken advanced ground in the demand for social justice.

Nevertheless, in such a time as this it is not enough for the churches to be a little ahead of the secular public in their concern and to contribute some slight amelioration to the dire condition of the world. The question still remains whether Christianity has in it the spiritual power to "save civilization" in these perilous times. For the times are perilous and the threat to the entire structure of Western civilization that has been built up through nearly two thousand years of thought and toil is imminent and unprecedented. It is beset by confusion within and by attack from without. No interpreter of recent and contemporary history fails to note the radical change from the tranquillity and confidence of the last years of the nineteenth century and the first years of the twentieth to the present sense of insecurity and crisis. The dream of peaceful progress toward a terrestrial paradise and an era of perpetual prosperity and universal brotherhood ("the kingdom of God on earth") was rudely shattered by a shot at Sarajevo. That was indeed "a shot heard round the world." Christian missionaries found their sermons mocked by the spectacle of Christian nations tearing one another to fragments. The "peace" from 1918 to 1939 was a long armistice in which moral relaxation accompanied preparation for future wars. The wave of disillusion that swept over the world did not abate when World War II, having extinguished one menacing madness, placed opportunity in the hands of another with an unlimited program of expansion.

While the "white" peoples of earth have been—and are— engaged in these titanic struggles, they have lost the proud position of dominance that had been theirs ever since they made effective contact with the darker peoples outside the traditional limits of Christendom. What the favored nations had slowly and painfully learned of human rights and independence became common knowledge among those who had enjoyed neither, and their smoldering discontent burst into flames of hope and action. With lines of transportation and communication spanning every ocean, crisscrossing every continent, and penetrating in a flash to the remotest corners, the news got around that there were whole nations where almost everybody had three meals a day. Resentment equally against the white man's assumption of racial superiority and against his rule, reinforced by plain and persistent hunger —for there are countless millions with whom hunger is a constant companion and from whom starvation is never more than arm's length away—brought on that rising of the dark peoples which is an ominous element in the world's present turbulence. These peoples are three fourths of the earth's population.

Can Christianity save civilization in such a time as this? There are those who say that Christianity's business is not to save civilization but to save souls, to pluck a few brands from the burning and let the catastrophic end come when it will. It has been saving souls for a long time, but it has done more than that. It has done what it could to save the social order. Can it do that now?

It may be said that Christianity alone can save the world, but

Christianity cannot save it alone. That is a gigantic and precarious task requiring the co-operation of many factors. Christians cannot but feel that their religion has an indispensable part to play. It can be an agency of reconciliation and a bearer of spiritual light and material help to peoples among whom Christianity is, and for centuries perhaps will be, the religion of a very small minority. It can influence the attitudes and actions of the powerful nations that call themselves Christian. It must do this, if at all, in spite of the tensions and divisions that exist within its own ranks.

Christians, as we have seen, have never been united in doctrine, polity, worship, or action except when they were united by the use or threat of violent compulsion. Union on those terms is a present impossibility. In the Christian world tensions exist between Protestant and Catholic, between liberal and conservative, between Christianity itself and a benevolent secularism that denies all its doctrines but accepts its moral principles without recognizing their source, as well as between the forces that make for man's spiritual and material welfare and those that make for moral chaos. If the resources of Christianity are to be effectively deployed to win the war against chaos, it must be by co-operation with all those who are on its side on the basis of those things that are relevant to the dangers it opposes.

A generation ago it was being asked, "Can Christianity survive the changing order?" It may now be asked, "Can Christianity survive the present crisis?" The answer is: It can, if the world survives. The world and Christianity have survived many crises. The world is very durable—unless we bomb it into obliteration— and there is that in Christianity which can never die. If Christianity is responsible for the character of civilization, then its task is hardly more than begun. The prevalent sense of spiritual needs among men is even more poignant than their economic needs and their political demands. The insufficiency of other answers to their deeper problems is obvious. These facts make this the hour of opportunity for religion. Freud and the neo-orthodox theologians are agreed in locating man's ills far below the outer layers of his life. Can the Christian churches now persuade him that the grace of God can penetrate deeper, and with more saving power, than any analyst's probing? Scholarship may despair of ever completely recovering the figure of the historical Jesus, but never has the figure of Christ risen higher or in more compelling majesty over the debris of human failure. Never has the cross stood out more clearly as the symbol of man's ultimate hope.

BIBLIOGRAPHY

Angus, S., *The Mystery Religions and Christianity*, Scribner, 1925.
———, *The Religious Quests of the Graeco-Roman World*, Scribner, 1929.
Aulard, A., *Christianity and the French Revolution*, trans. by Lady Frazer, Little, Brown, 1927.
Baillie, John, McNeill, John T., and Van Dusen, Henry P. (gen. eds.), *The Library of Christian Classics* (to be complete in 26 vols., from the early Fathers to the English Reformers), Westminster Press, 1953.
Bainton, Roland H., *Here I Stand: A Life of Martin Luther*, Abingdon Press, 1950.
Baker, G. P., *Constantine the Great and the Christian Revolution*, Dodd, Mead, 1930.
Bates, Ernest S., *American Faith, Its Religious, Political and Economic Foundations*, W. W. Norton, 1940.
Bettenson, Henry (ed.), *Documents of the Christian Church*, London, Oxford, 1943.
Bevan, Edwyn, *Christianity*, Oxford, 1932.
Bingle, E. J., and Grubb, Sir Kenneth (eds.), *World Christian Handbook*, 1957 edition, London, World Dominion Press, 1957.
Bolton, Herbert E., *Rim of Christendom: A Biography of Father Kino*, Macmillan, 1936.
Bouquet, A. C., *Everyday Life in New Testament Times*, Scribner, 1954.
Braden, Charles S., *Religious Aspects of the Conquest of Mexico*, Duke Univ. Press, 1930.
Brauer, Jerald C., *Protestantism in America: A Narrative History*, Westminster Press, 1953.
Bready, J. Wesley, *England Before and After Wesley*, Harper, 1939.

Case, Shirley J., *The Social Triumph of the Early Church*, Harper, 1933.

Cassirer, Ernst (ed.), *The Renaissance Philosophy of Man*, Univ. of Chicago Press, 1948.

Coulton, G. G., *Five Centuries of Religion*, Vol. II, 1200-1400, *The Friars*, Cambridge, 1927.

——, *Medieval Panorama: The English Scene from Conquest to Reformation*, Macmillan, 1938.

Craig, Clarence T., *The Beginnings of Christianity*, Abingdon Press, 1943.

Cruttwell, Charles T., *A Literary History of Early Christianity*, 2 vols., Scribner, 1893.

Cullmann, Oscar, *Peter: Disciple, Apostle, Martyr*, trans. by Floyd V. Filson, Westminster Press, 1953.

Dahmus, Joseph H., *The Prosecution of John Wyclyf*, Yale Univ. Press, 1952.

Davies, J. G., *Daily Life of Early Christians*, Little, Brown, 1953.

Duckett, Eleanor S., *The Gateway to the Middle Ages*, Macmillan, 1938.

Erasmus, Desiderius, *The Praise of Folly*, trans. with commentary by Hoyt H. Hudson, Princeton Univ. Press, 1941.

Fichter, Joseph H., *Man of Spain: A Biography of Francis Suarez*, Macmillan, 1940.

Foakes-Jackson, F. J., *The History of the Christian Church from the Earliest Times to A. D. 461*, 7th edition, Doran, 1924.

Fülöp-Miller, René, *The Power and Secret of the Jesuits*, trans. by F. S. Flint and D. F. Tait, Viking, 1930.

Garrison, Winfred E., *Intolerance*, Round Table Press, 1934.

——, *The March of Faith: The Story of Religion in America since 1865*, Harper, 1933.

——, *A Protestant Manifesto*, Abingdon Press, 1952.

——, *The Quest and Character of a United Church*, Abingdon Press, 1957.

Goguel, Maurice, *The Birth of Christianity*, trans. by H. C. Snape, Macmillan, 1954.

Goodspeed, Edgar J., *A History of Early Christian Literature*, Univ. of Chicago Press, 1942.

Greenslade, S. L., *Schism in the Early Church*, Harper, 1952.

Grimm, Harold J., *The Reformation Era, 1500-1650*, Macmillan, 1954.

Haller, William, *The Rise of Puritanism*, Columbia Univ. Press, 1938.

—— (ed.), *Tracts on Liberty in the Puritan Revolution*, 3 vols., Columbia Univ. Press, 1934.

Henson, Herbert H., *The Church of England*, Macmillan, 1940.

Highey, John D., Jr., *Religious Freedom in Spain, Its Ebb and Flow*, Broadman Press, 1955.

Hill, R. T., and Bergin, T. G. (eds.), *Anthology of the Provencal Troubadours: Text, Notes and Glossary*, Yale Univ. Press, 1941.

Hollis, Christopher, *Saint Ignatius*, Harper, 1931.

Hudson, Winthrop S., *The Great Tradition of the American Churches*, Harper, 1953.

Janelle, Pierre, *The Catholic Reformation*, Bruce, 1949.

Jordan, W. K., *The Development of Religious Toleration in England*, 4 vols., Harvard Univ. Press, 1932-40.

Kelly, J. N. D., *Early Christian Creeds*, London, Longmans, 1950.

Kenton, Edna (ed.), *The Jesuit Relations and Allied Documents, 1610-1791*, A. & C. Boni, 1925.

Kerr, Hugh T., Jr. (ed.), *A Compend of Luther's Theology*, Westminster Press, 1943.

Landis, Benson Y., *Yearbook of American Churches*, issued annually by Office of Publication, National Council of Churches of Christ in the U. S. A.

Latourette, Kenneth S., *A History of Christianity*, Harper, 1953.

———, *History of the Expansion of Christianity*, 7 vols., Harper, 1937.

Laymon, Charles M., *The Life and Teachings of Jesus*, Abingdon Press, 1955.

Lee, Umphrey, *John Wesley and Modern Religion*, Abingdon Press, 1936.

Lietzmann, Hans, *From Constantine to Julian* (Vol. III of *A History of the Early Church*), Scribner, 1950.

Macchioro, Vittorio D., *From Orpheus to Paul*, Holt, 1931.

Mackinnon, James, *Luther and the Reformation*, 3 vols., London, Longmans, 1925.

McNeill, John T., *Modern Christian Movements*, Westminster Press, 1954.

Madariaga, Salvador de, *The Fall of the Spanish American Empire*, Macmillan, 1947.

———, *The Rise of the Spanish American Empire*, Macmillan, 1947.

Mangan, John J., *Life, Character and Influence of Desiderius Erasmus of Rotterdam*, 2 vols., Macmillan, 1927.

Manschreck, Clyde L., *Melanchthon, The Quiet Reformer*, Abingdon Press, 1958.

Miller, Perry, *The New England Mind: The 17th Century*, Macmillan, 1939.

Mossner, Ernest C., *Bishop Butler and the Age of Reason*, Macmillan, 1936.

Mowat, R. B., *The Age of Reason*, Houghton, Mifflin, 1934.

Nichols, James H., *History of Christianity, 1650-1950*, Ronald Press, 1956.

Osborn, Ronald E., *The Spirit of American Christianity*, Harper, 1957.

Payne, Robert, *The Fathers of the Western Church*, Viking, 1951.

Peers, E. Allison, *Studies of the Spanish Mystics*, London, Sheldon Press, 1927.

Piette, Maximin, *John Wesley in the Evolution of Protestantism*, Sheed & Ward, 1937.

Reeder, Ralph, *Savonarola: A Study in Conscience*, Brentano's, 1930.

Rouse, Ruth, and Neill, S. C. (eds.), *A History of the Ecumenical Movement 1517-1948*, Westminster Press, 1954.

Sabatier, Paul, *Life of Saint Francis of Assisi*, Scribner, 1897.

—— (ed.), *St. Francis of Assisi, 1226-1926, Essays in Commemoration*, Macmillan, 1926.

Schaff, Philip, *The Creeds of Christendom*, 3 vols., Harper, 1877.

Schevill, Ferdinand, *History of Florence from the Founding of the City through the Renaissance*, Harcourt, Brace, 1949.

——, *The Medici*, Harcourt, Brace, 1949.

Schneider, Herbert W., *The Puritan Mind*, Holt, 1930.

Scott, Ernest F., *The First Age of Christianity*, Macmillan, 1926.

Shotwell, James T., and Loomis, Louise R., *The See of Peter*, Columbia Univ. Press, 1927.

Smith, Preserved, *The Age of the Reformation*, Holt, 1920.

Spinka, Matthew, *John Hus and the Czech Reform*, Univ. of Chicago Press, 1941.

Stokes, Anson Phelps, *Church and State in the United States*, 3 vols., Harper, 1950.

Stone, James S., *The Cult of Santiago*, Longmans, 1927.

Sweet, William W., *History of Religion in Colonial America*, Scribner, 1942.

——, *Religion in the Development of American Culture, 1765-1840*, Scribner, 1952.

—— (ed.), *Religion on the American Frontier*, 4 vols. of source materials: *Baptists*, Holt, 1931; *Presbyterians*, Harper, 1936; *Congregationalists*, Univ. of Chicago Press, 1939; *Methodists*, Univ. of Chicago Press, 1946.

——, *The Story of Religion in America*, revised edition, Harper, 1950.

Symonds, John Addington, *The Renaissance in Italy*, 7 vols., Holt, 1887-8.

Talbot, C. H. (trans. and ed.), *The Anglo-Saxon Missionaries in Germany*, Sheed & Ward, 1954.

Van Dusen, H. P., and Cavert, S. McC. (eds.), *The Church Through Half a Century: Essays in Honor of William Adams Brown*, Scribner, 1936.

Voragine, Jacobus de, *The Golden Legend* (legends of the saints), trans. and adapted by G. Ryan and H. Ripperger, London, Longmans, 1941.

Walker, Williston, *History of the Christian Church*, Scribner, 1918.

Weisberger, Bernard A., *They Gathered at the River: The Story of the Great Revivalists and Their Impact upon Religion in America*, Little, Brown, 1958.

Willey, Basil, *The Eighteenth Century Background*, Columbia Univ. Press, 1941.

——, *The Seventeenth Century Background*, Columbia Univ. Press, 1942.

Wolfe, Don M., *Milton and the Puritan Revolution*, Thomas Nelson, 1941.

Workman, Herbert B., *John Wyclif: A Study of the English Medieval Church*, 2 vols., Oxford, Clarendon Press, 1926.

Zweig, Stefan, *Erasmus of Rotterdam*, Viking, 1934.

INDEX